Studies in Childhood History
A Canadian Perspective

Edited by

Patricia T. Rooke
R.L. Schnell

Detselig Enterprises Limited
Calgary, Alberta

Patricia T. Rooke
R.L. Schnell
The University of Calgary

Canadian Cataloguing in Publication Data

Main entry under title:

Studies in childhood history

    ISBN 0-920490-27-1

    1. Children — Canada — History — Addresses,
essays, lectures. 2. Child psychology - History —
Addresses, essays, lectures. I. Rooke, Patricia T.
II. Schnell, R.L. (Rodolph L.)
HQ792.C2S88   305.2'3'0971   C82-091377-4

© 1982 by Detselig Enterprises Limited
P.O. Box G 399
Calgary, Alberta T3A 2G3

Appreciation is expressed for financial support from Alberta Culture towards the publication of this book.

Printed in Canada   ISBN 0-920490-27-1

Contents

Acknowledgment

The editors wish to acknowledge the support since 1979 of the Social Sciences and Humanities Research Council of Canada and the University of Calgary for research related to the history of childhood in Canada.

Notes on Contributors

Patricia T. Rooke is Editor, *Journal of Educational Thought,* at the University of Calgary.

R.L. Schnell is Professor and Head, Department of Educational Policy and Administrative Studies, University of Calgary.

Brian W. Taylor is Associate Professor, Division of Educational Foundations, University of New Brunswick.

Evelina Orteza y Miranda is Professor, Department of Educational Policy and Administrative Studies, University of Calgary.

Peter J. Miller is Professor and Chairman, Department of Educational Foundations, University of Alberta.

Norah L. Lewis is Sessional Lecturer, Department of Curriculum and Instruction Studies, University of British Columbia.

Leslie Savage is a doctoral student, Department of Educational Foundations, University of Alberta.

Rebecca Coulter is Assistant to the Vice-President, Learning Services, Athabasca University.

David C. Jones is Associate Professor, Department of Educational Policy and Administrative Studies, University of Calgary.

Introduction

Patricia T. Rooke and R.L. Schnell

The teaching of history of childhood to students of education is a somewhat different enterprise from that of teaching it to history students. The
courses in Faculties of Education are frequently senior options that attract
students who are in either general or specialized degree programs with the
result that they have had few or no previous history courses. Therefore, the
content must be organized and selected in such a way as to be appropriate for
students of education who, not unnaturally, are primarily interested in seeing
some relationship made between their interests which are related to classrooms and schooling and the historical study of childhood experience.
Fortunately, the subject matter itself — children and adolescents and their
past social reality — is immediately seen as relevant since these age groups
are the very "stuff" of school life. Moreover, with the de-emphasis since the
1960s on the great theoretical literature of educational ideas, students of education remain unaware of the relevance of many such ideas and the vast body
of material which can initiate them into a dynamic understanding of the con-
ceptual implications and limitations of childhood and teaching. We are
thinking, of course, of the *original* writings (rather than critiques) of the foremost educational thinkers such as Locke, Rousseau, Pestalozzi, Montessori,
Dewey and A.S. Neil, whose contemporary links with the transforming sentiment of childhood of their times provide us with an increased understanding
of the formal implications and consequences of such sentiment. Although a
complete history of childhood can be organized around these thinkers and
their original works, we appreciate that most instructors prefer to use such
material as background to more contemporary issues. The first section of this
work is designed to provide that background to the case studies, by illustrating
the importance of "ideas" to "childhood" by careful analyses of three influential strands of intellectual thought.

Bearing the above in mind, we emphasize at the outset that the purpose
of this collection of papers is, given the paucity of Canadian materials and
books suitable as either texts or for reference purposes, pedagogical and pragmatic. We do not propose that the following articles are "unified" in either a
contextual or a chronological sense but instead operate on the persumption
that as a pedagogical device the articles will be found useful to instructors who
will bring their own interests to play in transmitting the ideas and evidence
within each section. For example, the theoretical section illustrates only three
philosophical strands which are important to a modern understanding of
childhood and which indeed are crucial to an expanded knowledge of the

assumptions of classroom practice, teachers as "authorities," and children as sentient beings. Even then only particular emphases are analyzed regarding these philosophies — utilitarianism, psychologizing, and pragmatic progressivism. Even within these limits, there remains a great leeway in their exploration and their use and in how they can be supplemented or expanded by the introduction of other psychological viewpoints and theoretical models. Consequently, each article lends itself to a variety of approaches and, we hope, lively discussion. If the instructor is less interested in the psychological and philosophical contributions to the history of childhood — contributions which have substantially affected our attitudes towards and treatment of children in both the classroom and/or the household, the students will have at least benefitted from the discussions of utilitarianism, pragmatism and psychologism. Given the few works that include these significant intellectual shifts (the exceptions being John Cleverley and D.C. Phillips, *From Locke to Spock* [1976] and William Kessen, *The Child* [1965]), we maintain that no serious student of childhood history should overlook this background to the case studies. Moreover, the subjects covered are representative of three major stands of North American educational thought and their impact on child life has been felt and can be observed still despite their obvious adaptations and modifications to new curricular theories.

The second section consists of geo-cultural case studies which serve to illustrate some of the major research interests of historians of childhood and demonstrate the varieties of approach for those working in the area. These approaches which are part of "mainstream" historical concerns deal with matters such as child health and welfare, dependent children, institutionalization, illegitimacy and urban and country child life. Although all of these topics have international and theoretical perspectives, our original case studies have attempted to explore conditions within the Canadian context. Thus, they will provide the specificity with which to illustrate the more general concerns about such things as the origin and purpose of the juvenile justice system; the nature of dependency and charity organization; and the growing sensibilities regarding child life generally and neglected children in particular. Moreover, through the contrasts between urban conditions and rural experience, we come to understand the growing concerns of a society that increasingly values its children as "national assets." This socio-economic point of view, whose roots can be traced to the early Humanist educators, is in harmony with political traditions which see childhood as the "seedbed" of adult citizenship. Such a conception of child as potential citizen is as integral to totalitarian or socialist societies as to capitalist or democratic ones.

Part I

Theoretical Perspectives

Utilitarianism and the Child: Jeremy Bentham

Brian W. Taylor

> You have been so careful of me, that I never had a child's heart. You have trained me so well, that I never dreamed a child's dream. You have dealt so wisely with me, father, from my cradle to this hour, that I never had a child's belief or a child's fear.[1]

In *Hard Times*, the often quoted parody of Utilitarian theory particularly as it relates to the education of young people, Charles Dickens gives a clear indication of the popular notion of how the 'utilitarian' child would be brought up. The emphasis on factual information as the sole basis of education, for

> Facts alone are what are wanted in life. Plant nothing else, and root out everything else. You can only form the minds of reasoning animals upon Facts: nothing else will ever be of any service to them.[2]

The arid nature of the environment served to emphasize this, with "The plain, bare, monotonous vault of a schoolroom."[3] Above all, there is Coketown, a town of "unnatural red and black like the painted face of a savage,"[4] of machinery and tall chimneys, black canals and a river that ran purple with ill-smelling dye, with streets 'all very like one another . . . inhabited by people equally like one another".[5] Even the humans are hardly credible. The 'extremely clear-headed, cautious, prudent young man', Bitzer, whose "mind was so exactly regulated, that he had no affections or passions" believed that "all gifts have an inevitable tendency to pauperise the recipient".[6]

All of these things contain an element of truth; to be a successful parody, which they are, they have to. But the notions of utilitarian childhood and its education which Dickens presented in *Hard Times*, contain little more than a grain of truth. They are based on a fundamental misreading, if not perversion, of the utilitarian child as Jeremy Bentham,[7] (1748-1832), the founder of the utilitarian faith, conceived of such a being.

In this chapter I hope to redress the balance a little by bringing to the fore the essential elements of Utilitarian ideas about children and their upbringing and, by discussing the practices by which "education" (in the peculiarly broad way in which the Benthamites employed that term) would bring about the kind of moral and practical transformation of which children, and poor ones most of all, stood in need. In order to do this it will be necessary to explain Bentham's Principle of Utility on which everything that he subsequently thought, wrote, and did, is based. It is essential, also, to put all of this into some sort of historical context because Utilitarian ideas about children, and most other things too, are inextricably bound up with the social and political events of late eighteenth-century England.

The long life of Jeremy Bentham was passed at a time when English society was going through a period of profound change at a rate it had never before approached. Perhaps the most fundamental change was that of the rate of industrialization with its attendant problems of a rapidly increasing population, growing towns and cities, and the translation of English society from one with an almost entirely rural base into an urban one. One effect of this was to rupture the traditional and familiar, though clearly defined, relationships of society in which the gentry enjoyed an unchallenged position of social and political superiority. Henceforth, the various groups within society (it is too early to refer to them as 'classes'), would operate with increasing mutual independence and with increasing suspicion of each other. Political events, too, played their part. The French Revolution of 1789 exercised a profound effect on English society: it increased the fears of the emerging middle class as to its own security and that of its property and it intensified that mode of thought, shared by Bentham and the philosophical radicals, which perceived the increasing numbers of the poor as a problem and, above all, a threat. Such a 'threat' is easy to accept when one considers some of the political events that were then taking place. The mutinies in the English navy, the ongoing war against now republican France, the March of the Blanketeers, the riots at Spitalfields, the Gordon riots, the Wilkesite disturbances and, finally, the shame of Peterloo, all took place within a twenty-five year period. It was against such a background, and at least in part as a response to it, that the Utilitarian child came to be defined.

An entree into an understanding of the utilitarian child may be made by a brief comparison with the Romantic idea of childhood. It is perhaps ironic, but wholly understandable, that Romanticism and Utilitarianism should have developed at the same time for it is difficult to imagine two more diametrically opposed approaches to life. In all essential respects they are mutually exclusive: most certainly they held opposite views about children and childhood and the kind of society that was good for them.

The Romantic recognition of the innocence of childhood and its appreciation of this as a desirable state is a prominent feature of that philosophy's approach to childhood. So, too, is its frank delight in the total spontaneity of the child.

> Piping down the valleys wild,
> Piping songs of pleasant glee,

its hostility towards the increasingly automated and un-natural society which it saw developing around it, its desire for close and intimate and continuing contact with nature and natural things in which

> One impulse from a vernal wood
> Will teach you more of man
> Of moral evil and of good
> Than all the sages can.

And in which Blake's lament,

> Is this a holy thing to see
> In a rich and fruitful land,
> Babes reduc'd to misery,
> Fed with cold and usurous hand?

> [Whose] sun does never shine,
> [Whose] fields are bleak and bare
> [Whose] ways are filled with thorns . . .

strike a startlingly resonant note. All of this stands in marked contrast to the pro-industrial and pro-intellectual Utilitarianism which looked askance at emotions being given free rein, which applauded planning, system, order, and anything that could be described as 'scientific', and which was highly sceptical of the notion of childhood innocence and spontaneity.

In some respects it seems to be almost a contradiction in terms to speak of such a being as a "Utilitarian Child" since utilitarianism itself was such a materialistic creed and one that was seemingly adult oriented, appealing as it does, to a fully developed rational sense and one that had to be capable of functioning in some kind of emotional vacuum. However, it is precisely because of these qualities that the notion derives its sense, for the utilitarians were above all else, realists, and fully recognized that children were a part of the world they were about to attempt to transform. The main question became, therefore, what to do with them and to them to ensure that they, too, were governed by the Principle of Utility in their thinking and in their various acts. The net result of this was a view of childhood and education of children that was defined along social class lines. The Utilitarian child ought to be useful to society and that meant that he ought to be brought up in a way that would bring this about. Since the Utilitarian position accepted as a *sine qua non* that what subsequently became the social classes were an essential, necessary and desirable feature of society it followed as a matter of course that their upbringing and education ought to be structured in a way that would accommodate this. Utilitarian education, therefore, is to be conceived of in terms of clearly defined social groups and one should not be deceived by the name "philosophical radicals" (an alternative to "utilitarians") into thinking otherwise. Before

I pursue that line of thought, however, I think a brief word or two on the theoretical basis of Utilitarianism is needed.

Utilitarianism is an ethical system developed by Jeremy Bentham. I say 'developed' because although he is widely regarded as the 'founder' of it, he did not, in fact, originate it. Beccaria, Helvetius, Bacon, Gay, Locke had all written along utilitarian lines. Bentham's contribution was to distill and to synthesize their thought, refined by his own logical nature and humanitarian instincts, into an ethical system. The fundamental basis of that system is the Principle of Utility or, as Bentham frequently referred to it, the Greatest Happiness Principle. The Principle is most clearly defined in *An Introduction to the Principles of Morals and Legislation* as

> That principle which approves of every action whatsoever according to the tendency which it appears to have to augment or diminish the happiness of the party whose interest is in question.

In other words, the greatest happiness of the greatest number, a phrase universally recognized if not so universally associated with Bentham. In order to "approve of every action" it is necessary to erect a criterion and this Bentham did with his notion of a Felicific Calculus. This was a means of calculating units of 'pleasure' and 'pain' that would be created by any proposed action. Whichever course resulted in the least pain or the most happiness was the one that ought to be adopted. For Bentham, if not for his later disciples (notably John Stuart Mill), this was to be a purely quantitative analysis.[9] It is a sensible idea, something that we in any case do, but nonetheless one that has provoked a great deal of criticism and one must admit, I think, that it does have tinges of absurdity. The notion of the ascetic Bentham making such nice calculations in his hermitage does have its lighter side. That notwithstanding, Bentham did establish a number of criteria which he felt should be applied when judging the effect an action would have in promoting the greatest happiness of the greatest number of people affected by it. The intensity, duration, certainty, remoteness, fecundity (by which was meant the chance it had of being followed by the same kind of sensations) and the purity of an action were to be considered, their effects totalled up in terms of units and a fine calculation arrived at.

There is, yet, another important strand to Utilitarianism and that is the theory of Associationism. This latter aspect, developed to fine limits by David Hartley, aims to present a deterministic account of mental occurrences through a recognition of the association of ideas with other ideas and that of ideas with language. Both of these strands are important. Associationism aims at an ethical system and a code of laws designed to make men virtuous so that they will naturally eschew personal feelings and desire the greatest happiness of the greatest number. Utility is a necessary means to define virtue. It was this combination of Utility and Associationism which initiated, and continued to sustain, Bentham's work for law, prison and pauper management reform as well as his interest in economics and, above all, education which was to occupy him for the rest of his life.

The notion of Education is central to all of Bentham's schemes for the improvement of the lot of the mass of mankind. Education, however, is not to be equated with mere instruction though that was certainly a part of the process:

> Education is the conduct of the individual through the early part of life. The proper end of education is no other than the proper end of life-well being . . . [and that] . . . the field of education comprises the whole of the individual's time.[10]

Education, then, had to be useful in preparing a child for its future role in society, a much easier thing to predict in the eighteenth-century than it would be today. It must also be strictly regulated so that the beneficial effects could be maximised and the vitiating ones eliminated. It ought, therefore, to be carried on as far as possible under the right circumstances and in the right kind of, and specially constructed, institutions. For the poor those places were prisons and workhouses as well as the more traditional kinds of schools. For the middling ranks of society there were special schools — a topic which Bentham addressed in the one major "educational" scheme that he drafted, the *Chrestomathia*, of which more later.

It will be readily appreciated, therefore, that Bentham's ideas about childhood, children and their education were drafted along deeply-held notions of social class. Despite the name by which they are frequently known, the Philosophical Radicals, Bentham and his close associates were, and remained, members of the middle rank of society. They shared the concerns and fears of that group and they supported what they perceived to be its legitimate aspirations at a time when the whole notion of social class, described by E.P. Thompson,[11] was beginning to develop. For just as the lower orders were becoming increasingly aware of their commonality of interests, their increasing numbers and consequent political strength, so also was the middle group of society becoming increasingly reluctant to rely on the order that had traditionally ruled the country. Instead, the middle rank became increasingly conscious of the fact that it generated the greatest share of the national wealth, that it possessed the entrepreneurial skills, business acumen and above all the will and determination to succeed, and as it did so it became more reluctant to leave the power of direction in traditional hands. Alone among the members of that middle 'class' Bentham and his disciples were uniquely conscious of what he referred to as the "plastic power" of education to mold society in ways that were felt to be desirable. This is what, in the education of children and young adults, forms such a large part of Bentham's far-reaching plans for the transformation of society. *Panopticon* (the scheme for prison reform), *Chres-*

tomathia (a plan for the education of the middle ranks of society), the scheme for *Pauper Management Improved*, the criticisms levelled at the National Schools Society, the outline scheme for Irish Education and even the daunting Plan for the Moral Reformation of Irish Labourers in New York (Bentham, it would seem, enjoyed a challenge) are all evidence of his belief that education, well designed, consistently and systematically applied in the right kinds of institutions, and designed with that specific purpose in mind could achieve virtually anything at all. The one major factor, essential to its success and not yet touched upon in this chapter, is the involvement of the state either directly or indirectly. This was essential in order to counteract the apparent unwillingness of some parents, particularly those from the inferior ranks, to 'educate' their children. Education was designed to make men happy. For Bentham it went without saying that all men had a right to be happy, therefore, all men had to be educated. That did not, of course, mean that all would be educated in the same manner, since that would end up by making some men extremely unhappy by raising unreasonable expectations which could not subsequently be satisfied, and misery instead of joy would be the end result. Nonetheless, all men must be educated since that would give them increased control over their environment and so enable them to be useful to society. Only the state, Bentham reasoned, had the power to compel the education of children, consequently the increased involvement of government in the education of the governed was essential.

The aim of all this was to produce, in a way I intend to describe, an individual who would be useful to himself and to society through the development of his moral, intellectual, practical and physical skills, always bearing in mind the role in society he was destined to fulfill. The first would ensure good habits and respect, the second would improve the mind and provide a permanent source of pleasure and power over oneself and others, the third would enable them to be independent, and the fourth would contribute by ensuring a sound body to house the improved mind Bentham intended to develop. Let us now turn to a more detailed look at the theory and practice which was designed to bring about the transformation of men (and women!), starting with the education of the poor.

Bentham wrote about the poor and their concerns over a lengthy period of time, from 1796 or thereabouts until his death in 1832. His aim was to save them from the consequences of their own folly for it appeared to him that as a group they were particularly prone to a variety of moral weaknesses. There were too many of them and it appeared that their numbers were on the increase. They were idle: he wrote of the pauper child that

> Idleness is his first lesson, and this lesson (reckoning from 4 years old the age of commencing ability) fills up the measure of 8 or 10 years.[12]

They were prone to drink too much and

> . . . drunkenness affords an occupation at the same time the most gener-
> ally alluring and the most uniformly pernicious. With a full purse and an
> empty head nothing more difficult than for a man to avoid falling into the
> abyss of drunkenness.[13]

It was these weaknesses that was their undoing for it made them a threat to
the good order of society. A crucial part of that society was its security, and
particularly the secure holding of property, that most precious of middle class
tenets. This perception of the poor as a threat was certainly shared by Bentham who wrote that

> Property and the law are born and must die together. Before the laws, there
> was no property; take away the laws, all property ceases. With respect to
> property, security consists in no shock or derangement being given to the
> expectation which has been founded on the laws, of enjoying a certain por-
> tion of good.[14]

Bentham went on to justify the holding of property as a benefit to society as a
whole for

> . . . the laws in creating property, have been benefactors to those who
> remain in their original poverty. They participate more or less in the pleas-
> ures, advantages, and resources of civilised society; their industry and labour
> place them among the candidates for fortune: they enjoy the pleasures of
> acquisition; hope mingles with their labours.[15]

A proper upbringing, Bentham argued, would ensure that they would reap
their proper reward, the social order would not collapse, and society would be
secure.

Bentham considered the question of an appropriate upbringing for the
poor in a number of his schemes for prison reform, better treatment of paupers
and a number of minor works dealing with education in one way or another.
The most thorough treatment of the subject occurs in the scheme which he
called *Pauper Management Improved* which he drafted in 1797 and a version
of which appeared in Arthur Young's "Annals of Agriculture" that same year
and the one that followed it. I will, therefore, rely mainly on it in this explanation of the programme and the practices which Bentham believed to be
essential to the molding of the utilitarian child. Perhaps, though, one should
first define just what kind of child it was that Bentham was aiming to produce
as a result of his schemes.

There are, I think, five qualities that the utilitarian child would develop
as a result of his upbringing and which he would carry on into adult life. The
first is that he would learn to be independent, independent, that is, in the

economic sense. In this way he would not only gain in self-respect, but would also not be a burden on society. There was widespread concern in the middle and upper ranks of society in the last decades of the eighteenth century about what seemed to be a rapid rise in both the numbers of poor people and the cost to the parishes of maintaining them since the costs of poor relief in the absence of any system of poor assistance fell directly on the tax-paying members of society. The desire, therefore, to mold independent youngsters was at least as much motivated by self-interest as it was by disinterested theory.

The second quality aimed at was that of a morality. I have referred earlier to the widespread belief in the moral decrepitude of the poor which caused misery and pain and which was, therefore, quite obviously at variance with the Greatest Happiness Principle so dear to Bentham. The utilitarian child was, therefore, to be brought up in such a way as to produce a sober, industrious, honest, thrifty and literate adult who would work hard, save his money or spend it wisely instead of on drink or other pleasurable, but misery-producing, activities, and who would use his ability to read, write and cypher to improve his mind, his environment and his lot in life.

Bentham was well ahead of all his contemporaries in his belief in the virtue of physical fitness. It was a belief he put into practise himself: he used to exercise on a daily basis until the very end of his life. His neighbour in Queens Square Place, Westminster, the essayist William Hazlitt, derived wry amusement from the circumgirations of his garden at something between a fast walk and a trot which were a daily feature of Bentham's routine. But then, Bentham and his neighbour never did get along. *Mens sana in corpore sano* was, then, a *sine qua non* of the utilitarian child.

It was also essential that the child should develop the 'right' attitudes for only by doing so would he be happy. The right attitudes were predominantly those of a social nature and first amongst them would be an acceptance of the prevailing social situation and a respect for one's 'betters' for it was they who knew best, it was they who could be trusted to act, in a disinterested way, in one's own best interest. Coupled with this respect for people was a respect for their property, but that I have already referred to. In short, our child would respect the king and church (both of which Bentham himself did not at all respect and which he consistently attacked with all the considerable power of ridicule and scorn at his disposal), the squire and all his relations and all those in authority, he would work hard and above all else he would be content with the lot which fortune, if not the Good Lord, had ordained for him.

Finally, the child would study to be useful; what else would one expect of a Utilitarian child? He would be useful to himself because that would increase his chances of being happy and for the same reason he would endeavour to be useful to society. To be otherwise would be to subvert the notion of desiring the greatest happiness of the greatest number, and that, quite clearly, was unacceptable.

What Bentham proposed to help solve the problem posed by the poor in general and their children in particular was to set up what he intended to call the National Charity Company to run the special institutions, i.e., work-houses, in which they would be brought up. This would be a public company in which interested people would invest money and from which they would, since the Houses of Industry were intended to be self supporting, expect to receive a profit. Other funds would be derived from existing poor rates and from the profits on the labour of the inmates. Bentham's scheme was, by the way, only one of a number of such plans that were proposed in a decade in which interest in the poor was a subject of perennial concern: one of the other plans was the brain-child of no less a person than the Prime Minister of the day, William Pitt. The parish was to be the territorial unit for the houses and Bentham suggested that they be grouped together to form viable units with approximately four houses to each county: thus a chain of institutions would be formed all over the country under the control of the Company with a Director in charge of each house. A unique feature of Bentham's system was that there would be no 'out' relief, that is, admission would be denied to virtually nobody (prostitutes were an exception to his rule for Bentham considered them to be already gainfully employed), but they must live in the house. Bentham suggested that all be admitted

> . . . under the condition of remaining and working for the benefit of the Company until the expense of relief has been defrayed by the value of his labour.[16]

The administration of the houses was to be carried out in accordance with a series of clearly defined principles of management which were designed to ensure fair, uniform and disinterested administration. The various groups of inmates (sick people, the "corrupt" class, young children, etc.) would need to be kept separate from each other and the principles of management, in part, were to facilitate this. Of particular interest was Bentham's recommendation that, for the purpose of education, those children who had lived outside the establishment would need to be kept separate from those who were born in it since the former group would probably have been corrupted by their experience. They would, therefore, require a different kind of education in order to overcome that handicap. The principal means of achieving the necessary kind of supervision was an application of what Bentham referred to as the "All-Seeing Principle". This was achieved by means of an architectural device which permitted the supervisor to oversee all that was being done without being seen himself. Bentham reckoned that if people did not know whether they were being observed or not they would automatically behave themselves. This idea appealed to Bentham, after all, it was effective and cheap. Bentham borrowed it from his earlier Panopticon Plan for prison reform and was very proud of it since

. . . it rendered uncleanliness, drunkenness, oppression, idleness and destruction of life or property at once impossible.[17]

Reference has already been made to the importance given by Bentham to the notion of constant, if unseen, supervision. This requirement necessarily influenced the basic design of the houses; there were, though, a number of other considerations to be born in mind such as the health of the inmates, their potential for work, the reception and accommodation of visitors, safety against fire, and, of course, economy of cost. On each of these, in turn, Bentham elaborated in the greatest of detail. One example will suffice, I think, to demonstrate this. The buildings, as well as being home, school and a place of work, would also be used for religious services. Bentham, therefore, suggested that

. . . at the time of divine service, a stage, on which are placed the pulpit, reading desk, clerk's desk, and communion table, lets down through the ceiling upon the floor of the lodge. Balanced by counterpoises all round, a moderate force is sufficient to raise or lower it. The under surface of the stage, in form of a flattish dome, constitutes, as far as it extends, the ceiling of the lodge. The descent of this dome discloses a set of circular seats above, serving as a gallery for chapel visitors. The pauper congregation are ranged, on a set of forms backed by circumferential screens, which keep the implements of work out of sight. An interval of two feet all round, above the top of the circumferential screens, serves for the admission of light.[18]

A further unique feature of Bentham's plan, when compared to others, is that nobody would be turned away because of their inability to work and so contribute to the financial viability of the house. Bentham argued that

Not one in a hundred is absolutely incapable of all employment. Not the motion of a figure — not a step — not a wink — not a whisper — but might be turned to account, in the way of profit, in a system of such magnitude. A bed-ridden person if he can see and converse may be fit for inspection; or though blind, if he can sit up in bed, may knit, spin, etc., etc. Real inability is relative only.[19]

Whilst on the subject of work, Bentham took care to ensure that as far as was possible the work carried on in the houses should not be injurious to health. Unwholesome work was to be allocated to an individual in proportion as his constitution was able to bear it. Each inmate was to be taught two types of occupation, one active and one sedentary, one indoor and one outdoor, and females were to have a mixture of "ordinary family employment and other lucrative employment." It was Bentham's intention, by such means, to ensure that the inmates would be treated to a rigorous but fair, consistent, and above all, humane regime.

There are three further aspects of the pauper plan which are germane to this chapter. The first is the question of employment in the houses. The second is the important area of ancillary uses for them. The third is the question of schooling. I propose to turn to these now, having given at least some indication of the kinds of institutions that Bentham proposed.

On the matter of employment, Bentham had a number of considerations to satisfy. All were to be admitted and all would work. The work must not be injurious to health. The institutions were to be self-supporting by offering a wide range of employment and by making it suitable for all inmates. So far so good, but Bentham then proceeded to hedge them about with so many restrictions that the notion of profitability was all but eliminated. First, those who had skills in demand during war-time must not use those skills for more than two days out of six when there was peace. Second, the work done in the houses should not compete with that done by independent workers or the latter group would be pauperised and that would defeat the object of the whole enterprise. Third, the work was not to be more than usually lucrative as this would only increase the speculative nature of the enterprise and probably require more capital. Fourth, the work was to be clear of "impropriety." Given such circumstances, it is surprising that any work at all was possible. Indeed, there was little, beyond husbandry, that was acceptable.

In order to provide the maximum opportunity for the poor child to grow up into a useful member of society, Bentham drafted on to his scheme a number of "collateral" uses designed to enhance the quality of life of the poor and to better their circumstances. Such services, in this category, as were to be provided by the houses were to be available to the independent poor as well as the inmates of the houses. They would, as well, enhance the profitability of the enterprise. What, then, did Bentham have in mind? The houses would provide information about jobs that were available to the independent poor and provide cheap overnight accommodation for those obliged to travel in search of work. They would provide savings-bank facilities where the poor might leave their meagre savings in safety. They were to provide an inexpensive means by which such small sums of money as a poor worker might want to send elsewhere could be transmitted cheaply and in safety. They were to provide medical assistance for the benefit of the poor at minimal cost to them. Bentham also expected the houses to provide services of an obviously domestic kind: bad children and bad apprentices would be sent there to be reformed, they would provide a refuge for unemployed girls, repentant whores and "friend-less females at the approach of the perilous age," and they could act as 'nurseries' for boys destined to enter the army or the navy.

Finally, there is the explicitly educational purpose of the houses. Teach the children of the poor a trade and you increase their self esteem, enable them to be independent and you make them happy. Useful knowledge gave a man the means to pursue an objective and the ability to achieve it. Bentham proposed to go about the business of disseminating useful knowledge amongst the poor in two ways. The first was to teach the children useful skills whilst they were inmates of a house. The second was to admit the children of the independent poor to the courses to be instructed. By such means girls would, for example, learn midwifery (to be taught by the medical curator as part of his normal duties) and boys would be taught the elements of veterinary science.

The same principles and objectives (independence, morality, fitness, healthy attitudes and usefulness) were of course at the front of Bentham's mind when he came to consider the upbringing and formal education of the "middle-class" child. This Bentham did in his only major scheme that was specifically "educational" in the normally accepted sense of that word, the *Chrestomathia*.[20] This scheme, which was published by Bentham in 1816, was in part an application of the Lancasterian method[21] of instruction and was attractive to Bentham on a number of accounts: it was scientific, it was systematic and, above all, it was cheap. It was, too, a revolt against the traditional classical education of the times which Bentham considered to be irrelevant to the needs of the bourgeoisie since many of its members did not have the means to inform and qualify themselves to recognize good government and neither did they have the means and skills to read and understand what they read. It was a scheme which, though it was never put into operation in the way that Bentham expected it would be, was destined to influence the education of the radical middle classes for much of the nineteenth century.

For the time in which it was written, indeed for the present, too, the scheme is "progressive", encompassing as it did many pedagogical principles which were subsequently to be adopted by forward-looking and kindly educators. Such innovations included the replacement of corporal punishment by a system of rewards, the extensive use of what have come to be known as "visual aids" to reinforce learning, and "streaming" in the grouping of students according to their perceived ability. Bentham's implacable critics have refused to recognize the progressive and humane nature of any of Bentham's schemes, preferring instead to believe that

> His *Panopticon* and *Pauper Management* plans were no improvement over the existing system they were supposed to replace; and in the case of the latter (Bentham's proposal for poor relief) actually a step backward.[22]

I have attempted in my *Note*, etc., to indicate the absurdity of such criticism.

Chrestomathia is drafted in accordance with Bentham's customary attention to order and detail. It consists of two tables of content, one dealing with the proposed curriculum and the other with pedagogical principles, and a whole series of appendices. Bentham's program of education was predicated on the idea that children should, first, be taught those subjects which they would most readily master and those ideas which would be most easily understood by them. The programme was designed to last for seven years and a child would embark on it when he was seven years of age. The initial stage, of two years, was to be devoted to the three Rs, for Bentham reckoned, with obvious common sense, that without a thorough grounding in these basics children could scarcely be expected to progress to more difficult work. The remainder of the five year programme was to consist of the following subjects and in this order:

Stage I: Natural history, geometry, geography and drawing.

Stage II: Physics and chemistry, geometry, geography, history, drawing and grammar.

Stage III: The application of science to industry and agriculture, geography, history, grammar and drawing.

Stage IV: Medical science, geometry, geography, history, grammar and drawing.

Stage V: Mathematics, astronomy, history, drawing, grammar, technology, book-keeping and commercial subjects.

I think it is the courses that were excluded which are particularly significant here: these include religion, physical education, and the ancient languages. Religion is, perhaps, not so surprising. Bentham was an agnostic and devoted much of his life to criticising religion.[23] Some, at least, of this criticism originated with his own resentment of what he perceived to be the role of the king, George III, in the decision not to proceed with Bentham's cherished *Panopticon* scheme for prison reform. This was a scheme to which Bentham, encouraged by the government, had devoted not only a considerable amount of time but also a lot of his own money.[24] The clue to its omission from *Chrestomathia* lies, I believe, in the notion of usefulness when applied to social class. Religion was useful for the poor because it helped to impress on them their place in life and the advantages of not disturbing the ordained social order. Its usefulness to the middle orders of society, concerned as they were to improve their own social position vis a vis the aristocracy, was much less apparent. Whilst physical education was not left out entirely, it was given a surprisingly inferior degree of importance considering Bentham's own predilection for it and the time he devoted in his pauper scheme to a consideration of the most beneficial exercises that could be devised (he was particularly keen on swimming, by the way, as that sport exercised all parts of the body all the time). Here again, utility is the key. It was more important for the middle classes to have their intellectual and entrepreneurial skills developed in order that they would fulfill their designated role in society and since that and physical education could not both be accommodated, then the latter had to be dropped.

The omission of the classical languages, Bentham's ancient foes, is not at all surprising and the reason is readily apparent — they could not be justified on the basis of their usefulness. Latin and Greek were, Bentham believed, generally useless. There were no ancient Greeks or Romans around to speak the languages with, they contained stories and allusions calculated to corrupt morals, they took up time in the curriculum that could be more profitably devoted to other things (science, for example), and everything that was of value in them had already been translated into English anyway. There are also several other, minor, omissions worthy of note here: music was too noisy (and, also, too closely related to drinking for Bentham's liking), drawing and fencing were not useful. Such, then, was to be the basis of useful education for the children of the middle classes; its effectiveness was not, however, destined to depend solely on content. A variety of architectural and pedagogical devices were incorporated in the scheme to provide for its increased effectiveness. I would like to examine some of these, now.

There are three cornerstones, apart from the curriculum upon which Bentham depended for the success of his middle class utilitarian child. These are the design of the building, the method of instruction, and the extra teaching aids he intended to use; all were central to the success of the scheme and all were well in advance of contemporary thought and practice.

The design to which Bentham proposed to build his school incorporated the beloved "All-seeing" principle which Bentham had proposed for the prison scheme. The building was a circular one constructed in such a way as to permit a gaoler (or a school master) to observe his charges freely without, himself, being visible to them. In the school, the benefit of constant supervision was, to Bentham, self-evident: whether they were, or not, the pupils would believe they were being observed and so would apply themselves to their work. The school was to admit six hundred male, and four hundred female students, since

> According to the indications afforded by experience, the above number
> . . . is understood to be generally regarded as the greatest number that, in
> one and the same schoolroom, can be taught under the constant inspection
> of one and the same Master.[25]

The school was, therefore, to have a pupil to teacher ratio of one thousand to one. Certainly it would be cheap!

The method of instruction favoured by Bentham was that initiated by Bell and Lancaster: the monitorial, Lancasterian, or Madras system. At the time of its introduction it was hailed as a signal advance in teaching method. It promised to be efficient, it had the potential to be effective, and certainly it would be cheap. This, latter, was a virtue ever likely to commend itself to Jeremy Bentham. What happened, in practice, was that the teacher taught the lesson to be learned to a group of senior children who were called "monitors." Each monitor would then teach the lesson to a group of younger children. In this way one teacher could effectively control, at least in theory, virtually any number of students. Originally perceived as a method of instructing a large number of extra pupils it became, in Bentham's hands, a scientific application of the division of labour to the field of mass instruction and whatever defects it may have had it was, at least, successful in occupying in a profitable way the large numbers of children entrusted to schools. As with all of Bentham's schemes, *Chrestomathia* was drafted in strict accordance with well-defined principles of both teaching and management: in fact, there are no less than forty-three general principles laid down by Bentham. Three of these, in particular, relate to the method of instruction and its peculiar advantages as they occurred to Bentham. The scheme would be inexpensive since the pupil-teachers would not be paid. The scheme would save time since there was no reason why several different classes should not be carried on at one and the same time. The third would be an increase in what Bentham referred to as "relative aptitude." What Bentham had in his mind was that whereas a professional teacher might well hold opinions of his own which could be at variance with those of his employer, the pupil-teachers, owing to their peculiar situation, could afford no such luxury. Bentham regarded this as

> . . . an essential feature [of the scheme] operating to the complete and proposed exclusion of all such naturally reluctant and untractable subordinates.[26]

The principle which underlay the process of instruction was the "Proficiency-Promising" principle which stated that the level of instruction must be geared to the ability of the pupil to understand it; in other words, begin with the simpler concepts and progress to the more difficult ones as the pupil's ability to master these improved. This was of obvious importance at the elementary levels of instruction but was no less so at the later stages. Several of the other pedagogical principles (normally prefaced with the double-barrelled titles favoured by Bentham)worthy of mention here are the "Perfect-Performance Exacting" Principle which restricted the length of lessons to forty-five minutes, the "Note-Taking, Self-Service" Principle by which the pupil-teachers ruled the lines on the students' pages in order to save time and cut down on waste, the "Instruction-Preventing" Principle (perhaps not quite as progressive as the others) which stipulated that the windows should be sufficiently high as to prevent the pupils from wasting time by looking out of them, and the "Tabular-Exhibition" Principle which required the walls to be covered with charts, diagrams and other visual aids so that if a child finished a lesson ahead of his class-mates he could continue to learn from the charts instead of sitting idly by waiting for the others to complete theirs.

There are still two further principles which underpinned the teaching at the school: the "Place-Capturing" Principle and the "Punishment Minimizing and Reward-Economizing" Principle. The first of these combined exercise with reward for good, and punishment for bad, work and it worked in the following manner. The pupils would be arranged in line according to their proficiency in doing a lesson — the most successful at the head of the line, the place of honour where children will, in any case, strive to be. If a pupil erred in saying the lesson for the day his place would be taken by the next successful, and so on, in such a way as to determine the new order for each day: the disgrace, alone, of losing one's place was deemed to be sufficient punishment. Never was physical punishment to be inflicted. The question of punishment was one of recurring concern for Bentham and one which caused him some trouble on account of his adherence to the Greatest Happiness Principle, for a reward to one person would cause pain to others. It was a dilemma he was not totally able to resolve though in the "Punishment-Minimizing and Reward-Economizing" Principle he recognized that

> Never can the matter of reward be obtained, to pour into one lesson, but at the expense of suffering, however remote and disguised, inflicted upon others.[27]

Bentham's solution was to minimize the reward to such an extent that it still acted as an inducement but not an overwhelming one. In this way the pain inflicted on others, whilst it would not be eliminated, would be minimized, and the Principle of Utility would be partly mollified.

Much of what Bentham wrote in *Chrestomathia* he derived, in essence, from that other pillar of Utilitarianism, the associationist psychology of David Hartley: this is clear from the emphasis placed on repetition and "drill" which would form the association between ideas and other ideas and between facts and ideas that he wished to establish. Whilst the scheme was probably impractical (and it was never put into effect) it was certainly a more systematic, enlightened and humane approach to the education of young people than the kind of instruction it was designed to replace. As such, warts and all, it is to be welcomed.

So far, I have concentrated on the essential elements of Bentham's thought and his ideas on how that thought ought to be translated in practical terms. As we have seen, the Principle of Utility was the main motivating force and usually the sole criterion of action, and the programmes for producing the utilitarian child (or children, since there were to be different programmes for the different social groups) were to be carried on systematically in specially designed and constructed institutions. At this point it seems desirable to turn to a consideration of the anticipated attitudes, expectations, and mode of comportment of the child. Here, one need not emphasize the differences Bentham had in mind for the different social groups for the objectives are really the same for them all. It was just the method of attaining them that was to be different.

To start with, then, what legitimate expectations could the child entertain for himself? For the children of the poor, Bentham's expectation was that

> Instead of being bred up in ignorance and vice to an idle, beggardly and vagabond life, [they] will have the fear of God before their eyes, get habits of virtue, be inured to labour and thus become useful to their country.[28]

In more general terms, and above all, the child could expect to be happy: Bentham defined this state as "enjoyment of pleasures, security from pains". In drawing up his schemes he attempted to establish the objective and the means of attaining it. Thus, he was able to claim

> This is Utopia . . . In this Plan [Pauper Management Improved] happiness is provided for not by the unfounded assumption or confident prediction, but by the catch that is taken to bring together the means of happiness, and to exclude the efficient courses of unhappiness.[29]

The utopian aspects of Bentham's scheme may have eluded some of his critics but there seems to be general agreement that such an objective is desirable. Bentham believed that the "plastic power" of education applied in the ways he proposed would provide the means of effecting this.

An essential ingredient of happiness is security, and in pursuing happiness (of himself and society) the individual and those with power were also seeking to provide security: thus

> It has been shown that the happiness of the individuals, of whom a Community is composed, that is their pleasures and their security, is the end and the sole end which the Legislator ought to have in view: the sole standard, in conformity to which each individual ought, as far as depends upon the Legislator, to be made to fashion his behaviour.[30]

The kind of security which Bentham had in mind here was security of property, person and personal rights against thieves and the whims of arbitrary rulers (particularly, from Bentham's point of view, King George III).

There are, perhaps, four further expectations which the child could expect. The first is a store (and here Dickens is at least partly right) of practical knowledge for such knowledge placed its possessor in a more commanding position from which to control his own environment and so control his share of happiness. The kind of knowledge which was to be considered so useful would, as we have already seen, have to be closely related to his future function in society. Nonetheless, the objective was the same, and equally, it was amenable to empirical investigation (as the unfortunate Cissy Jupe was to find out) — a quality calculated to recommend it, on its own, to the utilitarian mind. Such knowledge had to be capable of being applied in a severely practical way on a day-to-day basis.

Second, the child could expect to be provided with a marketable skill. For the poor child this meant a trade which he could use to earn his living, or knowledge (usually of a practical and/or scientific nature) which would be of direct use to him in a job already selected: a knowledge of biology and natural history, for example, would be of use to gamekeepers. For the better-off child, destined for trade or commerce, a modern language or bookkeeping would suit the bill. In this way the child would not only be able to maintain himself without being a burden on society but would also be happier through his greater control over his own life.

Third, the child's mind would be improved (and here Dickens did miss the point). Of course, great care had to be exercised in doing this so as not to arouse unreasonable expectations:

> They [poor children] are not intended for historians, for Secretaries of State for foreign affairs or for trading in foreign countries in the character of Merchants.[31]

To improve their minds in such a way as to arouse such hopes would be, ultimately, to add to their stock of pain. No, the improvement of the mind was undertaken with the aim of providing the means for profitable use of leisure time, to provide "Security against inordinate sensuality and its mischievous consequences" and to provide the means of "admission into, and agreeable intercourse with, good company."[32] In other words, it would enable them whatever their social level, to withstand vice and temptation.

All of these would contribute to a state of independence. The utilitarian child would respect himself and enjoy the respect of others, he would hold his head high, he would be useful to himself and to society, he would, in large measure, be in control of his life: he would be beholden to no one — he was his own master. In short, he would be independent.

When one turns to look at the kind of behaviour which our utilitarian child would manifest, one is again struck by the fact that the same kinds of behaviour, the same characteristics, are demanded regardless of the social order from which the child came. Anything else would, of course, have contravened the sacred principle. Basically we are looking at five behavioural characteristics. The first of these (one which is, as Bentham would have put it, "self-evident") is that of industry. Idle people, no matter what class they belonged to, got into trouble and brought disrepute to themselves and they were, besides, a menace to society. Whilst the poor were particularly prone to this it was by no means their monopoly. That the devil finds work for idle hands is a *sine qua non* of Utilitarian belief: drinking, stealing, damaging property, begetting too many children, all of these are the products of idleness. All of them, individually, clearly contradict the Greatest Happiness Principle, collectively they nearly destroy it. Hard work was a virtue in itself (and certainly one that Bentham himself practised) and was productive of happiness: it was profitable, edifying, satisfying, natural and desirable.

Arising, at least in part out of the virtue of industry, is that of sobriety. Here, again, no one class had a monopoly of vice. Hogarth has provided us with records of the degradation drunkenness wrought on the poor driven to drink more through desperation than desire. The better-heeled indulged in the activity with no less enthusiasm but with more discretion. It was the excess which Bentham principally objected to: all things in moderation was his life-long working rule. Excess apart, there was the expense, and the temptation to commit crimes in order to obtain the money to drink, there were the debilitating effects and the deprivation of necessities for family. All in all, nothing was as good or as desirable or as productive of happiness as sobriety.

Closely allied to the virtue of sobriety is that of thrift: indeed, the two would seem to be mutually complementary. The Utilitarians viewed the careful use of money as a virtue in itself: they eschewed extravagance in any form and whilst Bentham was both kind-hearted and generous, he lived a life that was characterized by abstemiousness and plain living. Their belief that however much wealth one had one should use it carefully and quietly influenced many aristocratic families (the Russells, for example) during the nineteenth century. For the poor thrift was not only desirable in itself; it was also essential to happiness.

There are, I believe, two further behavioural characteristics which the Utilitarian child would possess. The first of these would be amenability or perhaps, more accurately, submissiveness. This was particularly desirable in the poor since there were so many of them, but it was also necessary in more fortunate children who should, too, know their place and do as they were bidden. The second characteristic is they should have "good habits": honesty was certainly high on any such list, so, too, would be reliability and respect for others, as well as the virtues of industry, sobriety, and thrift already referred to.

Finally, one should consider the question of attitudes. What sort of disposition would the child be expected to show? Once again, the same qualities would be expected of all children but the desirability of them among the children of the poor is that much stronger not only because they formed the vast majority of the people but also because the middle ranks of society (and that included Bentham and the other philosophical radicals) had most to lose by any change in the status quo that elevated the poor. The fear of the poor by the middle-ranks of English society is, perhaps, most clearly shown not by the Utilitarians themselves but by the Victorian Poet-Laureate, Tennyson, in his "The Northern Farmer — New Style" where he wrote, with some feeling,

Tis'n them as as munny as breaks into 'ouses
    an steals,

Them as 'as coats to their backs an toaks
    their regular meals,
Noa, but its them as niver knows wheer a meal's
    to be 'ad,
Toak my word for it, Sammy, the poor in a
    loomp is bad.

It appeared to Bentham and many of his contemporaries, and certainly to Thomas Malthus, that the loomp was getting rapidly bigger. A respect, then, for property was an essential attitude for the child to have. If it was your own property or that of your family, so much the better: that way it provided you with the necessities (and other things besides) of life and the means of happiness. Its careful preservation and security of tenure was therefore essential. If it was the property of others it had, equally, to be respected: that was how the social fabric of society was ordained to be, it benefited you indirectly because its owners paid taxes from which you derived benefit, and, as Bentham pointed out in his pauper scheme, even if it was seized and divided up amongst the poor the difference that would make to each individual would be infinitesimal, and even that would be quickly spent on ale or gin (or both). Whilst on the subject of the poor child perhaps mention should be made of one attitude that was definitely not to be expected, and that is gratefulness to their benefactors for any assistance given to them. Rather, the reverse: nothing but resentment could be expected. So, for Bentham,

> As objects of tenderness they ought to be treated as children; but as instruments ever in readiness for the hand of mischief they ought to be regarded as enemies.[33]

If the child was to respect property equally he was expected to be respectful to those whom God had placed in authority over him. For the middle-class child this would, of course, not only include his parents but also all adults with whom he came into contact. For the poor child it was a somewhat daunting prospect for besides parents there were the myriads of other adults who were his social superiors. Society had been ordered in this way, the gentry had been placed over him and there was no reason to wish to change a situation that had clearly been divinely ordered: he must, therefore, respect his betters and be content with his lot. In this process, the right kind of education had an important part to play, particularly, of course, for the poor. It would

> give their minds a right bias, a strong sense of religion and moral honesty; a horror of vice, and a love of virtue, sobriety and industry; a disposition to be satisfied with their lot; and a proper sense of loyalty and subordination.[34]

In the *Introduction*, etc., Bentham wrote

> The interest of the community is one of the most general expressions that
> can occur in the phraseology of morals; no wonder that the meaning of it is
> often lost. When it has a meaning, it is this . . . The interest of the com-
> munity then, is . . . the sum of the interests of the several members who
> compose it.[35]

This, I believe, indicates in a general way the nature of the attitudes which
utilitarian children of whatever rank or order in society were expected to strive
to attain: they were to endeavour to be useful. They were to be useful to
themselves. They were to be useful to society. They were to be useful to their
country.

In intention, if not always in act, Jeremy Bentham was the most practical
of philosophers. Not for him the starry-eyed musings of mere theorists. Certainly the theory was not lacking from his work but it was invariably tempered
by the realization that if it could not be translated into action in a practical
way so as to promote the greatest happiness of the greatest number then it
was of little value. The translation of the theory was undertaken with educational concerns (in the sense that we have come to understand that term in
the context of utilitarianism) in mind and also in terms of a social programme.
In other words what Bentham was attempting to do through education was to
produce reliable citizens.

In this context he was not overly concerned with the middle-classes: their
social and political reliability was, with few exceptions, largely beyond question. They produced the national wealth through their professional and
entrepreneurial skills and they had a consequent right to dispense it. The poor,
of course, were different. Their loyalty could not be counted on and they were,
as we have seen, prone to all sorts of moral weaknesses which rendered them
even more suspect. This was why Bentham made sure that when actually
pauperised they would be confined in institutions. His was to be a rigorous,
though fair, system of relief:

> . . . Compassion is one thing; relief, efficacious and unmischievous relief,
> a very different thing . . . it is not in the power of parishes to give King-
> doms . . . *Come in and give your all or stay out and starve* such is the
> harsh, though unavoidable alternative presented by Poor House charity.[36]

It was because he recognized that the poor would need practical and ready
help in regulating their own concerns that Bentham drafted onto his great
pauper relief scheme the provisions for savings banks, for transmitting small
amounts of money from place to place, and for providing not only information
about work that was available but also the means of obtaining it. In this way
the poor, too, would develop the habits of loyalty, thrift, honesty, industry and
so on which I have previously referred to. There is, however, one of Bentham's

schemes not dealt with so far, which exemplifies his concern that education should be seen to have practical consequences. Unfortunately for his students Bentham's work habits leave much to be desired: he frequently drafted his schemes in outline form only, returning to them at a later date himself or leaving some amanuensis to fill out the skeleton. Such, in outline form only, is Bentham's scheme for Irish Education.[37] The problem with the Irish, of course, is not only that they were mostly poor with all the vices that such a state necessarily implied, but they were also disaffected. Their education had, therefore, to accomplish more than its customary load of rewards, and consequently the scheme had a number of purposes. There are the anticipated ones, such as to improve the intelligence and good morals of the people and to teach them to read and write, one or two less anticipated such as to increase a love of agriculture in a predominantly rural country, to give increase to habits of economy and frugality, and several others reserved especially for Ireland by separating the people from the Catholic Church and, if possible, securing their affections for the Union. Here Bentham had a number of objectives in mind: these are

> Getting their clergy under the influence of the Crown Lessening the activity of the Catholic Church by lessening their interest in retaining proselytes [and] attracting them to the Government.

In doing these things Bentham was also concerned not to promote the influence of "Bishops from England — of Bishops brought up in arbitrary principles in a country where Dissenters form no portion of the nation" whilst at the same time dividing the facade of Catholic unity. In respect to the latter Bentham recommended it would be

> Good to promote land purchases among Catholics since Irish Catholics purchasing the forfeited estates are opposed by Catholics, the Catholic interest will thus be divided against itself.[38]

We may, therefore, add the virtue of reliable citizenship to the list of objectives which the upbringing of the utilitarian child would achieve. These objectives Bentham expected to accomplish by much the same kinds of principles he had set out in his earlier schemes. It may thus be seen that the notion of the "Utilitarian" child is not the absurd one it might originally have been supposed to be. Basically the same social virtues were aimed at in all cases; it was just the means of achieving them that differed. The objective in all cases was to produce a child who would be independent and who would work hard, who would be moderate in all his personal habits and who would conform to the expectations of the Principle of Utility. That aim was happiness and an absence of pain.

Notes

[1]Dickens, Charles. *Hard Times*, Penguin English Library, Penguin Books, Harmondsworth, 1981, p. 137.

[2]*Ibid.*, p. 47.

[3]*Ibid.*, p. 47.

[4]*Ibid.*, p. 65.

[5]*Ibid.*, p. 65.

[6]*Ibid.*, p. 150.

[7]Jeremy Bentham (1748-1832) is the founder of English Utilitarian philosophy and one of the greatest seminal minds of the eighteenth century. There are several good biographies of him, of which the following is recommended: Mack, M. *Jeremy Bentham: An Odyssey of Ideas*, London, 1962.

[8]Bentham, Jeremy. *An Introduction to the Principles of Morals and Legislation.* Ed. J.H. Burns and H.L.A. Hart, Athlone Press, London, 1970.

[9]For a fuller explanation of the differences between Mill and Bentham and the modifications made to the Utilitarian position, notably on the subject of a qualitative dimension to the theory, see Mills *Essay on Utilitarianism.*

[10]Bentham, J. Published in "The Annals of Agriculture and Other Useful Arts," ed. Arthur Young, V. 30, 1797, p. 268.

[11]Thompson, E.P. *The Making of the English Working Class*, New York, Vintage Books, 1963.

[12]Bentham J. The Bentham Collection, Library of University College London (hereinafter UCL), Box C111(a), Sheet 95.

[13]*Ibid.*, UCL, CLI, 23.

[14]*Ibid.*, *The Works of Jeremy Bentham*, ed. J. Bowring, London, 1843, Vol. I, p. 308.

[15]*Ibid.*, *Works*, Vol. I, p. 308.

[16]*Ibid.*, UCL, 154a, 18.

[17]*Ibid.*, UCL, 151, 1.

[18]*Ibid.*, UCL, 151, 16.

[19]*Ibid.*, *Annals of Agriculture*, Vol. 30, p. 145.

[20]Bentham, J. Chrestomathia: being a collection of papers explanatory of the design of an institution, proposed to be set on foot, under the name of the Chrestomathic Day School, or Chrestomathic School, for the extension of the new system of instruction to the higher branches of learning, for the use of the middling and higher ranks of life. London, 1815, Langue and Foss. For one discussion of it, see Itzkin, E.S., "Bentham's 'Chrestomathia': Utilitarian Legacy to English Education," *Journal of the History of Ideas*, Vol. 39, 1978, pp. 303-316, and the response by Taylor, B.W., "A Note in Response to Itzkin's Bentham's Chrestomathia, etc.," *Journal of the History of Ideas*, Vol. 43, No. 2, April-June 1982, pp. 309-313.

[21]The Lancasterian method of instruction (also known as the Madras system and the Monitorial system) was developed by Lancaster as a cheap method of instructing large numbers of children. The lesson to be learned was first taught to a group of senior students called "monitors" and each of these would then teach it to

a group of other children. In this way large numbers of children could be taught at little cost.

²²Itzkin, E.S., op. cit., p. 303.

²³Bentham's works on this topic include the following: Church of Englandism and its catechism examined, Mother Church relieved by bleeding or vices and remedies extracted from Bentham's Church of, etc., The Book of Church Reform, Not Paul but Jesus by Gamaliel Smith, Esq., and an Analysis of the Influence of Natural Religion on the Temporal Happiness of Mankind. It is a body of works that is consistently critical of organized religion.

²⁴For a full history of this project, see Hume, L.J., "Bentham's Panopticon: An Administrative History," Part One, *Historical Studies*, Vol. XV, 61 (October), 1973, pp. 703-721; and Part Two *Historical Studies*, Vol. XVI, 62 (April), 1974, pp. 36-54.

²⁵Bentham, J. *Works*, Vol. IV, p. 47.

²⁶*Ibid.*, *Works*, Vol. IV, pp. 46-47.

²⁷*Ibid.*, *Works*, Vol. IV, p. 48.

²⁸Taken from *An Account of Several Workhouses, etc.*, London, 1732. Quoted in Lawson, J. and H. Silver, *A Social History of Education in England*, London, 1973, p. 188.

²⁹Bentham, J., UCL, 107, 58.

³⁰Bentham, J. *An Introduction to the Principles of Morals and Legislation*, p. 34.

³¹Bentham, J., UCL, CLIII(a), 115.

³²Bentham, J. *Works*, VIII, pp. 8-12.

³³Bentham, J., UCL, 152(a), 7.

³⁴Colquohoun, Patrick. Quoted in *Class and Conflict 19th Century England, 1815-1850*, London, 1973, p. 333.

³⁵Bentham, J. *An Introduction to the Principles of Morals and Legislation*, p. 12.

³⁶Bentham, J. UCL, 153(b), 413.

³⁷*Ibid.*, *Irish Education: Marginal Outlines of a Plan*, c1800, UCL 106, 76-80.

³⁸*Ibid.*, UCL, 106, 76, 77, 79.

Pragmatism and the Child: John Dewey

Evelina Orteza y Miranda

John Dewey's pragmatic philosophy of education is the basis of the discussion of this chapter. It will be dealt with in three parts. Part I is a brief exposition of the basic tenets of pragmatism. Part II presents the educational implications of pragmatism and illustrates a teaching activity characteristic of pragmatic education. The concluding section portrays the reactions of a pragmatic child relative to the particular question of authority.

I

Introduction

What is pragmatism? Pragmatism, a twentieth century philosophy, is commonly said to be a distinctively American philosophy. Its development is associated with success in overcoming the harsh environmental experiences of frontier life and transforming them into instruments for social good, with the development of democratic ideas on government and society, and with the rise of industrialization and technology. The latter, as application of science, is evidence, it is said, of the ability of the Americans to master procedural matters. Correlating the American experience with the rise of pragmatism led to the conclusion that, indeed, strands of some of the tenets of pragmatism are characteristically American. For example, its workability principle (if it is true, it works), and emphasis on methodology, procedure, or know-how's, are all suggestive of the American ethos of practicality, given more to grappling with problems directly and with immediacy than to contemplating them. For the pragmatist, like the American, knowledge is not speculation or contemplation of what one is said to know, but rather it is an *instrument* to be used to design, redesign, or transform the environment/world nearer to one's desires. The pragmatist, like the American, deals with the life of man as it is lived in time.

Considering that the frontier life did not afford much time for luxurious meditations on ideas and may be said to have influenced the American ways of thinking, acting, and behaving, which are said to be pragmatic, still it can be shown that strains of pragmatic thought can also be traced to some Greek and British philosophers. Consider, for example, Heraclitus (540 - 475 B.C.), the theoretician of change. No one, he said, steps twice into the same river since it does not remain the same; what is constant is only the principle of change. Relativity of knowledge is often traced to Protagoras' dictum: "Man is the measure of all things." Change and relativity, or contextuality, of knowledge are central tenets of pragmatism. Other philosophers who may be said to have contributed, in one way or another, to the development of pragmatic thinking are Francis Bacon (1561-1626), with his inductive way of thinking; Jean-Jacques Rousseau (1712-1778), with his emphasis on understanding children as children undergoing certain developmental processes and not as miniature adults; Auguste Comte (1798-1857), with his social interest and positivistic view of the universe, namely, that it is composed of laws and relations, without metaphysical substance; and Charles Darwin (1809-1882), whose biological evolutionary theory of life provided an explanation of the continuity and unity of life in all its aspects. Pragmatic thinking did not originate with the American experience. It is, however, admitted that the American philosophers, namely, Charles Sanders Pierce (1839-1914), William James (1842-1910), and John Dewey (1859-1952) were responsible for its modern formulation.

Common to all three philosophers was their interest not in the theoretical question of the relation of the object of knowledge and the subject (knower) but in the more practical question of how propositions claiming to be knowledge can be determined or established to be so. This question of validation of knowledge claims may be termed the basic pragmatic theme. There were differences among them in the approach to answer the question, but they were agreed in general on the broad themes of meaning as future/anticipated experience, truth as verifiability, and knowing as leading to satisfactory experiences or consequences. And basic to pragmatic themes is the suggestion of the reliability of the method of science to settle matters of question or dispute.

Of the three philosophers, John Dewey was most aware of social problems and the need for social reconstruction. To be effective in meeting these problems, he suggested the employment of practical intelligence or the theory of social inquiry which is basic to his pragmatic philosophy. Philosophy, for Dewey, is not the contemplation of eternal verities, of suppositions derived from speculative thinking, but it is a method for dealing with the problems of men. It is relevant to the needs of the times. This means that there is a social dimension to philosophy. That is, philosophy is not an activity independent of its social matrix but, like any other activity, it is constantly involved in an interactive process with other societal activities, whether they be confrontation with politics, arts, religion, or education. Like any phenomenon in human culture, philosophy is intrinsically related to its social history. Dewey, therefore, applied his pragmatic philosophy to varied and diverse problems in different aspects of philosophy, in the social sciences and problems of society, and in education. He wrote forty books and over eight hundred articles on these areas. His popular works on education include *Democracy and Educa-*

tion, The Child and the Curriculum, The School and Society, Schools for Tomorrow, Experience and Education, and *How We Think.*

John Dewey was a dominant force and influence in the field of study and practice of education from the 1930's up to the time of Sputnik. Indeed, it could be said that contemporary understanding on schooling, teaching, curriculum, and education is, in many ways, indebted to John Dewey evidenced by the seriousness with which we have come to accept expressions associated with his pragmatism, e.g., learning by doing, child-centred education, problem-solving approach, integrated approach, critical inquiry, and interactive experiences, and which expressions have become or are taken to be central to the language of the teaching profession. Dewey's philosophy and thinking on education was chosen to be the basis of the discussion of this chapter for these and other specific reasons, namely, (1) Dewey systematically applied or translated his pragmatic philosophy to education. Unlike other philosophers, he believed in the close connection between education and philosophy: "If we are willing to conceive education as the process of formulating fundamental dispositions, intellectual and emotional, toward nature and fellow men, philosophy may even be defined as the general theory of education."[1] In other words, it could be said that philosophy is education in action; (2) His pragmatic thinking on education was influential in, if not attributed to be the cause of the development of the Progressive Education Movement which inspired many attempted reforms in education in the 1930's - 1950's. It developed the educational theory known as progressivism. Some of its principles are: active learning which must be related to the interest of the child, problem solving activity in learning, education is life/experience, the teacher as a guide and not as an absolute authority, emphasis on cooperative activities in schooling and not on competition, and on democracy as a way of life. The influence of this movement and, of course, John Dewey's teachings, was world-wide, reaching China, Japan, Turkey, and Mexico. It was felt directly in Alberta, Canada, with its curricular revision in 1936 known as the Enterprise Method, the Alberta version of the activity-type method of education.

To understand Dewey's thinking on education a brief introduction to his pragmatic philosophy is essential. Its central point, which will also be its definition for the purpose of this chapter, is the instrumental function of certain concepts, which are experimentally testable or have been tested, in resolving or transforming the unsatisfactory or indeterminate features of experienced situations into satisfactory ones. It is also known as experimentalism or instrumentalism. Like any philosopher, or any thinker for that matter, he conducted his thinking with certain assumptions about the nature of reality, of man, and of truth.

Pragmatism, Metaphysics, and Nature of Man

Metaphysics, simply put, consists of a unifying principle that underlies the connectedness of all things in life and illumines one's understanding of why things are what they are. Dewey in *Experience and Nature* and *The Quest for Certainty* labelled his metaphysics "naturalistic metaphysics" which may be translated "naturalistic humanism." It is also common to read that the metaphysics of pragmatism is Experience.

Dewey's naturalistic metaphysics means that all that goes on in the world of nature is part of the continuous evolving natural process. This continuity is true regarding the development of simpler, more complex organic forms and human beings and of thinking. Thinking and philosophy could begin as primary behaviours characterized by pre-reflective activities and end up as logical inquiries. It is the same kind of thinking employed in solving elementary problems in life, perhaps, even akin to the thinking of animals exhibited in their behaviours when in search for food and safety. The one explanatory principle that binds everyone and everything is the biological evolutionary theory. In short, Dewey was an empirical pragmatist and his metaphysics was limited to nature and humanity. Whatever statements there are about them could always be referred back to the world of natural and social phenomena for empirical verification. All that is in nature is all there is.

The world of nature is the experiential, empirical world, characterized by human conflicts and tragedies, by human habits and desires. It is a material, physical world existing on its own right. It is not orderly nor permanent but it is in order and at the same time in a state of flux and movement, process and change, knowing no limits either in its internal make-up or external boundaries. The direction of its dynamic development is dependent, not upon an outside force, but upon its interaction with humanity and its events. The evolutionary process suggests that all that there is in the world and what the world is now are the results of such interactions. The world could be other than what it is.

Man is continuous with nature and shares its traits. As nature evolves, so does man. His innate nature, if there is one, consists of impulses which activate him. Habits, which are acquired, give direction and provide a goal for impulses. Intelligence, which may also become a habit, is actuated when habits break down, due to certain lapses or lags, and are no longer capable of providing a smooth relationship with one's changing environment. To restore such a relationship is the task of intelligence. This is done when man transacts or interacts with nature resulting in problems being solved and new objects and features created. At the same time this also increases one's powers and control over the interactive processes and develops more insights into nature's traits, assuming that he has learned from his interactive experience. Given the changes, the next problems that confront man could be more demanding and complex necessitating changes in exploratory and searching activities. Life is enriched with new possibilities, broadening one's relationships. The necessary interaction between nature and man develops and enhances all truly human powers and imbues the environment with reason and intelligibility. Its *ultimate aim* is to improve the quality of man's interactive process, his practical intelligence, with his environment exemplified in his activities, whether they be aesthetic, religious, socio-ethical or scientific, thereby resulting in the transformation of raw materials of nature into social goods or beautiful objects.

Man is not, however, reducible to nature and subject to its processes. The existential world is, in part, predictable and, in part, ambiguous, full of contingencies and possibilities, providing man with sources of freedom in the world. He can act on and convert them into instruments for the creation of public social good. The exaltation of all potential human powers, pitted in creative tension against all that is uncertain and hazardous in nature is Dewey's humanism. Man and nature are necessarily dependent upon each other for nourishment and growth, hence, man-in-nature, but each one is not reducible to the other. Naturalistic humanism is the necessary interaction between man-in-nature resulting in intelligible growth or experience. In what way may experience be considered pragmatic metaphysics?

Pragmatic Metaphysics: Experience

If Experience is metaphysics, then Experience is logically prior, basic, to any and everything in the world. The undistinguished totality, named "Experience," is the matrix of all things. Objects and subjects are derived from or arise out of it as one engages in an interactive way with the environment. No interactions/experiences taking place means no creation of distinctions or differentiations. These distinctions, or outcomes of experiences, are not ready-made, existing on their own, independent of an agent. For them to arise, there must be an experiencing process involving man-in-nature. When a connection or relationship is established between man-in-nature, experience (outcome/ consequence) emerges. Experience is not in either man or nature but in the *relationship* that arises between them. But basic to the emergence of this relationship and other relationships (e.g., objects which are also constituted of relations) is the experiencing/interactive processes engaged in by man-in-nature. As soon as the experiencing processes cease, there is only the unanalyzed totality named "Experience." If the task is to establish connections/ relationships between man-in-nature, for their continuous development and growth, then basic to it is the experiencing process. *The experiencing process is the pragmatic metaphysical reality.* Not to bring about and engage in the experiencing or interactive process with one's environment is also not to engage in reality. For without the interactive process, brought about by man in the environment, there is no reality to speak of. There is only the *evolutionary process of nature.* Unguided, undirected by man's ideas and allowed to go on its natural ways, it will not yield knowledge, outcomes of inquiry, or objects of distinctions. There only remains the unanalyzed totality to which the name Experience is given.

Since there are no ready-made entities, not even truth, enjoying existence and reality outside of experience, so there are no antecedent conditions to matters of inquiry. In solving a problem, one cannot begin with the question "What is truth" but rather with "How do we come to know what is true of this problem?"

Pragmatic Notion of Truth

Pragmatic truth is man-made. It is the result of man's successful inquiry into his problems, which act of inquiry is characterized by careful investigation of matter of fact and by reason. Truth is an end of critical inquiry that is confirmed in its consequences. Truth means scientific or empirical verification. It is a result of the means, techniques, methodologies employed in solving a problem. That is, the way truth is arrived at is also the nature of its outcome, or truth. To say, e.g., that the nature of man is dual, one natural, the other spiritual, is difficult to accept because there is no way of establishing publicly the manner by which such a claim was reached. On the other hand, to say that man's nature consists of impulses which tend to develop into dispositions or set habits is also to say one can find out for himself if this is so or not. As a man-made product, truth is subject to public verification for its acceptance, suggesting a public way of showing whether or not a claim that something is true is true. This is usually taken to mean that the truth asserted "works." Based on evidence and logic, that which was problematic is now rendered determinate and the effects or consequences of the claim can be verified. This does not mean that the truth claim verified guarantees that it is settled forever. It could also be a resource employed to further inquiry or it could be subject to revision in further inquiry. Truth, like everything in the evolutionary process, is tentative.

Truth is also contextual, that is, it works in its own situation. This does not mean that it is not applicable to other situations. Granted that something is unique to each situation, nonetheless, there are common features among them, namely, the presence of some unsatisfactory conditions, doubts, etc., prompting inquiry and their being characteristically *natural* and *human* problems. If successfully solved, all inquiry reinstitutes the individual's harmonious relationship with his environment. The pragmatic point of *continuity of contexts, unity in nature,* suggest that if truth is truth, then it is applicable to other situations. The meaning of one experience grows out of a former experience, leading into a subsequent experience. To make one experience freely available in other experiences is the function of knowledge, says Dewey. What is emphasized in Dewey's contextualism is the actual setting of truth, showing its relationship with the process of inquiry, namely, that truth is not antecedent to it but arises out of it. It is a product, an outcome, of specific instances of inquiry. And all outcomes of experiences or truths, total experience, may be said to constitute different aspects of experience, each one related to and continuous with each other.

How do we come to know what is true (of a given problem)? First, it is necessary to find out if a claimed problem is a genuine problem. A genuine problem arises out of human and actual empirical situations characterized by "active contact with things and persons." It can be solved by employment of human intelligence or logic. Problems that remain outside, over, and beyond human experience are artificial problems. No one knows how to test for the acceptance or rejection of their solutions. The second step is to subject the problem to Dewey's theory of inquiry, commonly known to teachers as the problem-solving approach. Since this will be dealt with again, suffice to mention its different phases here: (1) The Indeterminate Situation; (2) The Institution of a Problem or Problematic Situation; (3) The Determination of a Solution; (4) Reasoning and (5) Experiment.

In sum, truth, for Dewey, is a *practical* instrument of thought. It functions to organize, reorganize, and extend the meaning of one's experiences in order that a more effective adaptation to one's environment could be made. This does not mean adjustment to what is, but to transform the environment by means of what is known about it into an instrument that secures individuals' socially chosen desirable ends. Truth is functional. If it is true, it works.

Given the above characteristics of pragmatic philosophy, how may a pragmatic child be described? A pragmatic child is an agent who acts and interacts with the environmment. Without his acting, experiencing, he ceases to develop and grow and, along with him, the environment. He is an intimate participant in the activities of the world, which he and the world together bring about. These activities, guided by ideas or previous experiences, bring about relationships or connections between the child and his environment. Such results may be termed outcomes of inquiry or knowledge. The knowledge he now possesses the child employs to solve problems of whatever kind, to explore further into his environment, the results of which could lead to the modification of the environment intended to secure desirable social ends. Knowledge to the pragmatic child is participating in the ways and processes of his environment, directing and redirecting them, to secure the greater good of all. So, he engages in popping corn, frying eggs, etc. in order to know the effect of heat on its objects. Knowing their relationship, he attempts to manipulate it in order to achieve his own ends, for example, cooking medium-rare steaks, boiling vegetables, soldering metals, candle-making, etc. To know how to take pictures is to know concepts of light, lenses, refraction, etc. and to use such knowledge to secure solutions to related problems. The pragmatic child knows that questions and answers derived from specific activities eventually would lead to activities in the broader social life, the setting of all human and natural problems. To know the policeman now as a community helper leads to questions of community organization, different community industries, social and political organizations, etc.

A pragmatic child, basically, a knower, is, in part, an active creator of the world which he inhabits. And that which he creates he also subjects to further inquiry, promoting more knowledge, connections with the world. This knowledge, in turn, increases his consciousness of his control over the conduct of inquiry. His intelligent employment of it could mean that the direction and outcomes of future experiences are secured.

To educate such a child, what would Dewey's pragmatic philosophy of education provide? How would his education proceed? The next section attempts to answer these questions in two parts. First, educational statements based on pragmatic philosophy will be made. Second, an illustration of a teaching activity which is characteristic of pragmatic education will be presented. The point in both is to show how the meaning of pragmatic philosophy of education is translated into what Dewey called "Education equivalents as to what to do and what not to do."

II

Pragmatic Philosophy of Education

As suggested previously, Dewey believed that philosophy must animate educational activities, aims, etc. or else schooling becomes "routine empirical affairs" or arbitrary set habits.[2] In translating his pragmatism to education, he arrived at this definition of education: "(Education) is that reconstruction or reorganization of experience which adds to the meaning of experience, and which increases ability to direct the course of subsequent experience."[3] What does this mean?

First: Education is concerned with experience. What constitutes experience? According to Dewey, experience has an active and a passive element, peculiarly combined. The active part is "trying" and the passive, "undergoing." When we experience something, we act on it in an informed way regarding the nature of the problem and our conduct of inquiry. No one experiences something if he does not do anything with it. There are no ready-made experiences existing on their own and waiting to be claimed experiences. One does not experience *experience* — but nature — its stones, plants, people, etc. This means two things. First, for experience to occur an agent and something upon which he acts are required. Whether or not his acts succeed, consequences follow which he may be said to suffer or undergo. That is, when he acts on something, it does not remain passive but rather it does something to him in return. What it does, the consequences that follow, either success or failure, harmony or frustration, etc., depends upon how successful he is in his manner of experiencing or experimenting with it. If guided by ideas, relevant knowledge, then his chances of successfully securing desired consequences are good. But if the experience is guided by habits or routine, then, it may not be a case of experience at all. But whatever the manner, risk is always involved with experience, noting that in pragmatic thinking nothing is absolutely guaranteed in advance.

Experience, in pragmatic thinking, is more clearly understood not as a noun but as a verb, to experience. To experience is to do something to or act in an informed way on the object of experience to bring about certain desired results. The desired results are connected with the process of securing them which was instituted on the object by the experiencing agent. All these constitute experience. If the manner of experiencing an object is correct the desired outcome could be secured. But whether or not it is secured, if the manner is characterized as experience, then the outcome is a learning experience. In Dewey's terminology 'experience' is always a learning experience, constituted of an agent, object of experience, manner of experiencing process, and outcome. The term 'learning experience' does not mean that what one has learned from it, either from his acting on it or from its results, one will necessarily apply to another happening or event. It means that the tendency of disposition to act in an experiencing/experimenting manner on objects, events, etc. could be developed.

Second, this means that experience belongs to nature, and is of nature, that is, characterized by it. What one is experiencing and the results that follow can all be subjected to inquiry, thus showing whether or not the consequences that followed from the experience were intended or predicted to follow. The theory of inquiry is applied to experience, as it is to natural and social events, in order to find out if its results can be warranted. To claim that one has experienced something which cannot be tested, verified, or publicly shown to be true or false, because it is derived from a transempirical world is to use the word 'experience" in the wrong way. It would not contribute knowledge to one's ways of controlling the direction and outcome of future experiences because it is not known whether it is true or false or how it was derived. If it is 'experience,' it is available to other experiences. Experience is in and of nature. To illustrate briefly. Suppose a child *chances* upon a dish of salt and puts lots of it in his mouth. If he cries, this may be taken to be a reaction to the awful salty taste he is suffering from. He sees a connection between his action of putting salt in his mouth and the consequences of his action. It may be said that this is the beginning of experience. However, if after removing all the salt grains from his mouth and he is now pacified he repeats the act, then, this is sufficient evidence that there was no connection seen between his act and the consequence of saltiness in his mouth. If the child desires the taste of salt, his problem is to figure out how to have it in a satisfactory manner. So to constitute experience he repeats the act but now with the *intention* of bringing about a pleasant taste of saltiness. His experience is now guided by such questions as quantity of salt intake, frequency, etc. It could, of course be that after so many experiences/experiments he concludes that to bring about a situation described as pleasant saltiness one must always take salt with something. To constitute experience there must be a connection made between doing (active phase of experience) and its consequences (passive undergoing). And the connection constitutes the *meaning* of his experience. To experience something is to know the *meaning/connection* of one's act and its consequences or the connection between cause and effect, means and consequences, and means and ends. Since for Dewey, the outcome of experience is equated with outcome of inquiry, which is knowledge, so, education is concerned with acquiring or achieving knowledge.

Experience suggests either success or failure. To fail is to repeat the experience in exactly the same way in the same condition. To succeed, or to have learned from the experience, is *to use* one's experience to transform a present condition to a satisfactory one. Taking into account one's previous action with something and its consequences one is led to modify the quality of one's experience with the same thing. Here, something is being done to the previous experience, and a change is exhibited in the person's actions by virtue of his suffering. One, for example, may now take a few grains of salt, eat it with something, say a lemon, etc. The change is not a mere trial and error or hit and miss affair but genuine discernment between the connection of the thing dealt with and its consequence. One has learned from the experience which means a reconstruction of one's experience.

Second: Education is concerned with the reconstruction or reorganization of experience. Granting that outcomes of some experiences could be considered true, this does not mean that there is no possibility of their being shown to be wrong in the future. The conclusion on the combination of salt and lemon may have shown to be satisfactory but further inquiry on the chemical structure of salt and lemon may show that it also induces kidney dysfunctions. Similarly, I know that the nearest route to point A from B is by way of point C. But this may not always be so. At one point in societal development, rugged individualism may have been the correct way of overcoming human and societal problems. But given the changes in society, knowledge of its changing and complex relationships, rugged individualism may have to be reconstructed if it is meant to secure desirable goods. The evolutionary process of natural and social life suggests that truth, outcomes of experiences, are tentative and subject to reconstruction. Of course, true outcomes of experiences could be instrumental to the growth of one's experience.

Third: Education involves cumulative growth in matters of experience. This does not merely mean that there has been a reorganization of experience but, more importantly, that there is increased meaning in one's experiences, that is, increased perception of connections of acts and consequences, means and ends. If one knows A and establishes a true connection between it and B and C and later finds out that B is connected to D and E, then, it may be said that one has increased the meaning of one's experience, or knowledge. A child experiences the connection between heat and light, then heat and combustion, oxidation, temperature, etc. One experience leads to another and both, in turn, could lead to their reorganization.

Growth in experience tends to increase one's capacity to control the direction and outcome of his experiences; expecting, anticipating the securement of certain ends. In one's experiencing, the intelligent element tends to be more explicit, such that even in the trying phase of experience the outcome is already predicted if not ensured. In acting in this manner, one may be said to have succeeded in controlling and directing his experience. This leads to Dewey's fourth point.

Fourth: Education is concerned with increasing one's ability to direct the course of one's subsequent experiences. This means that one can intend for certain consequences to come about; or, in its weaker sense, one can better anticipate what will happen. This ability could be brought about because of one's cumulative experiences in acting on something, in reconstructing the results of one's experiences, and in engaging in the inquiry process. One's increased knowledge of the connections of the different phases of experience and of the different objects experienced contributes to his learning to be competent in the conduct of his experiences. Whereas in a previous experience of being lost in the woods, for example, he panicked, he looked aimlessly at all directions, shouted and yelled for help, hoping that any one of these acts would help, now that his ability to direct his experience is increased, being lost in the woods means, among other things, to figure out where one is, to ask how he managed to arrive at the place, to find out the relationship of the place with the setting of the sun, to note botanical and zoological characteristics of the place as indicators of its location in relation to a place he knows, etc. He reacts in an informed way to the experience as it is and asks; "Where did I go wrong? What matters and ways are relevant to solving problems of being lost?" Along with employing relevant knowledge thus, geography, physics, etc. reasoning regarding the connections of things is controlled. To find that there are bears in the place does not necessarily mean that there are grizzly bears and he is in peril. Employment of relevant knowledge and sound reasoning increases the possibility of success of his experience: he will reach his intended destination. The previous situation of being lost in the woods has been transformed into an instrument for learning and increasing one's ability to direct and secure the consequences of one's experiences. Similarly, the place where one was lost was once a hindrance to his goals. Knowing it transforms it to a means to other future ends. As one increases one's knowledge of his experiences, so also is one's capacity to direct them to his intended goals increased.

Will the individual be lost in the woods again? Yes and no. If yes, it means that the experience will be more complex and demanding with more variables and factors to consider, such as, more people involved in it, most of them dying for lack of food, hazardous weather conditions, etc. But he will not be lost in exactly the same way and condition again because of cumulative experiences. To solve a problem is to be in control of the direction, outcome, and quality of one's experience in solving it. Pragmatic education intends to increase one's control over them. This simple illustration applies also to other problematic situations, simple or complex, social or personal.

Dewey's outcome of experience is also outcome of inquiry, or knowledge. Intelligence is also outcome of inquiry. To be competent in the conduct of one's experience is to be competent in one's conduct of inquiry. In turn, this means that one is intelligent. Pragmatic education is, therefore, concerned with securing knowledge and developing one's intelligence or expertise at conducting inquiries. In other words, to experience and to accumulate knowledge is to learn how to be and to be competent in subjecting it to further inquiry which, in turn, leads to one's growth or education and, in turn, leads to more inquiries and more growth, ad infinitum. Education concerned with experience enables one to continue one's self-education or growth.

In sum, experience is a "unified developing situation,"*an experiencing process.* If education is successful, then a qualitative change takes place in one's experiences, namely, presence of thinking/intelligence, hence, labelled *reflective experiences.* This means that one's life is not subject to the control of external events, is not at the mercy of happenings or guided by unexamined beliefs but subject to one's control by one's learning to control the process of inquiry. To be successful in doing so is also to be intelligent in the conduct of one's life.

Per the discussion above, for an experience to count as constitutive of education, the following criteria must be met: (1) it must be true empirically/ scientifically, (2) it is testable/verifiable, (3) it leads to growth, (4) it is continuous, and (5) it is an inquiring process. What does this mean for education?

Implications for Education and Teaching

Negatively, it means that education is not concerned with mere transmission of knowledge, absorption of information and factual matters, and master of subject matter in its systematized and logical form. The concept of experience, discussed earlier, judges the above to be short of fulfilling the condition of education. Positively, it means that the task of the teacher is to provide the learners with learning situations that could arouse their curiosities and which could be channeled into activities of inquiring that result in knowledge and its increase. And they must also be of the nature of genuine problematic situations in which the learners find themselves. Around them the teacher constructs learning situations or projects. Consider the following illustration on a discussion of drug taking.

Pragmatic Teaching Activity

The teacher begins by asking the class if anyone wants to share something which he has read from the newspaper, heard from the radio, or viewed on T.V., or if there is a need to review discussions on previous lessons. After some discussion interspersed with exchange of social amenities, agreement is reached. At this point the conversation is relaxed, ambiguous and anyone is free to say what he wants to say. This suggests that our thinking moves and develops from one level to another, from pre-reflection to technical thinking depending upon its object and manner of reacting to it. Sensing that there is no issue that is of apparent interest to the students and the discussion is not going anywhere, possibly creating boredom and restlessness in some, the teacher then directs and focuses the discussion on a topic which is of general interest to them, for example, societal problems. The students freely give examples of societal problems and comment on them. If drug taking is mentioned, the teacher could ask the class to dwell on it for the moment. If not, the teacher could raise it himself. Informal comments may be made, for example, recent news items that some movie stars have been found out to be addicted to drugs. Students exchange ideas, opinions, and comments on these items. Some would say: "It is nobody's business how I run my life." Others reply: "But it is illegal to take drugs." Others retort: "But what does drug taking have to do with the law if it means tranquility for one who takes it. When in a euphoric state, the drug taker does not harm anyone." Others try to inform: "When one is in show business, in rock music, or in any business that is under pressure, taking drugs enables one to make it." The curiosity of the class is by now aroused (even if the problem is still ambiguous and vague) especially when they hear some of their members tell of their experiences and reasons for having taken them. A sense of adventure pervade their story telling as they conclude: "Try and decide for yourself."

The comments above raise the question on consequences of drug taking. Disagreements on it easily involve the class in vigorous discussion. From a curious topic, now its transformation into a genuine problematic situation for them is beginning to set in. The discussion may be hypothetical, but the possibility of being confronted with the problem cannot be dismissed. The students reflect: "On what bases does one decide whether or not to take drugs? How does one go about dealing with the problem?" These are critical questions because the students do not know, at this point, how they would answer them. The discussion does not necessarily provide solid grounds for accepting or rejecting one side and not the other.

There are those who may not be bothered by the question because they have fixed and ready-made answers to it, such as fear of their parents/authorities, dislike for tastes of drugs, guilt feelings, etc. Their answers, however, are not quite related to drug taking. They are of no avail to others, contradicting pragmatic thinking that experiences are freely available to other experiences.

Given the disagreements on the consequences of drug taking, and sensing the need for sound suggestions on how to answer the question whether or not to take drugs, the teacher shows them the connection between the act of taking drugs and its consequences by analyzing the chemical components of drugs and their characteristics, for example, the reactions of the body to them. Given the consequences which are scientifically proven and empirically verified, the teacher proceeds to show that, *in fact*, some of these consequences of drug taking among adolescents have been established. The teacher is establishing the truth of the statement that certain consequences are connected with the act of drug taking. On the basis of this information, some answers previously given could be rejected as false, others as true. To provide palpable support for the truth of his statements, the teacher and the class observe actual experiments on these matters being conducted by hospitals, psychological centers, and chemical laboratories. In turn, the class could be challenged to conduct similar experiences, thus, verifying the results themselves. If they do not know enough chemistry to do it, they take time to read on it. If it requires further that a make-shift laboratory be constructed, this adds to the widening of one's perception of faulty thinking that one knows in advance how to go about inquiring into and resolving a problem. Both activities provide them with situations that increase their perception of the connectiveness of things, not only in drug taking, but also in other aspects of life.

All this, however, is only the beginning of the lesson that is being inquired, namely, the determination of the problem of drug taking. Suggestions, such as, societal pressures, family problems, emotional instability, identity crises, etc. could be offered. The teacher and the class elicit common features out of them in order to define the problem thus suggesting solutions. If no satisfactory definition of it is arrived at, the discussion may deal with related topics, e.g., alcohol, pills, tobacco, cigarettes, etc. The history of drug taking may be considered, which, in turn, could suggest that the nature of contemporary society is conducive to drug taking. To test this suggestion it is narrowed to the problem of family situations. Testing means to find out if the suggestion is a result that arises out of the process of inquiry into the problem. To do this, some members of the class may decide to visit drug centres and interview their administrators and some of their patients; others search for ex-drug addicts, and some may engage in reading cases of drug addiction, drug cure, and the history of drug taking. Branching out into community resources means that school interests and problems are related to the larger societal setting. The school and society are not independent of each other. If their findings uphold the suggestion that family situations are primary factors for one's taking of drugs, this means the problem is defined and solutions could be offered. Questions such as who is responsible for helping those in trouble, in problematic family situations, what is being done for them, what laws are legislated regarding sale of drugs, etc. are raised to elaborate on the problem. Having some understanding now of the problem, some members of the class could propose ways to combat the attractiveness of drugs, for example, by promoting lectures on it, dramatizing the problem by a class production of a documentary film on it, or by writing a play about it. These activities, in turn, could raise another question: whether or not they can secure intended consequences. The answers, in turn, create another question, ad infinitum. Of course, it is also possible that one solution after another may fail, because of faulty formulation of the problem. Given knowledge of drugs and their effects, perhaps, the question is not "whether or not to take drugs," but when may one consider taking drugs, when may one never consider taking drugs, who could take them, who should not, never take them, for what reasons, etc. The *old* way of thinking in an *either or* manner is not informative of given problems, hence, not suggestive of appropriate solutions. Reformulating the problem means inquiring into it again, hopefully, to gain insight and develop one's ability in inquiring into a problem and resolving it. The reconstruction of experience leads to growth. Drug taking started as a problem and the process of inquiring transformed it into an instrument for the possibility of creating social goods. This constitutes education as experience.

Observations on the Teaching Activity

The entire exercise touched on the disciplines of science, sociology, law, government, and social welfare. They were employed to enable the learners to understand their problem and help them evolve a solution. They entered into what the learners were doing, hence, participated in their personal experiences. They could not be transmitted in their organized, systematized, and abstracted forms because the growing child is unable to appreciate them in these forms. It is not that the logical organization of knowledge and the psychological process of learning are in opposition of each other but that in learning, unless the child rediscovers what he is learning from his experience, much would be meaningless. The hardships and difficulties of the weavers and spinners which a child may read makes sense to him as he experiences them by actually constructing looms and actually weaving.

Similarly, the need for adult knowledge must be felt to be necessary to facilitate the on-going of what one is doing or experiencing. Interests, for example, may lag in class, especially if no one is learning anything new *and* correct. When this was so the teacher stepped in and directed the class to scientific knowledge on drugs. Likewise, when engaged in popping corn, the child loses interest in it and asks: "what causes corn to pop," he is ready for

simple scientific explanations. Or, when in the process of drawing and drawing, a child is dissatisfied with his product, then he is ready for some instruction
in form, design, technique, relationships, etc. The teacher, as an intellectual
leader, entered the activities at critical points when the students, limited in
their experiences, do not seem to know what to do next.

According to Dewey, to understand correctly the place of subject matter
in teaching is to know how to relate the growing mind of a child to the accumulated minded experiences of humanity. It means the coordination of
psychological and social factors. The former refers to the powers and capacities of a growing child that need to be developed and released so that he can
freely use them; the latter refers to the factors of his social environment which
must become part of the disciplinary realities of use of his powers. That is, he
freely uses his developing powers even as they are being disciplined to meet
and realize social ends. This is to say that an individual is a social individual.
His distinctiveness and uniqueness as an individual could only be developed as
he, in association with others, participates in and contributes to the social
community. So, to develop the powers of a child they must be in the context
of certain activities that require fulfillment of social ends or cooperative activities, thus contributing to a child's sense of social being.

To unite these two factors successfully, it means (1) that the materials fit
the natural capacities of the child at a certain age, (2) that the manner of
presentation is such that what he learns in one situation is carried over to the
next, creating a bit of experimentation in the sense of prediction, whether or
not his success in the past will secure future success, and (3) that a sense of
continuity in experience is established to ensure growth.[4]

The first point simply means that for teaching to be effective it must take
account of matters of fact, established scientifically and psychologically,
regarding all aspects of child development. In this sense the school is child-
centred. It does not mean that the child is the final arbiter of standards or
ends of teaching. Nor does it suggest that the schools should be permissive,
allowing the child to do as he pleases. This means that in teaching and schooling, the materials selected, its manner of presentation must be in accord with
the habits of mind, the tendencies and attitudes of a child given his development. To encourage a child to learn to read at age 4, for example, when his
tendency is to explore his surroundings, to play, and engage in direct personal
interests, is to waste one's time. The curriculum to be meaningful to a learner
must be psychologized, so advises Dewey.

Drug taking is not a suitable topic to a child but it is suitable to teenagers.
But whatever the age and topic, the manner of presentation, as illustrated
here, secures the second point above. Consider the drug taking example again.
If the discussion observed strictly the problem of drug taking as understood
by the pharmacologist, the chemist, the law-makers, the social welfare coun-
sellor, more likely, only interests that related necessarily to their individual
professions and specializations could have been discussed. Nothing new

emerges or evolves. When, however, the learner's stage of development and his interests are taken into account in discussing drug taking, encouraging interaction between the learner and the subject, some *new* items for discussion evolve. These items do not belong strictly to the subject but to the learner's present experiences. The subject matter, however, is instrumental in eliciting them out of the learner making a possible connection between him and the subject. The relationship established is what was previously termed *experience* emerging out of the interaction of subject and object. For the growing child to make sense of drug taking is not to understand it as the pharmacologist, the chemist, the police, etc. understand it but to feel its effect on his on-going experiences. The process of discussion, characterized by conflicts and disagreements, indecisions on how to go about resolving the question, vacillation on the rightness or wrongness of the act, etc., all these throw the learners right in the midst of what must be a traumatic experience of a drug taker. The pressing reality of the question "whether or not to take drugs and why?" and the loneliness that one feels as he himself must answer the question are simply overwhelming. The problem is felt and becomes part of their experience as they undergo certain experiences in trying to understand the magnitude of the problem.

The lesson in verifying test results is carried over to testing whether or not the hypothesis on family situations is acceptable, illustrating points (2) and (3) above. Whatever its results, it could always mean a more thorough and careful formulation of a problem another time. Or, when children experience difficulties in actually weaving and spinning, they learn to question the statement on the evils of the machine age and inquire into its truth. They could say that the benefits of the machine age are not understood, leading to inquiry on its truth or falsity.

The importance of reconstructing one's plans in order to meet certain needs that arise in the process of interacting was evident in the class' decision to read chemistry and to build a make-shift laboratory. They recognized their own need and they learned to secure practical control of methods of work that would help them to obtain their own ends. Reconstruction of experiences goes on even as some experiences are assumed.

A sense of continuity is noted as members of the class branched out into their own interests initiated originally by the drug taking discussion. The employment of different disciplines in solving a problem suggested a continuity and interrelatedness among them. Pragmatically, this means that an activity is not important in itself except as it is a means that enables the learner to begin to experience and continue to experience his self-identity and to identify with interests and objects in an ever-widening environment. From personal interests in drugs, the thinking, now informed by sociology, family situation problems, drug addiction, etc., moves on to social concerns. For the child, there is free play, games, and work, which is a progression of attempts, increasing in complexity, to relate to the environment, to emphasize techniques and rules as well as to plan and figure out how to secure desirable consequences. As an educative experience, consisting of attempts to define the problem, of suggestions for solutions, and tests for the suggested solutions, back to defining a problem, etc., it will lead to growth, more growth and, in turn, to inquiry, further inquiry, etc.

In what way may a growing mind of a child relate to the accumulated minded experiences of humanity (subject matter)? The discussion shows that they participate in the life of a child as instruments that enable him to continue with what he is doing. The adult's understanding of art facilitated the continuance of his activity of drawing. The child participates in humanity's funded knowledge when he employs it and as a result of his experiences with it finds it questionable and subject to inquiry, e.g., the statement on the evils of the machine age. Here, one notes a rudimentary expression of the adult mind, namely, critical inquiry. Achieving this is evidence that the portion of adult material presented to the child was in accord with his on-going experiences and developmental growth. Contact between the child and adult world is made, facilitating his entry into adult life. This requires a pragmatic teaching activity.

In pragmatism, trying and experiencing are always guided by knowledge, ideas, and reasons. No one experiences something blindly. To try something which one does not know and decide on its consequences later is to be subject to something one is not in control of. This can be perilous. The advice "Try and decide for yourself" is accordingly rejected. Pragmatic education is concerned only with *educative experiences*. Throughout the teaching activity, the pragmatic concern for validation of knowledge claims was evident. It is not enough that a teacher transmits something that is true but, more importantly, the question is how it can be established that it is so independent of the teacher's saying so.

Relationship of Pragmatism and Pragmatic Education

The above example suggests that pragmatic education consists mostly of *activities* being engaged in by the learners. How is this related to pragmatic philosophy? Recall that basic to pragmatism is the notion that unless man acts on the environment, directs its development, the natural evolutionary process alone will not yield knowledge, truth, and values. Man, left to himself, builds his own world of thought. His thinking may be logically consistent but irrelevant to his surroundings. He could atrophy and die. It is when man is acting on or interacting with the environment, and the environment, in turn, reacting back at him, that minding, intellectual curiosities are taking place and being developed. Discovering and creating knowledge, values, and truths, and testing them in turn, life is being directed toward certain evolving ends, judged socially desirable and characterized by truth. In their interactions, man and his environment transform the world from being undistinguished in form or problematic, into a set of complex human and social relationships permeated by reason and intelligence. The learners, in the drug taking example, guided by their knowledge of drug taking, are trying to transform a situation that is denying of growth into one that encourages possibilities for creating social goods and growth. Where there was drug taking in their social environment, now different social activities, channeling their energies into socially desirable directions, characterize it. If they are successful, the problem is not merely gotten rid of but transformed into an instrument to transform a disruptive situation into one that encourages experiential undertakings.

Based on the evolutionary theory of life, pragmatic philosophy suggests that there are more or less established truths which can be trusted now but they will not always be true. As evidences relative to knowledge claims of the truth change, so does knowledge of the truth. So the more significant activity in education as experience is not accumulating knowledge but using it as instruments for knowing and learning how to go about assessing truth claims and knowing how they are established. Since truths are man-made, pragmatic education engages the learners in inquiring activities so they will know how to go about creating truth, which, in turn, suggests that they know the process of truth making, know how to direct it such that its outcome is acceptable. *One interacts with his environment not merely for the sake of interacting but for generating and discovering new truths.* Continuous practice in these activities enable the learners to know how to inquire and to manipulate the process of inquiry in order to arrive at or secure one's intended ends. One does not merely wait to see what happens to an experience/experiment but one brings about certain intended results by controlling the inquiring process. The teacher does not merely see if the children will desire to learn to read. He manipulates the situations and places the children in situations which he hypothesizes and judges will bring about the necessity to read. If his intended end is secured, then his manner of inquiring into the question and controlling it is upheld. Similarly, if the solutions to combat drug attraction are successful, this means correct employment of inquiry process.

Pragmatic education insists that life, in itself, does not have meanings, ends, values, or truths. They arise only as man in connection with his environment intends to create them. *In creating them, he is experiencing reality.* Man, of course, could accept whatever is doled out to him by societal authorities, by traditions, etc. and remain inert. This means he is incapable of intellectual exercise and growth. His life is no better than that of any of the lower forms of life, which is one of instinct and reflexes and absence of intelligence. Pragmatic education challenges the learner to experience, to inquire and so to discover and generate truth, create meaning, and experience reality.

Pragmatic Education Distinguished

Pragmatic education differs from other kinds of education in two significant ways. First, its central activities do not consist of learning matters of fact but knowing and learning the rules in making true statements, for example, that the cause of drug taking is the family situation, and the rules in assessing their truth. Subject matter distinction is minimized and each one is viewed as a source for potential projects for classroom learning situations.

Second, the learners do not merely come to know these rules, how they are applied, etc. But they learn to employ them on whatever they are learning. This is popularly known as "learning by doing," meaning that one learns to do something by actually doing it. One learns to cook by cooking; to teach by teaching. The learning consequence is a direct result of one's activity (it is presupposed that one knows what cooking or teaching is). This is common sense, however. Dewey's concern was with *learning by means of problem solving/inquiring*. How may this be related to "learning by doing?"

"Learning by means of problem solving/inquiring" means that the process of learning is problem solving/inquiring and what is learned is an outcome of it. To learn something that is true, for example, that family situations could cause drug taking behaviour, but which learning did not arise out of the process of problem solving could hardly qualify as learning in Dewey's sense. The learning outcome must be the result of the process of inquiring, suggesting a strong connection between process and outcome, means and ends. If outcomes and ends are necessarily part of the process, and without it, there would be none of them, pragmatic education suggests that its basic concern is for learners to learn how to inquire and learn to inquire/problem solve. How is this done? If to learn how to and learn to inquire is by inquiring into something, pragmatic education consists of inquiring into problematic situation activities. Learning to inquire by inquiring into them increases one's ability to master the inquiry process and to control it such that it brings about certain intended ends. The expression "learning by doing" means not merely learning something as a direct consequence of whatever one is doing but learning something by means of doing/engaging in the activity of problem solving/inquiring.

Central to pragmatic philosophy and education is Dewey's theory of inquiry. It was illustrated briefly in the teaching activity and presented in summary form below.

Theory of Inquiry

Inquiry, says Dewey, is "the controlled or directed transformation of an indeterminate situation into one that is so determinate in its constituents, distinctions, and relations as to convert the elements of the original situation into a new and unified whole."[5] Simply put, inquiring is solving problems. The phases of inquiry are:

1. Indeterminate Situation. Thinking/reflecting begins when there is something in the indeterminate situation that perplexes or troubles us. Things do not seem to go the way they should. Our actions fail to secure certain intended consequences. Life is disrupted. This could apply to any aspect of one's total environment. Apart from it there could be no inquiry.

2. The Institution of a Problem. The recognition of and the attempt to solve a problem is called the institution of a problem, the first step of which is to recognize the indeterminate situation. This phase attempts to organize and transform the confused elements into some kind of unity in order to scrutinize it better. This is an important stage because the way a problem is defined already suggests certain solutions. When the class agreed on family situations to be responsible for drug taking behaviour, they instituted the problem.

3. The Determination of a Solution. Stating a problem involves observing and ordering the "facts of the case" of a situation. Some of them, although present, may turn out not to be a part of the problem. Studying them leads to a clearer perception/conception of the problem, resulting in a suggested possible solution, meaning, idea, or hypothesis. Cognitive elaborations on and examination of them, as studied possibilities or plans of action, take the form of reasoning.

4. Reasoning. Reasoning is an examination of the meaning of an idea or hypothesis proposed, that is, to account for all its possible implications before it is accepted. Before any of the hypotheses offered to combat drug attraction is accepted or acted upon, it is subjected to questioning, for example, how relevant is it to the problem, how adequate is it to meet the magnitude of the problem, how does it compare with other suggestions, etc. Whatever the results of the reasoning process, it must show that the hypothesis accepted has a good chance of fulfilling its promise.

5. Experimentation. This means a plan acted out on the basis of the accepted hypothesis. If it fails, inquiry may continue, reexamining the facts and ideas of the case, redefining the problem, etc. If it succeeds, confusion is removed and harmony between the individual and his environment is reinstituted. The person lost in the woods is now on the way to his destination.

As stated, for Dewey, education, concerned with experience, is concerned with inquiry and its outcome is knowledge. Inquiry is part of an on-going natural process of evolution. To engage in it when settling a problem is also to engage in a never-ending process of inquiry. Education as experience/inquiry is continuing one's self-education.

In sum, pragmatic education is concerned with the development of such dispositions as inquiring, questioning, assessing evidences, counter-arguing, testing results, concluding, etc., in short, critical mindedness. The attitudes that tend to be developed are tentativeness, cautiousness, deliberation, or, healthy skepticism. To secure these dispositions, pragmatic education provides problematic learning situations (drug taking lesson, for example,) which require resolution necessitating learners to question, assess, argue, test, etc., that is, to do what they are learning or have learned to do. In continually being disposed to act in this way on whatever one is acting on, hopefully, the inquiring disposition becomes habitual to the pragmatic child.

Given these dispositions, how does a pragmatic child react to authority?

III

The Pragmatic Child, the Teacher, and Authority

The question of authority was chosen because it is often supposed that pragmatic education encourages a negative attitude or disrespect toward authority. A pragmatic child knows no authority other than his own wants and desires. This is a wrong understanding of pragmatic education. The following discussion and illustration will show why this is so.

The illustrated teaching activity showed that the teacher, although in control of the situation, rarely teaches matters which he knows are true of drug taking directly to the class. When he does, his purpose is to remove a difficulty which is inhibiting the activity of the class. The information he provided enabled the class to continue with their learning activity. The teacher is more of a guide to a class than a teacher who teaches items that must be known regardless of their instrumental value to the on-going activities.

The teacher is an authority, because of her position and knowledge of what she teaches. In pragmatism, however, what is taught is not automatically accepted to be true simply because the teacher said so. In the illustration, the class verified the statements of the teacher by conducting their own experiments. Had the experiment contradicted his statements, further inquiry would have been required to determine, not *who* is right or wrong, but, more importantly, *what* is right or wrong scientifically. An appeal to a standard external to both teacher and learners could have been made in order to make a right decision, in this case, to scientific/empirical knowledge of chemistry and drugs. Authority does not reside *in* the person of the teacher if this means standard of correctness derive from him and not from knowledge external to him. He could, of course, be an authority of something over someone because of his knowledge of it. But pragmatic authority is not interested in exercising power over someone but in being instrumental to meeting his needs and to further inquiry. When the learners did not know what to do next, they recognized their need for the teacher to say something which would enable them to go on with their tasks. There is authority in pragmatic education. Its nature and function, however, has to be understood.

Nature and Function of Pragmatic Authority

As illustrated, the teacher's authority, right, to say something, is open and testable. He did not impose or intrude. Noting the learners' frustrations, the teacher's right to say something is publicly upheld. And what he said was testable. Pragmatic authority knows no dogmas and is open to public scrutiny for questioning anytime. It is also transitory. In the process of conducting their interviews and experimentations, it is possible that the learners will come to know more about drugs than the teacher. They are authority over the teacher in this regard. So, one does not always have the right to exercise authority over someone simply because one did so before. Pragmatic authority does not reside in the person. It is not a given, fixed and external, but is acquired and transferable to someone else.

Appealing to scientific knowledge for a correct decision on drugs and its effects, suggests that pragmatic authority is not personal or private. It is organized or collective intelligence which consists of verified/verifiable statements on matters of the world, and human/social relationships, or, products of methods of inquiry. To this organized intelligence one submits one's expressions of intelligence for its acceptance or rejection. In sum, pragmatic authority is constituted of collective intelligence and methods of inquiry.

The illustration showed that the exercise of authority by the teacher was conditioned by critical moments in the activities of the class, of the child popping corn and the child engaged in drawing. The teacher exercised authority only when something blocked the learner's activity and the learner could not transform it into something instrumental to achieving his goal. This means that an authority need not be exercising his authority over the learners on all things all the time. An authority functions only to meet certain critical needs that arise out of particular situations.

For the pragmatic child, authority functions to provide grounds for facilitating the conduct of on-going meaningful activities. It judges areas of freedom to curtail because in so doing it expands, enlarges, and encourages other areas of freedom which are more meaningful to present direct experiences of the learner. The teacher stopped the discussion and exchange of views on drug taking when it was going nowhere and directed them to scientific knowledge. Curtailment is justified because necessary and relevant freedom to do what is meaningful to do was secured. The class could move on to the resolution of the problem. Authority functions to liberate and release those in his care from unnecessary encumbrances, whether they be rules, doubts or perplexities, customs, etc. and to enable them to go on with the conduct of their activities in a meaningful way.

An important function of pragmatic authority is to develop learner's competency in the conduct of the inquiry process so that he knows how to arrive, *on his own*, at warranted conclusions which could become part of collective intelligence. So learning situations that require the employment of pattern of thinking by means of inquiry are provided. As the learner increases his capacity and develops his ability to employ the inquiry process he also develops independence from an authority. When there are no critical needs in the class this means that it is carrying on with its activities guided and directed by the authority or order of the pattern of inquiry, unhampered by unnecessary intrusion of the teacher as authority.

It may be said that a pragmatic child is his own authority in the sense that he is learning to direct and redirect his own experiences utilizing changes or hindrances as instruments for realization of his chosen goals. In another sense, he is not his own authority. There is authority external to him constituted of methods of inquiry and collective intelligence which judges the acceptablity of his products of inquiry and which authority is binding on all. The pragmatic child's freedom is limited to and conditioned by such an authority. He acts toward or on something in an informed way — not just in any way. The task of the pragmatic teacher as an authority is to facilitate this development of the learner's sense of authority by meeting his critical needs when they arise and to enable him to be competent in the conduct of inquiry, which is authority.

Pragmatism suggests that authority, like other relationships, is not a given. It arises in the context of relations and is instituted to meet and fulfill certain needs. When the need is met, authority ceases to function. How may authority arise?

A Case Illustration

Suppose a group of children, varying in age from 8-12, are in a plane crash which landed in a jungle. They are unharmed. All other passengers are dead. There is enough food to last them for a month. How may the children react to this situation after their fears have been calmed down?

The children knowing that they are by themselves, with no adults to interfere, do anything they want to do. Freedom and adventure characterize their reaction. It is another camping spree!

After a few days, however, some of them fail to return during the night. No one seems to know where they went. Some one suggests: "For our safety, we should organize as a group with a leader to guide our conduct. In this way, we will be safe. It is dangerous to be lost in the jungle." Another asks: "But how do we choose the leader?" "By election," is the quick retort. A question is raised: "What qualities should a leader in our case have?" A child, tending to be pragmatic in his ways, joins: "Why is the question of leadership crucial? What is our problem?" His point is that a solution is being offered in advance of knowing and instituting the problem. So, an assessment of their situation begins.

They are in the jungle, no one knows where. What should they do to secure help, build a fire, fly white flags, etc.? How long will they survive? Conclusion: they are lost and they need help. Meanwhile, the lost members have returned. The leadership question is taken up again, arguing that the questions above could be solved if there were one to direct in answering them. An election is held, accompanied with proper speeches and make-believe music. In the midst of merriment, the pragmatic child butts in: "All these are irrelevant to our case. If the problem is to find a leader who can lead us back to civilization, election and fine speeches will not do. Is there anyone here who has had experience in dealing with a situation similar to ours?" A response is made.

The leader begins by exercising his authority over them. They are divided according to duties he perceives necessary, e.g. kitchen staff, food gatherers, and guardians. A secretary is appointed to record their meetings and his first appointive act. At the first meeting, it was suggested that the leader should be seated on a dais so as to distinguish him from them. Someone discoursed on history: "There was once a lost tribe that managed to develop a high degree of culture and civilization. Alas, this tribe has vanished forever. But what they did was splendid!" He noted that in Parliament, there are symbols of authority, a gavel, a mace, etc. The pragmatic child chides: "Having determined our problem, the next thing to do is figure out an appropriate solution. All this talk is not related to our problem." A child agrees: "Yes, I perceive that there are mysterious things going on which we are not in control. I see them clearly in my vision. If we look within ourselves, you will know what I am talking about. I am afraid." His comment, although perhaps perceptive, does not contribute to the resolution of their problem because it is too metaphysical, thus, irrelevant. The pragmatic child suggests: "First, we take account of our food supply. Second, we make a study of the place. This could give us clues as to where we are. And we may find things to eat as well. The question of survival must be secured; then we look for help."

While the pragmatic child makes sense, the leader suspects that his power is being eroded: "I have been acclaimed as leader. It is my duty to see to the welfare of the group. From now on, what I have to say must be obeyed." The pragmatic reply: "What if your acts bring about disastrous consequences?

Should we obey you?" The leader: "How can you tell in advance whether or not consequences are disastrous? We must simply try." The reply: "This is faulty reasoning. Before we act out something, it must be subjected to reasoning and questioning. Our chosen plan of action, at least, could promise that it will secure our ends: to find help. It is dangerous to act on something blindly." The leader: "Again, I insist that I must be obeyed." The pragmatic child: "I disagree with you. Your authority is not in your person. It arose out of our particular need but you misunderstood it to mean authoritarianism, to uphold your authority because you are authority. Proper authority facilitates the resolution of a problem by removing hindrances or making them instrumental to the realization of our goals. For example, we could use the place to increase our capacity for survival by investigating it as thoroughly as we can." The leader: "These are worthy suggestions. But you could be wrong." The pragmatic child: "I admit. But if we exercise reason and inquire into our plans of actions, we could ensure that only certain consequences are brought about. The point is that we act on something in an informed way, not blindly or irrelevantly."

Sensing the futility of their discussion, the pragmatic child addresses the group: "What in your judgement should we do now?" The reply: "Perhaps, we have been carried away by our imagination regarding our situation. We tried to bring over practices that are meaningful in other places and they have failed to work here. They did not arise out of our problems. The gavel used in the meetings is out of place and the secretary is a joke! So, we suggest that we redefine the problem, think of a plan of action, subject it to reason, and depending upon the results of reasoning process, we act on it. Knowledge and reason must control our inquiry." The leader cuts in: "What of the leadership?" The pragmatic child: "the right kind of leadership or authority is one that enables us all to increase our capacity for participating in and contributing to the solution of our problem. Authority facilitates the fulfillment of social goals, our survival, which are the grounds for developing our individual distinctiveness. Having done so, we make a *social return*, that is, participate in and contribute to our social good. Your authority arose out of our situation. Its practice must be relevant to our situation. You have failed. It is not important who authority is but whether or not authority enables us to overcome difficulties at critical points in our attempts at inquiring into and solving our problems. Authority guides our reasoning and thinking. In so doing, true connections between ourselves and our environment could be established. This means we will survive and be rescued. What should discipline us is what we collectively know to be true of our situation and of the process of inquiring into things. This is our authority, not persons." On this note, the group sits down and interacts with each other, subjecting offerings to question, etc., in an attempt to arrive at a true definition of their situation. Whereas their previous experience was uncontrolled and uninformed by knowledge and reason, now the theory of inquiry is the controlling qualitative difference to their experience. The reconstructed experience has led to growth.

Whether or not the children will survive, or be rescued, depends upon their mastery and control of the inquiry process. What is sure, however, is that the children will not revert to savagery or animism. In their conduct of inquiry is the controlling presence of intelligence and rationality which, in turn, characterizes their disposition.

Conclusion

How does a pragmatic child act? A pragmatic child acts in response to a problematic situation that he senses, feels, and discerns in his relationship with his environment. He acts in a manner characterized by reflective, critical inquiry the intentions of which are to transform a problem into a possibility for realizing human social goods and to direct and redirect future experiences into desirable social ends. A pragmatic child inquires into what he is experiencing and, in turn, inquires into the inquiring process itself. In so doing, he creates and secures knowledge and transforms it into an object of inquiry and so he continues his self-education. The world of a pragmatic child is characterized by a realm of inquiry inquiring into objects of inquiry and into inquiry itself. Toward what end? To establish true connections between himself and the world around him and in the process both are transformed into relationships expressive of that which pragmatically true, good, and beautiful.

Notes

[1] John Dewey, *Democracy and Education* (New York: The Macmillan Co., 1964), pp. 331-328.
[2] For a direct application of pragmatic education to an actual school situation, see: Katherine Camp Mayhew and Anna Camp Edwards, *The Dewey School* (New York: Atherton Press, 1966).
[3] *Democracy and Education*, p. 76.
[4] See Katherine Camp Mayhew and Anne Camp Edwards, *The Dewey School*, pp. 20-36.
[5] John Dewey, *Logic: The Theory of Inquiry* (New York: Henry Holt and Co., pp. 8-9; 140.

References

John Dewey, *The Child and the Curriculum* (Chicago: The University of Chicago Press, 1902).
_____*Democracy and Education* (New York: The Macmillan Co., 1964).

_____*Logic: The Theory of Inquiry* (New York: Henry Holt and Co., 1938).
_____*The School and Society* (Chicago: The University of Chicago Press, 1943).

Katherine Camp Mayhew and Anna Camp Edwards, *The Dewey School* (New York, Atherton Press, 1966).

Psychology and the Child: Homer Lane and J.B. Watson

Peter J. Miller

As an academic discipline and as an experimental science, psychology is now a little over one hundred years old. In that period, it has come to exert an increasingly important influence on almost every aspect of western culture; our political and economic life, our literature, art, music and sport all have been transformed by the findings of psychology and their applications. By far the more important contribution of psychology, however, has been its enrichment of our understanding of childhood and the provision of a scientific knowledge base for radically new systems of childrearing.

Interestingly, despite an increasing acceptance by scientists of evolutionary theory and a widespread interest in discovering the origins of man, in the initial period of the development of the new science little interest was shown in the problems of childhood and child development. Indeed, the generally acknowledged father of modern psychology, Wilhelm Wundt, explicitly rejected the possibility of there being a scientific experimental and distinctive child psychology.

> Since in the investigation of children and of savages [he wrote in 1897] only objective symptoms are in general available, any psychological interpretation of these symptoms is possible only on the basis of mature adult introspection which has been carried out under experimental conditions.[1]

Wundt, in fact, "staked the future of psychology and the definition of the experimental procedure itself on introspective mental analysis. There was no place for child or animal in such a scheme. . . ."[2]

Within a few years, however, Wundt's particular view of experimental psychology had been swept aside, and child psychology was not only a fully integrated dimension of psychology in general, but perhaps its most controversial, vital and socially influential branch. Wundt's objections had been overcome — and from two quite different directions. On the one side, the associationists and behaviourists insisted that "introspective analysis" was entirely a subjective process and thus had no place in a genuine science of psychology. For them, Wundt's "objective symptoms" required no introspective mediation and in themselves constituted the raw data which a science of psychology could utilize and exploit. From this point of view, the various behaviours of mature adults, of children and, indeed, of animals were not dissimilar in kind to that of other objects in nature; all could be subjected to investigation, analysis and explication. Indeed, since the behaviours of animals and children were less complex than those of adults and thus more easily investigated and understood, the study of both had a particular significance. Childhood, in fact, was at once the seedbed of adult behaviour and a laboratory for the investigation of its causes.

From the other side, Wundt's views regarding the possibility of a child psychology were assailed by the findings and beliefs of psycho-analysis. The discovery of the existence and significance of the unconscious as a source of behaviour; the insistence that the unconscious could be probed and its effect on the personality understood; the belief that in the conflicts of the inner life of the child were to be found the answers to the questions which beset man in his attempt to understand the mature human being in his relationship to society — all these elements in psycho-analytic theory tended to make the study of the child indispensable. Seen alongside such beliefs, Wundt's objections were but trifling ones. For both psycho-analysis and behaviourism the child was seen as "father to the man." And for both an investigation and understanding of childhood was a necessary precondition for any successful attempt to investigate and understand the adult personality and adult behaviour.

Both associationism and psycho-analysis had a European origin, and, in this origin, demonstrated a distinctively European lack of optimism about man and society. Pavlov, who is generally regarded as the most important of the early associationists, was deeply skeptical and thoroughly pessimistic about the possibility of his work being of any value to psychology, or indeed of psychology to man and society.[3] And Freud, the founder of psycho-analysis, remained throughout his life deeply pessimistic about the possibility of societal progress or improvement.

In the young and vibrant atmosphere of early twentieth-century North America, however, a quite different mood prevailed. Here man had already escaped his past and the errors of his ancestors; here inherited tendencies could be discounted; here man could overcome his own and others' weaknesses. And provided the environment was a healthy one, provided he was reared (and schooled) properly, then the constant improvement of both man and society was not only possible but inevitable. Health, prosperity and, of course, happiness all lay within the grasp of man.

There were a number of sciences which provided insights into the origins and character of human behaviour. Biology, the emerging medical sciences, even the new science of sociology — all in one form or another helped strengthen and broaden the base of the optimistic view of man and society current in early twentieth-century North America. But it was psychology, the queen of sciences, which seemed to promise most success in explaining, predicting and, above all, helping to control man's behaviour. Of course, scientific theory, even psychological theory, was in itself of little value. Theory must be made relevant, must be translated into concrete directions for action and into specific program proposals. In short, theory had to be viewed and treated pragmatically.

Given its reductionist tendencies, it is, perhaps, not surprising that it was associationism rather than psycho-analytic theory which held most potential for this transatlantic shift in orientation from skepticism and pessimism to strident dogmatism and optimism. Indeed, the 'new psychology' of behaviourism was to become the dominant and most distinctive school of American psychology, one which was to play a "prominent role in the cultural and social life of the time."[4] As Bergman has correctly pointed out, North American psychology, particularly behaviourism, tended to become social philosophy and even prophecy.[5]

Psycho-analytic theory, on the other hand, contained no such social gospel and, perhaps for this reason, had little impact on North American psychology. Even now, it retains a European character. For while psycho-analysis carries with it the hope of personal reformation and salvation, it offers no such promise to society. Indeed if it can be said to possess a social mission, it is radically to criticise society for its failure adequately to meet the needs of the individual. It is, as A.S. Neill often asserted, optimistic about the child, pessimistic about adults.[6]

Despite these differing orientations and the different basis of their appeal, both behaviourism and psycho-analytic theory had this in common — that their findings were easily popularized, even vulgarized, and could be translated into general theories of childhood and systems of childrearing. Behaviourism tended to buttress, if not provide a fresh inspiration for, an already powerful existing social control philosophy deriving from nineteenth-century Benthamite utilitarianism, and to provide a rationale for a more systematic control of the child in the name of social progress. Psycho-analytic theory, on the other hand, assumed a primarily reactive and protesting stance towards societal conventions and norms, and especially towards its childrearing practices. As such it spawned childcentred and libertarian educational theories.

In the important task of creating rival systems of childrearing from the findings of contemporary psychology, two men are of particular significance. They are Homer Lane, perhaps the most significant figure in psycho-analytic progressivism, and J.B. Watson, the father of behaviourism. In their lives and work are revealed at once the characteristic strength and characteristic flaw of psychology and its influence on contemporary childrearing — on the one hand, the high expectations it has generated concerning the possibility of producing model children and model adults; on the other its consistent failure to produce what it has promised.

Homer Lane (1875-1925)

In no sense can Homer Lane be said to have been a professional psychologist or to have made any contribution to the development of psychology as an academic discipline. Intellectually his theory and practice were entirely derivative, incorporating many of the concepts and discoveries of psycho-analysis, developmental psychology, and the psychology of learning that were current in his lifetime, although he applied them in his own unique way to the problems he himself faced in education. He was according to Perry "perhaps the greatest man thrown out by the [progressive education] movement on the side of personal relationships."[7]

He was born in 1875, in a small town in Massachusetts.[8] Like several other well-known progressive educators, notably Dewey and A.S. Neill, his parents were of strict evangelical leanings. After leaving schools at an early age, Lane pursued a number of occupations in Massachusetts, eventually deciding upon a teaching career. He attended the Sloyd Training College in Boston where, in all probability, he attended lectures by John Dewey, who was then teaching at nearby Harvard. The central ideas in the Sloyd system were the respect it sought to engender in children for physical labour and its almost complete lack of coercion of the child who was, as much as possible, to be self-regulated both in his work and his play. Lane's studies in the Sloyd Training College and his subsequent experiences in school teaching convinced him that coercion bred anti-social behaviour and delinquency in children, and that only freedom and self-regulation could result in the child's acquiring a sense of responsibility.

In 1901, Lane had his first contact with convicted juvenile delinquents in the Pennsylvania State Reformatory where he attempted to apply his ideas of work and self-regulation to prison education. From there he moved to Detroit where, for several years, he was employed as a teacher and as Superintendent of Playgrounds for the city. Once again, he took advantage of his position to apply his philosophy of freedom for the child — once again, with notable success. In 1906, he was offered the Superintendency of an experimental residential institution for wayward boys, the Ford Republic. Here he instituted a much discussed and very successful system of complete self-government among the inmates. Lane's reputation as an innovative educator was growing and increasingly over the next few years he was invited to lecture on problems of delinquency and education.

By 1913, his work was so highly regarded among advanced thinkers in the field of child delinquency that he was invited by George Montague, the Earl of Sandwich, to come to England to advise on the establishment of an institution patterned after the Ford Republic.[9] The establishment was to be known as the Little Commonwealth and, following its creation, Lane was appointed as its Superintendent. This unique community consisted of some fifty individuals, eight or nine children, four or five grownups, and some forty boys and girls between the ages of fourteen and eighteen. The young people had been sent there either by magistrates or by parents who found them simply too difficult or inconvenient to handle. Most of the time the community was divided into two families, each containing about twenty boys and girls, together with a house mother and one or two adult helpers. Each family lived together and, equally important for Lane, worked together. As much as possible, the Commonwealth was to be economically self-sufficient. Both boys and girls were expected to look after the cottages, tend the gardens, take care of the laundry and work on the farm. The farm work was extensive, involving the care of dairy cattle, pigs, sheep and horses. Plowing, sowing, harvesting, hedging and ditching, timber-felling, building, carpentry, all were part of the yearly round of work in the Little Commonwealth. It was, in many respects, a North American frontier farm transported into the gentle English country-side of Dorset. Lane's philosophy of education, of course, would not permit any coercion to be used in getting children to work in the community. As Lane explained to the citizens of the Little Commonwealth, "We came here to do as we like, and so long as we like to break windows, yell, take fruit and live at the expense of others, we would do so. If at any time we felt like doing something else that was more fun we would do that."[10]

This wholehearted commitment to the principle of freedom for the child led inevitably to the principle of self-government, that is to the right of the citizens of the Commonwealth to make their own laws and to elect the authority they agreed to obey. In the Little Commonwealth there was thus no authority to defy except that of the whole community. Meetings of citizens fourteen years and older were held at least twice a week. Here the community could debate policy matters, elect its officers, hear complaints and grievances, and, where necessary, dispense punishments.

Instruction was offered daily in a number of subjects and the children were encouraged to attend whatever classes interested them. Lane found this aspect of the work of Little Commonwealth somewhat disappointing and in 1917, just before its closure, was making plans to introduce a more systematic form of intellectual and particularly aesthetic education. On alternate Sundays, the local vicar held a service in the assembly hall which was generally well attended. A.S. Neill, who dined at the Little Commonwealth almost every Sunday night for a period of two years or so, was impressed with the behaviour of its 'citizens', noting that they were "quiet, social, gentle young men and women."[11]

Although Lane tried desperately and generally successfully to avoid the appearance of an authority figure, he could not prevent himself from becoming the emotional cornerstone of the community. Upon him were focussed all the hopes and fears of his adult co-workers for the success of the experiment. More importantly, he quickly became the centre of the immature emotional life of the children and adolescents. It was, perhaps, inevitable that the emotional intimacy generated between Lane and the rest of the community would become so highly charged that it would explode and eventually destroy both it and Lane himself.

Within a year or so of Lane's appointment as Superintendent of the Little Commonwealth, his approach to educational issues became increasingly influenced by his readings in the area of Freudian theory. Soon, he had succeeded in creating a unique brand of psycho-analytic theory, one which drew equally upon Freudian concepts and his own teacher training and experience. At this time he began to apply his theories in group therapy sessions with the inmates. Lane's tendency to treat every relationship with an inmate of the Little Commonwealth in therapeutic terms resulted in a number of stormy incidents and crises. Eventually in 1918 two of the girls accused Lane of improper behaviour and the subsequent inquiry, although vindicating Lane, resulted in the closing of the Institution.

Lane then moved to London where he lectured and practised, apparently very successfully, as a psycho-analyst. Among his "students," as he called his patients, were a number of influential figures, among them the Earl of Lytton, later Viceroy of India, and A.S. Neill. At this time Lane was perhaps at the height of his popularity and influence. In 1925 at the very height of his success, however, another scandal broke out when the family of one of his patients brought charges against him of improper behaviour. Although, again, it seems that Lane was entirely innocent in the matter, the pressures that government officials brought to bear against him were so great that he offered to leave the country in return for the dropping of all proceedings. Within a few months, while in Paris, he contracted typhoid which led to pneumonia and his death from heart failure.

Despite his revolutionary educational philosophy and enormous energy, Lane was not a writer. Indeed, he produced not a single book in which he presented his ideas on education. As A.S. Neill rather spitefully noted, "Lane could not write for he was not an "educated" man. His correspondence, written on postcards, abounds in mis-spellings."[12] He was, however, always willing to talk about his ideas, either informally or formally. He was, moreover, a forceful speaker, able to project his strong personality and to capture his audience both heart and mind. And, of course, he did have something to say about childhood and childrearing that was new and exciting.

These ideas he had developed over the course of his lifetime. Hemmings notes three stages in the development of Lane's educational thought.[13] The first stage was formulated shortly after his initial contact with juvenile delinquents, in whom he quickly recognized "a tendency to do right which had been twisted by the environment into what had the appearance of wrong." In a situation where the child was denied any freedom for self-expression, only two alternatives presented themselves, to become a criminal or to be a failure. According to Lane the former is the expression of the human soul still fighting against domination, and the latter that of a soul defeated. Lane's program at the Ford Republic was based upon this belief in the central importance of freedom, self-reliance, self-government and self-respect. The second stage in the development of Lane's philosophy of education was reached after he left the Ford Republic and arrived in England to take up work at the Little Commonwealth in Dorset. There he increasingly fell under the influence of psychoanalytic theories and formulated the central message of his subsequent teaching, that those who would help the child must not only be on his side but must fully accept and love him for what he was. The final and mature stage of Lane's thought was reached just as the Little Commonwealth was on the point of collapsing. Lane realized that his "failure" at the Little Commonwealth was not due to the theory he had subscribed to but rather his refusal to accept all of its implications. It was not enough for the teacher to accept or love the child; just as important the teacher must be willing to accept the love that the child had to give. And what was true for the child was equally true for the adolescent. There could be no backing away from what Lane referred to as the "transference phenomenon," which inevitably occurred in all teacher-pupil relationships. Lane's final position regarding childrearing may be characterized by the words total freedom, total trust, total support, and total love.

Lane's final recommendations concerning childrearing were thus based upon a mixture of North American environmentalism and progressivism, Freudianism, and developmental psychology, which he expressed in a series of talks and lectures to whomever would listen. Many of these were collected after his death and published in the book, *Talks to Parents and Teachers*, which is now regarded as the major source of his ideas concerning childhood and childrearing. Somewhat ironically it was the enquiry into the scandal at the Little Commonwealth that forced Lane to prepare his clearest exposition of his theory of education. Following the report of the commission of inquiry in June, 1918, Lane formally addressed the founders of the Little Commonwealth in an attempt to explain the theory he had been employing and the reasons why things had not worked out as they should.[14] From these sources can be pieced together and constructed Lane's fully developed theory of education.

Lane constantly acknowledged his debt to Freud, "the pioneer in the science" of psycho-analysis. And indeed Lane's 'theory' employs a number of key Freudian concepts. It is doubtful, however, if Freud would have recognized, let alone approve, the particular version of his ideas developed by Lane. The fundamental instinctive drive in man, that which lies at the base of all his motive forces, Lane identified as a deep seated impulse to create, which was, in his view, sexual in nature. By accepting this 'Freudian' insight, Lane claimed that he had been able to utilize Freud's technique of psycho-analysis for educational purposes.

> I have tried [claimed Lane] to use his technique in education, in the build-
> ing up of lives of joy and usefulness. He corrects insanity, I am trying to
> create sanity . . . So far as I am aware, no other teacher has attempted to
> employ the Freudian method systematically in any school, I have not had
> the benefit of any other teacher's experience in a parallel effort.[15]

Lane thus saw himself as "a pioneer in psycho-analytic education."[16]

Lane's practice of psycho-analytic education was based upon a particular
developmental theory which, he claimed, was also derived from Freud. Affec-
tive and cognitive development as well as social and moral awareness were all
intimately and inextricably related; moreover all were built upon deep seated
instinctive and unconscious processes in man's mental and emotional life. The
first stage in what Lane saw as a developmental cycle is infancy, which lasts
from birth to about the age of three years. It is characterized by the "craving
to create life or sexual hunger"[17] and this instinctive drive to express sexual
energy and carry it onwards to a higher form must never be thwarted. Of
course, the wise parent will make the right thing very easy for the child to do
and the wrong thing very difficult. But the infant's desires must always be
satisfied, his will never crossed. At this stage of his life, the child is wholly
amoral and no moral judgements can be made about any of his behaviours,
all of which arise from his naturally good instinctive drives. According to
Lane, "a prescription for utopia in the nursery — abandon three adjectives:
naughty, nasty, dirty."[18]

With the growing awareness of physical and emotional dependency upon
significant adult figures, at about the age of three years, the child enters the
"age of imagination." At this stage the child seeks a new way to express his
creative impulses, that of fantasy. Using the power of imagination, the child
can transcend his real world and his inherent weaknesses, and enter a world
where he is great, strong and significant. During this period of childhood,
libidinal impulses are directed towards love of parents. Once again, no behaviour which springs from the child's instinctive needs or his creative impulses
can be considered inappropriate or immoral. Thus lying, a characteristic
behaviour of the child at this age is either "creative lying" or "lying for self-
protection", and both must be accepted by the wise parent as appropriate at
this stage.

From about the age of seven until the age of eleven, the child is in the
"age of self-assertion," a period of heroism and almost total disregard for
danger. Here sexual energies express themselves in enormous mental and
physical activity, and the child is frequently noisy, blatant and disagreeable.
In order for the child to assert his selfhood, it is necessary that he confront
authority and manifest a certain degree of aggressiveness. Both these apparently anti-social tendencies are necessary for the redirection of the child's
libidinal impulses and the development of social instincts. Allowed to work
themselves out at this stage in freedom, they will not survive childhood. Free-

dom is thus necessary for instinctive tendencies to be developed and their demands outgrown and carried to a higher level.

Lane's message to parents and teachers concerning the nature of childhood and childrearing is beautifully illustrated in his parable of the rabbit and the dog.[19] Lane contrasts the emotions of a rabbit with that of a dog who is chasing it. The dog feels happy because he lives in the hope of achievement — that is, catching and presumably eating the rabbit. The rabbit, on the other hand, is unhappy because it fears the very thing that the dog is out to achieve. Sometime later the situations are reversed. The dog lies panting outside the rabbit's burrow, frustrated and disappointed that the rabbit got away. At the same time the rabbit lies deep and safe in the ground, happy and contented in the knowledge that it is safe and no longer danger. Lane terms the happiness of the rabbit in the burrow possessive happiness. It arises from the fear of death and the desire for security, and is essentially negative and destructive of all forms of creativity. Yet it is the happiness that is normally held out to the child as being most worth having. Traditional teachers and traditional parents produce 'rabbits,' who will crouch contentedly in the womb of society. The happiness of the dog Lane terms creative happiness. It arises from the pursuit of an instinctive drive and the desire to achieve and create. And although it inevitably involves an element of danger, surprise or uncertainty, it is the only kind of happiness worth having. What parents and teachers must do is clear; they must avoid developing the rabbit in the child and allow the dog free development.

At about the age of eleven the child begins to develop a social consciousness during "the age of loyalty." The non-reflective love of parents has now been supplemented by the love of neighbours. In the early period of this stage, up to the age of fourteen, the child seeks to merge his individuality in that of a group. He is ready to cooperate with others for a common purpose and realizes his own goals in those of the group. The major tasks facing the parent and teacher at this stage of the child's development are to help the child maintain his unique self-identity, to keep alive his instinct for play, and to prevent his curiosity being deadened by the constraints of institutions. These tasks are best carried out by giving the child freedom, including the freedom of conscious wrong-doing. Above all, where groups of children have been formed, it involves democratic self-government.

During the stage of adolescence, from roughly fourteen to eighteen years, the emotional content of the child's relationships is at a height and earlier attitudes towards the father and mother will be projected onto the teacher. Nevertheless, the teacher must resolutely refuse to become an authority figure; instead he must himself become a member of the crowd. He must, in fact, resign his own position of authority and exist only as a member of the group itself. And if this involves him in joining in what to him may appear to be anti-social or destructive behaviour, so be it. Thus when Lane's class decided, probably at his suggestion, to build a brick wall, Lane joined in and contributed his labour and experience to its construction. When the class afterwards decided to demolish the wall, Lane joyfully joined in and was as destructive as any of his classmates.[20] Only by this total identification with the group could the teacher demonstrate unequivocallly his love and support for each one of its members.

Finally, in adulthood the creative drive achieves its craving for perfection and fullest spiritual realization in sexual awareness and a fully developed moral sense in the consciousness of God. This Lane sees as at once the end and the beginning of the cycle, the realization of a deep seated instinctive spiritual craving for life and love, a kind of second birth.[21]

The blueprint for this cycle of human development, which Lane sees as an intention both of Nature and of God, lies deep within the unconscious, which is responsible for seven eighths of all human thought. The unconscious, in turn, is dominated by an instinctive craving for love, the libido,

> a positive dynamic force for love always seeking to attach itself to some object or purpose or person within the scope of the sense comprehension of its owner. Its most peculiar characteristic is its continual effort to gratify the conscious mind of its owner, irrespective of the moral and ethical code that exists within the consciousness.[22]

It is, of course, wholly unmoral and is thus easily rebuked by moral consciousness. But while libido may be repressed, it cannot be entirely suppressed and will emerge in another form at another point as a mania, a phobia or some form of hysterical obsession. Indeed,

> every human being is to a greater or less extent victimized and thwarted in the pursuit of his life purposes by the libido in his unconscious mind . . . But thanks to the brilliant and profound research of Professor Freud and his colleagues, there is now a definite technique by means of which the content of the unconscious mind may be analyzed, the libido brought out into the open, and its tremendous forces directed towards the service of the life purposes of the individual and the welfare of society.[23]

Thus does Lane create out of various Freudian concepts a new basis for North American progressive ideals of individual and social improvement through education.

In this curative and ameliorative function of education, there are two major tasks. First the educator must diagnose the student's or patient's difficulties — that is, he must explore the unconscious mind and bring the individual to as full an awareness as possible of the "thousand and one inclinations of his libido."[24] The second task is that of sublimation, "a process of redirecting libido, now freed from unwholesome futile pursuits, into channels of activity that will serve the life purposes of the conscious mind."[25] For Lane, all education was essentially sublimation, although only the teacher who had been trained in psycho-analytic techniques could make effective use of the process and avoid inefficient and damaging conflicts between moral consciousness and the unconscious instinctive cravings of the libido.

In his lofty expectations of the power of the teacher to do good, Lane reveals once again his North American progressive ideals of human and social improvement and perfection. In the following passage, this optimism is so strong that it borders upon educational megalomania.

> Does your boy hate arithmetic? He can be made to love it by analytic pedagogy. Is he rude and ungracious? It is conflict easily removable. Is he purposely annoying? He is suffering from an inferiority complex. His libido can be detached from its unwholesome goal. Does he bite his nails? Fidget in his chair? Has he an obsession for drumming with his fingers? Sucking the end of his pen? Teasing his brother or sister? Whistling? Throwing stones? Does he have a morbid interest in ghostly sights? Is he afraid of ghosts, burglars or goblins? All these things and thousand of others are inevitably the manifestations of unconscious conflicts raging within him and as such can be dealt with certainly and scientifically by analysis.[26]

For Lane, then, all human weaknesses, all human inefficiency, all human viciousness could be removed by the efforts of teachers who had been subjected to and trained in the technique of psycho-analysis.

Of course, Lane noted, no one could be successfully analyzed against his will, and the phenomenon of 'resistance' must always be faced. To breakdown this 'resistance' and to make possible the essential task of sublimation, there must occur first the 'transference' of the pupil's libido or 'interest' to the teacher. In other words, before a teacher can redirect the libido or life desire into appropriate professional, social or academic channels, he must gain and accept the affection, esteem and life-desire of the pupil. No effective education could take place, therefore, without there being involved a strong love connection between the three elements of education, the teacher, the pupil and the subject matter. According to Lane,

> The teacher who is coldly critical towards his pupil — does not love him, can never 'sublimate' that pupil's interests . . . The teacher who does not love the subject he is teaching will find his lack of love reflected in his pupil's lack of accomplishment. Any 'analyzed' teacher may 'sublimate' to love any subject that he thinks will benefit his 'first love' his pupil. Ergo: no one should teach who has not been himself analyzed and through the process gained that true psychological insight which produces the 'Art of teaching.'[27]

It was, Lane believed, his failure to accept fully the transference of the love of his pupils to himself that had caused him to fail in his attempt to sublimate their libidinal energies to the love of the community. He had emotionally drawn back from them, had failed, in fact, to love them and had thus inevitably failed educationally. Thus Lane refused to lay any of the blame for the scandal at the Little Commonwealth upon the girls who had wrongfully accused him. Their accusations were the result not of his involvement in a sexual relationship with them but of his failure to accept and to return their love.

Assessments of Lane's significance as an educator have been many and varied. Generally, however, they have tended to focus either on the character of Lane himself or upon his impact upon the life and personality of the individual making the assessment. Thus the Earl of Lytton sums up Lane in the following terms:

> A man who was so simple that only children could understand him, so good that his work was more apparent to the foolish than to the wise, so generous that no one could injure him, so modest that no one could praise him, so trusting that no one could deceive him, so happy that nothing could depress him, so great that no one could for long feel small in his presence.[28]

Miss Bazeley, Lane's co-worker in the Little Commonwealth, summed up the significance of his work in essentially autobiographical terms. "The result and the reward Homer Lane's life was to have made others better and happier, more certain of themselves and more certain of the creative spirit, which moves and experiments in all living beings towards a great design."[29] A.S. Neill noted that

> Homer Tyrell Lane, of all men I have known, was the one who inspired me most. . . . He introduced me to child psychology, he was the first man I had heard of who brought depth psychology to the treatment of children, something official treatment rarely does. It was also from Lane that I obtained the idea of self-government at Summerhill. He showed me the necessity of looking deep for the causes of misbehaviour.[30]

Such comments are interesting but they tell us more about the commentator than about Lane and tend to obscure the real historical significance of the man and his work. For despite his unique personal and professional qualities and the undoubted innovativeness of his work, Lane's educational ideas and practice are important because they are representative of a once very important if little studied movement in European education, the search for a psycho-analytic pedagogy.[31] And if writers like Melanie Klein and Anna Freud were the main theoreticians of the new psycho-analytic movement in education, it was Lane who, more than anyone else, succeeded in translating the theory into a practice that caught the imagination of his contemporaries and set the extreme libertarian parameter within which future discussions of childrearing would take place. The opposing extreme regulatory parameter of authority and control was to be set by a contemporary fellow American, J. B. Watson, 'the father of behaviourism.'

John B. Watson (1878 - 1958)

Homer Lane, like other educators in the psycho-analytic movement, had consistently used the method and findings of psychology to get at the inmost feelings and motivations of the child. He was, therefore consistently on the side of the individual and, indeed, upheld the child's right to free and full development even against the claims of civilization. But society, too, in its constant search for more effective means to bring its members under control and direct their energies aright, had need of the findings of psychology. In J.B. Watson it found its most forceful champion, a psychologist who not only revolutionized the methodology of his science but who, in the process, "invented a new kind of child."[32]

J.B. Watson was born in 1878 in Greenville, South Carolina.[33] His mother Emma was a Baptist and, in the eyes of his father, Pickens, insufferably religious. Although his mother doted on her son, it was upon Pickens that the young Watson centered his affection. And when the somewhat irresponsible Pickens could no longer put up with his wife's 'goodness' and left home, the thirteen year old John not surprisingly became something of a problem child. Not only did he frequently miss and do poorly in school; several times he ran afoul of the law.

He was, however, able to educate himself and at fifteen entered the Baptist College in Greenville, where he worked hard at odd jobs and at his studies. Despite the fact that he disliked its restrictive moral code, he earned an M.A. degree before he was twenty-one, and, shortly after the death of his mother, left for the University of Chicago to seek a doctorate degree in the area of Philosophy under the tutelage of John Dewey. Like many other of Dewey's students, Watson found his lectures incomprehensible and before long had switched his attention to psychology and in particular to the work of James Angell who became a mentor and something of a father figure.

Watson's earliest research was in the area of learning theory, a branch of psychology which was in its initial stages of development in the first years of the new century. Of particular interest to Watson was the problem of discovering the mental abilities and learning powers of animals, and this was the topic which he selected for his doctoral research. By 1902 he was the most experienced researcher in the United States in the area of 'rat psychology.' The following year his dissertation on animal education was accepted and he became the youngest person to gain a Ph.D. at the University of Chicago. In his thesis and later articles Watson pointed out that animal behaviour could be studied and successfully explained without any reference to the notion of consciousnesses or the mind of the animal and clearly without the aid of an animal's introspective powers.

In 1908 Watson accepted a promotion and a new position at Johns Hopkins University where his controlled experiments in the area of animal learning continued to impress his colleagues. Within a year or two he had published a number of well-received articles and was the editor of two journals. In 1912, his ideas about the appropriate method and scope of psychology had crystallized sufficiently for him to agree to present them in a public lecture. That lecture, which Watson titled "Psychology as the Behaviourist Views It" may be taken as the manifesto of a new science and, in some respects, a new social order. It begins:

> Psychology as the behaviourist views it is a purely objective, experimental branch of natural science. Its theoretical goal is the prediction and control of behaviour. Introspection forms no essential part of its methods, nor is the scientific value of its data dependent upon the readiness with which they lend themselves to interpretation in terms of consciousness. The behaviourist, in his efforts to get a unitary scheme of animal response, recognizes no dividing line between man and brute. The behaviour of man with all of its refinement and complexity, forms only a part of the behaviourist's total scheme of investigation.[34]

Psychology, then, was a natural science dealing with behaviour, both that of man and of animals. The old psychology together with its concern to study consciousness and all of its old concepts could now be abandoned. "I believe," wrote Watson, "we can write a psychology . . . and . . . never use the terms consciousness, mental states, mind, content, introspectively verifiable, imagery, and the like . . . It can be done in terms of stimulus and response, in terms of habit formation, habit integrations, and the like."[35] Not only will such a science yield reliable knowledge; it would eventually enable the investigator to reach the ultimate goal of predicting and controlling behaviour, including human behaviour. Psychology, more than other science, ought to yield useful results, in the field of law, in education, in business, in advertising, in testing — in fact, in every situation where the control and direction of behaviour was desirable and needed. Although anything like a social philosophy can scarcely be said to exist in Watson's initial lecture, a ground work and a rationale for one had been laid, and within a few years Watson was to give the development of this philosophy precedence over his work in the experimental natural science of psychology.

Watson's first book, *Behaviour: An Introduction to Comparative Psychology* was published in 1914 and was essentially an elaboration of the methodological principles outlined in his lecture. The book was well-received and the impact of his ideas so wide-spread that, in the following year, he was elected President of the American Psychology Association. By the time he joined the army, in 1915, he had already begun to move from a general theory of animal behaviour to a particular view of personality formation in man. This concern he pursued after the war in the first experimental studies of children and children's behaviour. By now the implication of the power to predict and control behaviour had become more apparent and their clear spelling out more urgent. In 1919 he published *Psychology from the Standpoint of a Behaviourist* which gave a complete account of his work and thought, and made considerable use of his studies of children. The book is, in effect, an attempt to map a complete behaviouristic program and contains discussions of research findings in the areas of instincts, habits and reflex actions in all manner of individual and social contexts. Its basic conclusion may be stated as a simple truth about man — that his personality consists primarily of a set of habits acquired through a process of reacting rather than acting, of responding rather than initiating. And despite Watson's disclaimers that his was not a strictly deterministic or strictly reductionistic position, both deterministic and reductionistic conclusions are present on virtually every page. Man, in effect, is portrayed as a product of his environment or rather of the history of his reactions to his environment. To understand him, to be able to predict and thus to control his behaviour, one needs to know this history — his education, his life experiences, his illnesses, his triumphs and his failures. Watson had thus finally spelled out the full implications of the view of psychology outlined in his initial public lecture on behaviourism, in which he had claimed, "In a system of psychology completely worked out, given the response the stimuli can be predicted; given the stimuli the response can be predicted."[36]

In 1919 Watson's career was at its height. He had almost single-handedly established behaviourism as a reputable scientific method in psychology and had set underway what seemed to be successful experimental procedures in the study both of animal and of children's behaviour. For those who believed that only in science lay man's salvation, his approach and work represented the most legitimate and promising school of psychology. Thus Bertrand Russell commented in 1919 that "Watson had made the greatest contribution to scientific psychology since Aristotle."[37] Tragically, however, the enormous promise of Watson's early work was never to reach full flower. For sometime his marriage had been unsatisfactory, and in 1920 he announced his intention of divorcing his wife and marrying one of his former graduate students. This was bad enough but when several of Watson's love letters somehow made their way to the President of the University, Watson was asked to resign. He was never to work in University again. In 1921 he began a new career, perhaps not surprisingly as a junior executive in an advertising agency. Characteristically, his drive, intelligence and energy carried him quickly to the top and within three years he was appointed Vice-President. He was to remain in the advertising world until his retirement in 1945.

The impact of the new career on his work in psychology and particularly on his work in the area of children's behaviour was, of course, disastrous. As Kessen has pointed out,

> Barred from his laboratory and the audience of his professional colleagues, Watson could not extend and modify the beginnings he made in the study of children. As a consequence, his work grew only in bulk, and rancour, never in form, and his dogmatism imposed constraints on academic child psychology that it did not throw off for many years.[38]

Nevertheless in the 1920s Watson maintained contact with the discipline of psychology. He lectured at the New School for Social Research in New York and produced several popular articles in periodicals. In one sense, it could be argued that Watson's enforced retirement from professional psychology freed him, allowing him to pursue the path which was already laid out in his earlier works — that is the move into social philosophy and the drawing up of a blueprint for a model society.

In 1925, he published his controversial book, *Behaviourism*. It is in many respects, an oddly compiled and far-ranging book moving from a discussion of the old and new psychology, through disquisitions on comparative anatomy and physiology and detailed descriptions of the human body and its functioning, to a treatment of the development of personality and a design for social engineering. Yet the book possesses both clarity of vision and a single purpose. It begins with a powerful condemnation of the old psychology of consciousness which Watson sees as a legacy of a magical and superstitious attachment to the body-soul dualism. The advent of behaviourism represents a final break with the past and has made possible, finally, a discrete natural science of man's behaviour. Such a science must be motivated by much more than mere curiosity. For Watson,

> The interest of the behaviourist in man's doings is more than the interest of the spectator — he wants to control man's reactions as physical scientists want to control and manipulate other natural phenomena. It is the business of behaviouristic psychology to be able to predict and to control human activity. To do this it must gather scientific data by experimental methods. Only then can the trained behaviourist predict, given the stimulus, what reaction will take place; or, given the reaction, state what the situation or stimulus is that has caused the reaction.[39]

Man's failure to act on the basis of such scientific data has meant that all his attempts at social reform have been pitifully unsuccessful. The 1914-18 war, prohibition, the Russian Revolution — all represent attempts to effect "changes in social situations," and all were examples of "blind experimentation." All were thus inevitably dismal failures.

In this type of social experimentation society often plunges — does not feel its way out by means of small scale experimentations. It works with no definite experimental program in front of it. Its behaviour often becomes mob-like which is another way of saying that the individuals composing the groups fall back upon infantile behaviour.[40]

Only when the science of behaviourism is seen as "basal to the organization and control of society"[41] can man hope to achieve the expected results of his attempts of social reform.

And what is true of society is even more true of man as an individual. Man's behaviour and his personality can be shaped in the same way as his social organizations, that is scientifically and successfully. Indeed, as Watson puts it,

Give me a dozen healthy infants, well-formed, and my own specified world to bring them up in and I will guarantee to take one at random and train him to become of any type of specialist I might select — doctor, lawyer, artist, merchant, chief and, yes, even beggarman and thief, regardless of his talents, penchants, tendencies, abilities, vocations, and race of his ancestors . . . Please note that when this experiment is made I am to be allowed to specify the way the children are to be brought up and the type of world they have to live in.[42]

The major part of the book is therefore given over to a discussion of exactly how the human body functions, and how this functioning produces particular behaviours, referred to as instincts, emotions, manual habits, talking and thinking; in short the book deals with the formation of the individual human personality. In these discussions, Watson refers frequently to the results of his experimental work with children. Thus, in the final chapter Watson is able to claim that "personality is the sum of activities that can be discovered by actual observation of behaviour over a long enough time to give reliable information. In other words, personality is but the end product of our habit systems."[43] Upon the appropriateness and efficacy of these habit systems depend the well-being and happiness of the individual. Clearly, then, they cannot be left to chance or to the working out of some intention of nature or plan of God. Indeed, it was clear from Watson's observations of his fellow men that "human nature has so many weaknesses in it that it is difficult to make a start pointing out the chief failures."[44] Inferiority complexes, susceptibility to flattery, the constant search for power, the carrying over of infantile modes of thought and behaviour into adulthood — all were characteristic weaknesses of modern western man.[45] Yet all were treatable. A personality had been constructed; it could also be dismantled and reconstructed. Given an understanding of the origins of personality, the rebuilding both of individuals and of the society they made up became possible. "We can," argued Watson, "change the personality as easily as we can change the shape of the nose, only it takes more time."[46]

The most dependable hope for the future, however, lay not so much in reforming adults as in forming children. And while Watson did not, in this particular book, supply any advice on childrearing, he concluded with the following plea:

> Behaviourism ought to be science that prepares men and women for understanding the principles of their own behaviour. It ought to make men and women eager to rearrange their own lives, and especially eager to prepare themselves to bring up their own children in a healthy way. I wish I could picture for you what a rich and wonderful individual we should make of every healthy child if only we could let it shape itself properly and then provide for it a universe in which it could exercise that organization — a universe unshackled by legendary folklore of happenings thousands of years ago; unhampered by disgraceful political history; free of foolish customs and conventions which have no significance in themselves yet which hem the individual in like taut steel bands . . . Will not these children in turn, with their better ways of living and thinking, replace us as society and in turn bring up their children in a still more scientific way until the world finally becomes a place fit for human habitation?[47]

From 1926 on, Watson's energies and interests were more and more focussed on this "more scientific way" of rearing children. In 1928 he brought together six articles he had written for McCalls Magazine and published them as the *Psychological Care of Infant and Child*, a behaviouristic childrearing manual and, appropriately, Watson's final book. He had moved, in a way logically, from the study of the behaviour of rats to a general theory of animal (including human) behaviour, to a particular view of man, to a personal view of the possibilities of social engineering, and finally, as a culmination of all his previous work, to the creation of a system of childrearing.

Watson's aim in writing the *Psychological Care of Infant and Child* was, according to Cohen, to shock the American public into a realization that most parents were a menace to their children's well-being. The American family, rather than regulating a child's personality development in a scientific fashion, inculcated absurd fears and all too frequently turned out invalids rather than healthy, happy and productive adults. It and its childrearing methods badly needed to be debunked, and in his book Watson set out to do just this. Interestingly, the American public, ever eager for expert advice, immediately made the book a best seller.

Watson's concern to debunk, if not destroy, existing patterns of childrearing meant that the book contained as many cautions about what not to do as it did advice about the proper procedures to employ. Current practice, based as it was upon prejudice, superstition and the infantile emotional needs of parents, was invariably seen as harmful to the child. Indeed, suggested Watson,

> No one today knows enough to raise a child. The world would be considerably better off if we were to stop having children for twenty years (except those reared for experimental purposes) and were then to start again with enough facts to do the job with some degree of skill and accuracy. Parenthood . . . is a science, the details of which must be worked out by patient laboratory methods.[48]

The advice in the book was thus designed to make professional child care workers out of amateur mothers. For it was upon the shoulders of mothers that the responsibility for the future welfare of society lay.

It was mothers, for example, who determined the "emotional life plan" of the child.

> At three years of age the child's whole emotional life plan has been laid down, his emotional disposition set. At that age the parents have already determined for him whether he is to grow into a happy person, wholesome and good natured, whether he is to be a whining, complaining neurotic, an anger driven, vindictive, overbearing slave driver, or one whose every move in life is definitely controlled by fear.[49]

The appropriate shaping of the fear life of the child was a principle task of the mother. This she must do by building in rational fears using "appropriate common sense, negative reactions," such as rapping fingers or spanking both dispensed as "an objective experimental procedure — never as punishment."[50] What must be avoided at all costs was the haphazard accidental conditioning of irrational fears — of the dark, of furry animals, etc.

Even more hazardous to children's and adults' well-being than the responses brought about by irrational fear conditioning were those resulting from too much mother-love. Indeed, the most distinctive weaknesses of American life, invalidism, the inability to face reality, and emotional dependency, were the direct results of mothers' kissing, coddling, and caressing their children. Until mothers could be prevailed upon to act as well-trained nurses or, even more unlikely, to rotate their babies and avoid the development of too close an emotional bond with their children, this "over conditioning in love" would doubtless continue. But, Watson warned the indulgent mother,

> remember when you are tempted to pet your child . . . mother-love is a dangerous instrument. An instrument which may inflict a never-healing wound, a wound which may make infancy unhappy, adolescence a nightmare, an instrument which may wreck your adult son's or daughter's vocational future and their chances for marital happiness.[51]

As an alternative and corrective to such damaging treatment, Watson recommended that children be treated sensibly.

> Treat them as though they were young adults. Dress them, bathe them with care and circumspection. Let your behaviour always be objective and kindly firm. Never hug and kiss them, never let them sit in your lap. If you must, kiss them once on the forehead when they say good night. Shake hands with them in the morning. Give them a pat on the head if they have made extraordinarily good job of a difficult task. Try it out. In a week's time you will find how easy it is to be perfectly objective with your child and at the same time kindly. You will be utterly ashamed of the mawkish, sentimental way you have been handling it.[52]

Of the positive habits to be developed in the young child, that of independence, both physical and emotional, was by far the most important. From the beginning the child was to be trained to do things for himself. In turn this required a carefully structured environment designed to permit a child to succeed in his efforts at independence. Toilet training should, for example, be begun early and from the age of nine months the child could safely be left alone on the toilet seat to 'work independently.' Children's clothes should be designed so that the child could get into and out of them without assistance.

The goal of early childhood training was the fostering of independence. But this did not imply a libertarian upbringing in which the adult exercised little control. Indeed, in Watson's plan for the training of the two to five year old, all was adult ordered, adult controlled, and adult regulated. Bathing, toilet and bedtime rituals, early morning activities, lunch procedures, play activities and social conduct were to be treated in strictly regulatory terms and all were to be determined in the context of the need to condition appropriate habits in the child. The sum total of all these habits would be a personality fitted to the demands of a given civilization, that is a person with customary manners, "as free as possible of sensitivities to people and who, almost from birth, is relatively independent of the family situation."[53] Above all, stated Watson, "We have tried to create a problem-solving child."[54]

Together with his new wife Rosalie, who incidently helped write the *Psychological Care of Infant and Child*, Watson had plenty of opportunity to put into practice his system of childrearing. In fact, he raised his two sons according to its precepts. As might be expected, both respected their father but neither felt very close to him. In 1936 Rosalie died and Watson retired from active participation in public life. He died after a short illness in 1958.

Watson's criticisms of the emotional bonding in the nuclear family and particularly of mother-love were hardly calculated to endear him to the majority of American parents. Nevertheless, although his sins were doubtless scarlet, his books were certainly read. Watson, in fact, must be considered one of the most important childrearing theorists of the twentieth century. He had set underway the systematic and experimental study of children and children's behaviour. More importantly, he had argued powerfully that for the proper upbringing of the child, love and good intentions were not enough. Child care must be based on scientific knowledge applied with clinical detachment and a resolute lack of passion. Child care, in effect, whether dispensed by a parent, nurse, teacher or social worker, was a professional responsibility, one not to be undertaken lightly and certainly not in order to gratify the personal emotional needs of the adult.

In this latter respect, Watson was an important contributor to the twentieth-century cult of the expert and to the professionalization of child care. And if parents were understandably reluctant to give up the care of the very young child to professionals, they were certainly more and more inclined to consult them about the proper way to go about caring for their children. Indeed, the good parent is now, almost by definition, one who seeks advice from someone who knows better, that is from a professional. Interestingly, the United States' Department of Health, in its very popular series of pamphlets for parents, incorporated many of Watson's ideas on early childrearing.

Perhaps the greatest testimony to the influence of his ideas is the virulence with which his ideas were attacked by his critics and especially by noted literary figures. Aldous Huxley's *Brave New World* and George Orwell's *1984* both attempt to portray a world driven and dominated by a perverted version of the Watsonian view of man and society. And certainly there is truth in Cohen's comment that Watson stands in the succession of Plato, with this major difference — that "his chosen ruler is the scientist and, in particular, the psychologist."[55]

Conclusion

Homer Lane and J.B. Watson are no longer familiar figures in the landscape of contemporary theorizing about childrearing. Both have been overshadowed by their followers. Yet it is important to remember that A.S. Neill, perhaps the foremost contemporary advocate of permissive methods of child care, consciously modelled his Summerhill upon the Little Commonwealth and constantly paid tribute to the influence of Lane upon the development of his educational thought. B.F. Skinner, on the other hand, who has exerted an equally powerful influence on the side of objective regulation and control of the child, owes a similar debt to Watson. His elaborate experiments in operant conditioning are clearly a continuation of the work of Watson, and his Walden II is an attempt, albeit a literary one, to create a utopia along the lines of Watson's psychological and social thought. In attempting to assess the significance of the work of all four men, it is, perhaps, significant that in the 1970s the books *Summerhill* and *Walden II* were the most frequently prescribed texts in North American educational theory courses.

And yet despite the freshness of their ideas and the undisputed impact of their recommendations, when one attempts a final judgement on the life and work of Lane and Watson and the contribution of their two very different approaches to psychology to child care, one is left with a feeling of disappointment. It is a disappointment that stems not so much from the significance of the contributions themselves as from the enormous gap between the extravagantly optimistic claims they made on behalf of psychology and its actual achievements. It is no doubt true that our contemporary treatment of children, both in the home and in the school, is more informed and certainly more humane than that of previous centuries, and that the discipline of psychology has played an important part in this process of enlightenment. It has vastly increased our store of information about childhood and given us greater sophistication and reliability in the application of this knowledge to the modification of children's behaviour patterns. But the initial high hopes for social progress based upon the science of psychology are as far from fulfillment as ever. Indeed, in the last seventy-five years we have seen psychology employed in the service of all manner of dehumanizing and socially reprehensible enterprises, including many involving children. Perhaps the most important lesson to be learned from a study of the impact of psychology on the practice of childrearing is that while the findings of experimental psychology should be accorded the respect due to all valid scientific data, any theory of childrearing which appears to contain even an element of a theory of social progress should be treated with the utmost scepticism and with the most modest hope.

Notes

[1]W.Wundt, *Outlines of Psychology* (1897), quoted in W. Kessen, *The Child* (New York: J. Wiley & Sons, 1965), p. 130.

[2]Kessen, *op. cit.,* p. 130.

[3]D.P. Schultz, *History of Modern Psychology* (New York: Academic Press), pp. 162-163.

[4]*Ibid.,* p. 182

[5]G. Bergmann, "The Contribution of John B. Watson," *Psychological Review* Vol. 63 (1956): pp. 265-266.

[6]See, for example, A.S. Neill, *Summerhill, A Radical Approach to Child Rearing* (New York: Hart Publishing Co., 1960), p. 103.

[7]L.R. Perry, *Bertrand Russell, A.S. Neill, Homer Lane, W.H. Kilpatrick — Four Progressive Educators* (London: Collier-Macmillan, 1967), p. 14.

[8]The only biography of Homer Lane is D.W. Wills, *Homer Lane: A Biography* (London: Allen & Unwin, 1964).

[9]The best account of Lane's work in the Little Commonwealth is E.T. Bazeley, *Homer Lane and the Little Commonwealth* (New York: Schocken Books, 1928).

[10]Bazeley, *op. cit.,* p. 39.

[11]*Ibid.*, p. 132.
[12]A.S. Neill, *Neill! Neill! OrangePeel!* (New York: Hart Publishing Co., 1970), p. 183.
[13]R. Hemmings, *Fifty Years of Freedom* (London: G. Allen & Unwin Ltd., 1972), pp. 25-26.
[14]The full text of Lane's 'Address' is given in Wills, *op. cit.*, pp. 253-267.
[15]*Ibid.*, p. 255.
[16]*Ibid.*
[17]*Ibid.*, p. 256.
[18]H. Lane, *Talks to Parents and Teachers* (New York: Schocken Books, 1969), p. 56.
[19]*Ibid.*, pp. 121-122.
[20]*Ibid.*, p. 12.
[21]H. Lane, "Address" in Wills, *op. cit.*, pp. 256-267.
[22]*Ibid.*, p. 259.
[23]*Ibid.*, p. 260.
[24]*Ibid.*, p. 261.
[25]*Ibid.*
[26]*Ibid.*, p. 262.
[27]*Ibid.*, p. 265.
[28]Bazeley, *op. cit.*, p. 24.
[29]*Ibid.*, p. 170.
[30]A.S. Neill, "Introduction" to H. Lane, *Talks to Parents and Teachers*, p. 8.
[31]See the interesting account of this movement in Sol Cohen, "In the Name of the Prevention of Neurosis: The Search for a Psychoananalytic Pedagogy in Europe 1905-1939", in B. Finkelstein (editor), *Regulated Children/Liberated Children* (New York: Psychohistory Press, 1979), pp. 184-219.
[32]Kessen, *op. cit.*, p. 288.
[33]The best account of Watson's life and work is to be found in D. Cohen, *J.B. Watson, The Founder of Behaviourism* (London: Routledge and Kegan Paul, 1979).
[34]J.B. Watson, "Psychology as the Behaviourist Views It," reprinted in Schultz, *op. cit.*, p. 187.
[35]*Ibid.*, p. 193.
[36]*Ibid.*
[37]D. Cohen, *op. cit.*, p. 145.
[38]Kessen, *op. cit.*, pp. 231-232.
[39]J.B. Watson, *Behaviourism* (Chicago: Phoenix Books, 1966), p. 11.
[40]*Ibid.*, p. 43.
[41]*Ibid.*, p. 44.
[42]*Ibid.*, p. 104.
[43]*Ibid.*, p. 274.
[44]*Ibid.*, p. 287.
[45]*Ibid.*, pp. 287-288.
[46]*Ibid.*, p. 302.
[47]*Ibid.*, pp. 303-304.
[48]J.B. Watson, *Psychological Care of Infant and Child* New York: Arno Press, 1972), p. 12.
[49]*Ibid.*, p. 45.
[50]*Ibid.*, p. 64.

[51] *Ibid.*, p. 87.
[52] *Ibid.*, pp. 81-82.
[53] *Ibid.*, pp. 186-187.
[54] *Ibid.*
[55] D. Cohen, *op. cit.,* p. 137.

Part II

Geo-Cultural Case Studies

Guttersnipes and Charity Children:
Nineteenth Century Child Rescue in the Atlantic Provinces

Patricia T. Rooke and R.L. Schnell

Introduction

In the first decades of the nineteenth century the Atlantic colonies saw little rationalized and organized relief for their pauper populations that included dependent children. Although dependent children were seen as part of the "worthy poor," initially there prevailed an ambivalence regarding the degree of difference between adults and "infant paupers" which meant that such children were neither morally nor physically protected from adult abuse, exploitation, or vicious example.

The attitudinal shifts, which made childhood a distinct social category defined by criteria of protection, segregation, dependence, and finally delayed responsibility, resulted in the withdrawal of children from the general pauper population and the emergence of the institutional forms which dealt specifically with the problems of dependent child life. The four criteria — separation, protection, dependence, and delayed responsibility — make up in a heuristically interrelated way the modern concept of "childhood." For the nineteenth century child saver, "childhood" became synonymous with child rescue, which had moral as well as physical dimensions.[1]

The following paper examines the evolution of the first three criteria in Atlantic Canada during the nineteenth century by discussing the treatment of dependent children and the rise of children's institutions which were, in fact, the visible and palpable manifestations of the criteria. Included in this discussion is the common practice of binding out of such children, a practice emulated by the new institutions, and which offers a contrast between modern consciousness and past attitudes.

I

In the eighteenth century, one of the first attempts to segregate children from the generalized pauper population occurred with the establishment of the Nova Scotia Orphan House in 1752. A colonial institution, which bound out children "so very young as to be unable to do any serviceable work," employed the older girls in the carding and spinning of wool or the knitting of stockings while the boys picked oakum in the winter and "gathered stones" or performed "other little offices" in the gardens and Crown hospital in the summer. Correspondence from Jonathan Belcher to the Lords of Trade in 1761 indicates that during a nine year period 275 children, mostly orphans, had been cared for by this Royal Charity and if they were between eight and twelve years of age they had been indentured from it. The Orphan house, however, fell into disarray and the children were taken over by the poorhouse so that by 1832 a committee before the House of Assembly examining the condition and conduct of the Poors' Asylum commented on the absence of "comfort and cleanliness" and observed that 74 orphan children slept with male or female adults "without any regard to fitness of health or morals." Moreover in 1851 "all paupers" including children were advertised in Dalhousie and Perot for public auction "to the lowest bidder" in return for five to twelve months of service with no supervision and no guarantees for their protection except by verbal agreement.[2]

The records of the Poor House of New Brunswick in the late eighteenth century deal with the aged, infirm, and widows with children, that they might not suffer from "hunger and privation" as well as with the "idle and the disorderly." The first Poor Law Act of 1786 stipulated that if such persons had children "in a suffering condition, the said overseers with the consent of the said justices, are hereby empowered to bind such poor children apprentices," males until they were twenty-one and females until they were eighteen or married.[3] Newfoundland, not being an official settlement, had no crown policy for the relief of its dependent poor; however, children, having been auctioned to the lowest bidder once they reached the age of eight, were bound if boys until they were twenty-four, and if girls until twenty-one or married. Until they were that age, children were boarded in private homes.[4]

Prince Edward Island, which seemed to operate as a large rural parish (with absentee landlords in the nineteenth century), maintained a casual system of relief well into the twentieth century. The municipality made no provision for the relief of its poor and expected private charity to alleviate distress although a "pauper's fee" of $5 per month for the destitute and indigent, by order-in-council, could be made after application. The recommendation for such assistance could be made by a citizen, clergyman, or social agency. However, it certainly cannot be construed that lack of formalized relief represented a true state of prosperity on the island for in 1852 the Ladies' Benevolent Society of Charlottetown, after only fifteen years of harried service, was compelled to dissolve because it could not keep up with the amount of relief required. Apart from isolated examples the evidence concerning dependent children is so scarce that it can only be assumed that informal arrangements and binding practices dealt with nineteenth century problems of dependent, orphaned, and neglected child life. These *ad hoc* arrangements prevailed until the founding of the Children's Aid Society (CAS) in 1909 and the passage of the Neglected Children's Act the following year.[5]

The lack of detailed references regarding the treatment accorded to last century's dependent children is in itself telling and supports the ideas regarding an absence of any special status or the recognition of special needs. Despite the relative disinterest in "childhood" for the offspring of paupers or deceased parents, we can nevertheless discern two trends. The first trend indicates a growing concern regarding their institutionalization and the second concerns the custom of binding out, both of which we shall examine in greater detail.

The absence of differentiated facilities for dependent children is observable in their general inclusion in poorhouses, houses of refuge and industry, penitentiaries and asylums in the nineteenth century. Although the poorhouses varied in size and in design, general public apathy prevailed concerning their upkeep. Halifax was not exceptional in sheltering transient persons and whole families on relief in the municipal refuge at only a cost of twenty-four cents per diem in 1898. The pittance itself reflects the public's attitude toward the whole affair. As one inspector noted in 1900, "rigid economy is practicably discreditable parsimony."[6] Various descriptions cannot but compel us to see municipal institutions as disconsolate environments for the most insensitive adults let alone children. Some, such as in Nova Scotia, were so verminous that it was noted of a poor farm in that province that despite "eternal vigilance, the bedsteads [were] occupied by other than sleepers"; while others like the Pictou Poors' House were so decrepit and rudimentary that the inmates were compelled to haul water for their use in puncheons from the town some distance away.[7] Since the forbidding concrete structure that was St. John's Poor Asylum proudly boasted a "liberal plan" in 1910 which included spray baths, a laundry for "a foul wash house," and a mortuary, we might assume that none of these amenities existed for previous generations of paupers or their children. Even then, there was to be no quarantine shed or facilities for medical examinations and the segregation of infected cases on admission. The custom of searching, stripping, and disinfecting was to be retained although uniforms were discarded. Classifications of inmates still included the aged infirm, aged able bodied, consumptive, and able bodied.[8]

In 1900 the Halifax Poor Farm included inmates who were "destructively inclined," "uncleanly," and "epileptic," while the Poor House, a two storied ramshackle farm house, was quite without bolts, locks, and handles in its twenty rooms. Subsequently the 57 lunatics among its inmates could roam at will and children, who were included among the others, were not separated according to sex, sanity, social or age distributions. One patient was reported to be subject to violent outbursts and was, therefore, immobilized by handcuffs and lay exposed without a shirt.[9] In short, almshouses made little or no attempt to classify adults in a rigorous manner and the governors saw nothing inappropriate in having young children promiscuously mixing with the disorderly and incontinent.

Pauper and dependent youngsters were not considered to require the same decorous solicitude as other children in society whose sensitivities were assiduously protected in their families and in the public schools. It is for instance ironical that at the same time as ordinary children were being carefully segregated according to sex in Newfoundland schools in the 1830's the children of the indigent and desperate poor had no separate facilities provided them in public refuges. Dr. Michael Fleming, the Roman Catholic primate, insisted on "withdrawing female children from the tutelage of men, from the dangerous associations which ordinary school intercourse with the other sex naturally exhibited." He, therefore, supported the Presentation Convent in 1833 which provided education for girls, so that they might not lose "that delicacy of feeling and refinement of sentiment which forms the ornament and grace of their sex." The sisters were to train them into "virtue and innocence" and "integrity and morality." As for the boys, he expressed grave anxiety that they were demonstrating a total independence of their parents once they were trained into the fishing trades at a young age. He further observed that being "free from every domestic restraint" each was accustomed to drinking "a yellow belly" [of rum] from his own "brown jug" three times a day.[10]

The irony is further compounded when one realizes that in Nova Scotia as well as Newfoundland, sexual separation was unthinkable as in the case of the poors' asylum in Halifax although the governors of the Annapolis Poors' Asylum made separate provision for "coloured" inmates in a most precipitous manner.[11] At the same time, insane women in the Yarmouth County Asylum were reputedly in charge of young children. The report of the Inspector of Public Charities observed in a remarkable understatement the this practice was "a very risky business." Fourteen years later, William Hattie, the Inspector of Humane institutions, was able to comment that

> under the most favourable circumstances, institutional life is not ideal for the child, and the building which houses a considerable number of inefficients, and degenerates, most of them well advanced in years, must surely be a most undesirable environment for the rearing of children.

Already "handicapped by hereditary," he continued that they spent day and night "in the company of irritable and complaining old people, of mischievous and profane lunatics, and of drivelling and unclean imbeciles." He noted that children were in the Home for the Poor, Truro, and the Yarmouth Poors' Asylum, Arcadia — and this in the year of our Lord, 1914![12]

This lack of segregation is startling to those now accustomed to protecting children from participating in baser adult preoccupations and from the sadness of grinding poverty, terminal illness, death, insanity, or degeneracy. But it is even more startling to realize that some of this still persisted in New Brunswick in 1949 when a Canadian Welfare Council (CWC) survey lamented that 29 children were retained in the nine existing poorhouses with eleven of these children between 3 1/2 years and 13 years of age. Although not strictly within our time period, the survey's remarks is equally apt for the nineteenth century.

The CWC survey, after observing that Section XIX of the Elizabethan Poor Law of 1601 had provided that the "Act shall endure no longer than the end of the next session in Parliament," continued:

> It would doubtless be as surprising to the members of Elizabeth's parliament, as it is to many Canadians, that many of the actual provisions of those early poor laws and many of the social and political ideas that lay behind them had endured into the middle of the twentieth century and are embodied in some of the social legislation of the province of New Brunswick.[13]

The survey was merely reiterating a similar one conducted by the same Council under the direction of Charlotte Whitton in 1928-29.[14] Although few children by the mid-twentieth century were found in the municipal homes, Whitton, when writing to a child welfare associate in 1943, was again able to observe that mentally defective children were "herded into almshouses" and noted that New Brunswick alongside Alberta, (although for quite different reasons), fell below all other English speaking provinces in the care of its dependent children.[15]

The lives of very young children, and especially infants, were in constant jeopardy in the poor houses, especially if they were also foundlings. Many of these children were sent out to wetnurse at the municipality's expense, a practice that did not guarantee them either long life nor adoption. Two year old Lilla M. Martan's case must not have been uncommon. This toddler died in the same year that she had been returned to Cornwallis poorhouse although she had apparently thrived at wetnurse before her return. One cannot tell what happened to tiny Blanche Doorstep who was delivered to be wetnursed by a Mrs. Best in 1903.[16] Doorstep babies were usually illegitimate and were not destined to survive their first weeks unless wetnursed or placed out to board. If they survived their initial tenous origins the records for infant mortality rates in the poorhouses indicate that a majority of them failed to withstand the physical and the psychological deprivations of the experience. Saint John almshouse recorded many "bastards" on its rolls and many deaths of these same bastards.[17]

Unmarried mothers unable to keep their babies as well as husbands whose wives were in asylums, or wives whose husbands were in prison or had been deserted, had little recourse but to surrender their children to the overseers for nominal monthly fees especially as the infants homes were scandalously overcrowded and the orphan asylums frequently refused illegitimates. Under the penurious circumstances of the poorhouses, the overseer's reluctance to receive infants was understandable although regrettable. Yet "baby farming" was a costlier business and notoriously negligent of the lives of infants. The Halifax Protestant Infants' Home was started in 1875 partly to counteract the pernicious consequences of the practice. Curiously, however, this home declined to admit coloured infants and we are left to speculate on the fates of such children before the founding of the Halifax home for coloured children in the twentieth century. The Halifax Infants' Home committee found itself in a quandary when it hired its first wet nurse because of a rule that "no woman [mothers of inmates] that is not of respectable character" was to be admitted into the home. Yet it seemed tautological, given nineteenth century structures on morality, that women forced into wetnursing would be unwed or deserted therefore not "respectable." The dilemma was resolved after lively discussion that a second-timer at wetnursing would not be admitted![18]

Some poorhouses were known to discourage unwed mothers and their "bastard children" with an increase in Johnny and June Doorsteps. In 1843, the Board of the Halifax Asylum returned an illegitimate child to the doctor who had admitted it with the observation "that whilst the Commissioners deem it their duty to extend the charity of the House to foundlings . . . they are anxious in no degree to cloak vice, or diminish natural affection."[19]

Unmarried mothers were driven, however, to the poor houses to deliver their babies and the registers of the institutions had an inordinate number of "bastards" recorded as inmates. At the end of the century, James Dowe, superintendent of the Halifax Asylum expressed the ease with which unmarried women could "hide their shame" at provincial expense.[20] Such distressing cases had few alternatives in a society that provided no cash relief to carry them over their predicament. Unwed mothers and their infants therefore were quickly identified as suitable objects of female philanthropic rescue in both the actual and the moral sense.[21] The Foundling Homes and Infant Homes that developed out of Women's refuges were melancholy places that received the most wretched and ostracized of the poor — the unwed mother and her unwanted child.

It was customary for pauper children's services to be advertised on the doors of almshouses or in the local press as can be seen in the case of the Charlottetown *Daily Examiner* which advertised a ten year old boy "for adoption" in 1883 to "any respectable farmer" on application to the Poor House.[22] Commissioners of the Poor reserved the right to reclaim children if the conditions of their indentures were not met. These conditions usually included board, religious instruction, and some education although there is little indication that any particular vigilance was given to such conditions. When Bridget Cody's case of mistreatment was reviewed by the governors of a Cornwallis poor house in 1845 they expressed "perfect abhorrence and disgust" at the inhumane treatment the child had received at the hand of her master. Nevertheless Bridget was summarily indentured again to another. It was common for poorhouses to indenture children without parental consent as happened in 1855 to Alfred Rooks. In this case the parental protest was so discomforting that the boy was hastily returned to the asylum. Between 1832 and 1847 in Halifax 301 had been bound out as apprentices.[23]

The custom of binding out into the care of private families had a long history; however, in the nineteenth century, it became increasingly reserved for dependent children. Private families became less inclined to indenture their own children into service, which required that they live in another household, and more inclined to replace such service with schooling or day-time apprenticeships. Institutions, benevolent societies, child savers and poor law commissioners continued to replenish households with servile/juvenile labour drawn from the ranks of dependent and neglected children. Since they were uniformly placed as domestic servants and farm labourers, these young servants were not actually trained into occupations according to the indenture arrangements for normal children of previous decades.

The difference between former agreements and those made by guardians of pauper and home children was the difference between a legal contractual form and a very loose arrangement hardly worth the paper upon which it was written. There was, moreover, little surveillance of the household to which the apprenticed child would be put either before or after the agreement. In New Brunswick, for example, there was a similarity between these loose forms and the conditions of service in the case of a seven year old *coloured* boy named Dick who was apprenticed to Joseph Clarke. He was to train "in the business of husbandry" and of "house servant."[24] Like Dick, most pauper children were put out to agricultural or domestic service and rarely apprenticed into trade, business, or other occupations. However, young Henry Forrester, at only five years four months, was apprenticed into the household of a printer in 1837. The indenture clearly stipulated mutual duties. During his service, Henry was to serve faithfully "his master and his secrets faithfully keep, his lawful commands everywhere readily obey."

> He shall do no damage to his Master, nor see it done by others without letting or giving notice thereof to his said master. He shall not waste his Master's goods, nor lend them unlawfully to any; he shall not commit Fornication nor contract Matrimony within the said Term: At cards, dice, or any other unlawful Game he shall not play, . . .[25]

Neither was young Henry allowed to "haunt the ale houses, taverns, or playhouses" until his apprenticeship expired at age 21 years.

Similarly in 1815 a yeoman of New Brunswick put out and bound his daughter Jane to "serve him [the Master] from the day of the date hereof and during the term of ten years from the seventh day of February lastpast or until she arrives at the full age of eighteen years." Like Henry, Jane was allowed to neither fornicate nor marry, nor absent herself day or night from the household without leave. Henry was to be trained in the art, trade or mystery of a printer, to be provided meat, apparell and board, as well as a complete set of clothing over and above his common working clothes at the end of term. Jane had to be trained into housewifery, cared for as a member of the family in sickness and in health, sent to school until she was literate, and be given a heifer with all the profits and advantages of ownership. At the end of her term she was to be provided with two suits of clothing for common and Sunday wear.[26] The significance of Henry's case lay in the fact that his parents retrieved him after two years and filed suit against the master for the "heartless and brutal treatment" he rendered his apprentice. He had been whipped, bedded in rags, and insufficiently nourished. It must be noted that similar "heavy and severe chastisement" was frequently the lot of pauper and home children but their plight was met with apathy.

While the treatment of pauper children did not appear to produce much controversy, the problems presented by the presence of so-called "street arabs" in the towns did. Indeed, these children's very independence seemed to be perceived as an insolent affront to that part of the citizenry which was determined to embrace them under the rubric of an appropriate "childhood" even if it meant imposing the three criteria on the street arabs. Boys were seen as potential criminals and girls as potential prostitutes.

II

If the protection of dependent children had not changed at all since the end of the eighteenth century, even poorhouses were preferable to prisons. Between 1846 and 1857 for example, 305 children between twelve and under eighteen were found in the New Brunswick provincial prison while in 1858 there were ten males between twelve and under eighteen with one sixteen year old girl among the 115 inmates. Few were incarcerated for violent crimes, the majority being apprehended for vagrancy and drunkenness. Along with the adult inmates the male children helped in the manufacture of brooms, brushes and nails, while the girls were engaged in cooking, washing, mending and making clothes. Oakum picking, brick making, and hammering granite were other recommended occupations. In this decade too, a nine year old boy, the progeny of parents of the class of "broken down drunkards and worn out prostitutes" had died of cholera while many young lads were sentenced from three to six months for theft and vagrancy.[27]

The first session of the New Brunswick House of Assembly in 1857 duly noted that these boy prisoners were "without parents or friends to instruct and guide them, and without homes to attract and improve them." Consequently they "were thrown into circumstances" of exposure and temptation and thus "become an easy prey to vice." Previously in 1845 the Journal of the House of Assembly had publicized at length the provisions in Great Britain that accorded special treatment for juvenile offenders and suggested similar action be taken while again in 1857 it was urgently recommended that immediate arrangements be made to provide "for the improvement of this class of offender." Segregation was to be ensured for boys in a special building with a school and special keeper while young girls were to be protected from vicious influences by segregated quarters in the almshouse. Nevertheless the New Brunswick Boys Industrial Home was not established until 1895 on the premises of the former Saint John penitentiary while in the meanwhile vagrant and delinquent children were bound out, usually in the country, under the appropriate clauses of the Poor Acts.[28]

A letter to the editor of *The Standard and Conception Bay Advertiser* at Harbor Grace in 1860 articulated the popular concern of the respectable middle classes regarding children roaming "lawless" about the towns. The writer, under the pseudonym of "Humanity," deplored the numbers of "guttersnipes" in the streets who were, it seems, "expressing their extreme felicity in a language made up of most extraordinary noises very like a bad street organ." The belief that such guttersnipes were destined to become the criminals of the future was as pervasive as it was compelling. Ideas that related criminality with pauperism spread the assumptions of child rescue which were grounded on the belief that children could be reclaimed from paths of vice, or better yet, prevented from walking them. By mid-nineteenth century, "the hulks, the prison, and the lash," no longer were seen as appropriate means of dealing with young and old alike. The rhetoric that prevention was better than cure was imbedded in child rescue sentiment which said that not only was reclamation wiser and more humane, but, as the Halifax Industrial School report asserted, it was economical too. Reformatories were cheaper in the long run than Bridewells.[29]

The Day Book of the Church of England orphan asylum in St. John's quoted from an extract in the *Daily Mail*, 15/2/1862, which warned against the evil influences surrounding street children. It advised the rescue of "those human waifs who are scattered over the country" and encouraged their protection in orphanages lest they be "snatched into error and ignorance and into a most dangerous future."[30] By the second half of the century children were clearly seen as in dire need of protection from adult society and if not in the bosom of their own homes, whether middle class or respectable labouring class, then segregated into artificially created surroundings. The 'child institutionalized' was synonymous with the 'child rescued.' Families, schools, or orphan asylums — these were deemed appropriate institutional settings.

In Newfoundland, concern for St. John's street arabs, as well as the drinking habits of young fisher lads, led to the island's philanthropic societies repeatedly drawing attention to the plight of its destitute children. In the 1840s, the St. John's Orphan Benevolent Society had been incorporated to bind out "proper objects for relief and protection" which included children of the indigent population; however, the Society could not effectively meet the demands of Newfoundland's poverty. The St. John's Factory Committee, which trained poor women and girls into earning an independent livelihood during the seal and cod industry failure, had sold manufactured garments in the year 1835 that consisted of 656 cotton shirts, 114 pair of hose and socks, and 43 pair of cuffs and gloves. The Society for Improving the Condition of the Poor had set the example of using a ladies' visiting committee which put dependent girls under 12 years of age into service while the male committee apprenticed lads to the fisheries and several trades. Other boys were set to net making and mending while girls were encouraged into carding, spinning and knitting in a school of industry which operated similarly to the St. Vincent de Paul school for poor female children.[31]

Disreputable family settings and the freedom of the streets were both antithetical to the changing ideas of child savers. The Halifax Poor Man's Friend Society had been concerned since 1820 about the children of the poor and had employed street boys in the manufacture of nails. Its second annual report pleaded that the juvenile poor be given special attention because of "the abominable practices associated with street begging such as theft and seduction." The first annual report of the Halifax Industrial and Ragged School insisted that unsupervised "street arabs" be "snatched from certain ruin." It further noted that

> In all large cities there is a number of boys and girls growing up under influences that mould and shape them for evil and not for good. . . . These are the heathen at our own doors, and worse than heathen; Arabs in the city; the standing reproach to our Christianity. These form the dangerous class in every community.

Between 1840 and 1860 the "climbing boys" of Halifax received much sympathy and attention from philanthropists and the press. An argument fulminated in 1862 as to the public's preference for chimney sweeps over machines which were "inconvenient and dirty." So much for any over-riding commitment to ideas of child protection.[32]

The "street boy" problem was undoubtedly the reason behind the establishment of the Industrial school in Halifax in 1864. The street boys' lot was seen as "a sad and melancholy" one because, according to their critics, they came from drunken parentage, earned their living by "begging and stealing or playing tambourine at some low public house." It was also observed that they lived in sewers, outhouses, dog kennels, or wherever they might find shelter in the inclement weather. It is less obvious that the street boys themselves, despite their precarious existences, agreed to their reclamation into "the paths of industry and virtue." Paper bag making and the manufacture of nails must have been confining activities when compared with their previous independent careers. The 1866 report of the school observed that the boys seemed less than enthusiastic about their incarceration for they were insubordinate and discontented and "the whole place looked comfortless." Nevertheless later in the century the Society for the Prevention of Cruelty to Animals continued to "snatch" such lads and force them into the paths of rectitude.[33]

To prevent girls growing up in Halifax under "noxious influences," a ladies' visiting committee established the St. Paul's Almshouse of Industry in 1867. The girls were trained into household tasks with "systematic regularity" and taught the three Rs. Miss Isobella Binney Cogswell, a Halifax philanthropist, was involved in this endeavour as she was involved in the establishment of the Industrial school which had emerged from a Ragged school. The second report of the Halifax Protestant Orphans' Home, on whose board sat Dr. Cogswell, said that the home protected twenty-six fatherless and friendless children otherwise exposed to temptation "in a cold and infectious world."[34] Thus institutions, whether for neglected and dependent children, or for "pre-delinquent" and "delinquent" children can be understood as physical manifestations of the concept of childhood which either rescued dependent children from unsuitable conditions or reclaimed children from unsavoury environments and occupations. Curiously, reformatories and industrial schools rendered previously independent children dependent by categorizing many who were neither destitute nor orphaned as in need of rescue. Such children were effectively isolated and protected in institutional settings.[35]

III

From the outset, the clienteles of the fledgling asylums except Saint John's, included fee-paying part-orphans, and although the homes insisted that the priorities of admission be granted to orphans, the part-orphans and the non-orphans soon were in the majority due to the inability of certain sectors of the labouring poor to maintain them in times of extremity, unemployment, or bereavement. Although one might argue that the institutions provided "a last resort" for desperate parents and burdened relatives to provide for their offspring until they were in a position to reclaim them, that this was not universally the case is suggested by the fee requirement. Consequently, these institutions, in fact, were not last resorts for poverty and despair but an intermediary step before the last desperate step had occurred. Many homes actually refused to receive children if both parents were living, believing this would encourage parental irresponsibility, just as they perceived remarriage of one parent, most often the mother, to be reason to give the child back to the parent.

The privately maintained orphan asylum, which required nominal monthly payments, therefore, became custodial residences for those children who were approved of by Ladies' committees for admission, often on grounds of the respectability of the families seeking assistance and of the probable ability to pay the requisite sum on a regular basis, and not on appeals of sheer destitution. Thus, when compared with the desolatory nature of the municipal houses in the Maritimes, or many of the Catholic institutions which usually operated an open-door policy, the Protestant Orphans' Homes (POHs) remained generally smaller and more intimate although depressingly poor. They were, therefore, without being gratuitous, relatively "elite" institutions which catered primarily to that category of people labeled "the worthy poor," with the poorhouses catering for the children of the less worthy. The almshouses along with the Catholic institutions therefore were truly the "last resort."

In the 1890s, J.J. Kelso, Canada's first Superintendent of Neglected and Dependent Children, was dismayed at Canadian orphanages' powers "to put out or bind out as an apprentice to domestic service or to any trade," and he grimly asserted that orphanage children were

> . . . moved about all day like pieces of machinery and their education consisted chiefly of scolding, fault finding, and lectures on behaviour, humility and respect for the good ladies who were doing so much for them. No real attempt was made to find homes for the children until they reached the age of twelve when they were apprenticed out as servants.[36]

The various orphan asylums in the Atlantic provinces which provided the first institutionalized settings for the special needs of children also utilized the commonplace practices of binding out. These homes collected part of the child's paltry wages to be put in trust until the indenture was completed. The records indicate that this was often inefficiently and negligently carried out and the child, once placed, was rarely adequately supervised unless a protest was lodged concerning his treatment. Supervision was given much lip service but rarely practised. Private funding could scarcely provide the home and its superintendents with other than the bare necessities and there was little money to spare to ensure a regular and systematic supervision of children placed in country homes.

Not surprisingly, pre-adolescent boys were easily placed on farms and girls between ten and fourteen years were also in great demand. The peculiar sexual vulnerability of such girls makes the situation all the more poignant. Curiously, part of the anti-juvenile immigration campaigns against the importation of young Britons under the auspices of child rescue societies, hundreds of which came to New Brunswick and Nova Scotia, was premised on the perceived unfair competition such children presented to domestic dependent children for whom homes and apprentices were zealously sought by institutions. Mr. Middlemore of Birmingham used the Halifax Industrial School to receive boys before they were placed in the countryside and Mrs. Louisa Birt of the Liverpool Sheltering Home used Nova Scotian Homes as distributing centres for her young children. Dr. Cossar's Boys Club of Glasgow and his farm in Scotland, provided New Brunswick with cheap labour consisting of several hundred boys. All the criticisms about the importation of British waifs, however, were no less applicable to the domestic institutions because few of these could scarcely congratulate themselves on having superior methods. The psychological and biological distance of the families in which they were all placed was no greater but the cultural and geographical distance was, thus aggravating the young Britons' loneliness and alienation.[37]

Records of various homes indicate distraught parents who lost track of, or control over, their children because the home had arbitrarily adopted or indentured them solely on grounds of non-payment and without parental permission. Such terms led to abuses in the system of indenture because although orphans could be smoothly bound out into service or "adopted" (which did not mean last century what it has come to mean in this) without fear of parental claims or legal reprisal, such a practice was more tenuous in light of the numbers of non-orphans whose custody was maintained through contract. Indentures were rarely altered to adjust to changing socio-economic conditions.

The orphan asylums' claims to guardianship, *in loco parentis*, were ordinarily absolute in the case of the orphan children although even then the principle was more one of custom than of law for provincial legislation was not uniform and was often ambiguously defined. It was only after the passage of the 1893 Ontario Children's Protection Act and related provincial legislation that such absolute authority on the part of the institutions over the guardianship of the orphan class began to diminish in favour of the principle of state wardship or that parental rights became gradually more articulated and defended.[38]

The most flagrant abuse of the agreements made for pauper and home children was in the area of schooling which was commonly compromised or totally neglected. Rarely were wages included and the indenturing of dependent children became merely a subterfuge for cheap labour or the perpetuation of a social system that saw the poor, and the children of the poor, as temperamentally and socially suited for menial occupations. As the first report of the Halifax POH sententiously noted, "They are trained to habits of order, cleanliness and industry and taught all kinds of household work and whatever may fit and prepare them for useful stations in life."[39] Pauper and home children had none of the recourses to justice that Henry Forrester had through his parents. Pauper, surrendered, orphaned and neglected children, therefore, both psychologically and objectively, felt the onerous burden on their young shoulders of their dependence and their destitution and were rarely encouraged to transcend this condition. The assumption that children in the institutions were from the lower orders and therefore suited for menial occupations both in status and in disposition was not only reaffirmed through the indenture system but also was operative within the homes themselves. The training of children "into usefulness" was a common theme and some homes such as the Halifax POH entirely operated on the children's contribution to household tasks under the supervision of the matron with no other domestic help from its founding in 1857 until 1871. The children's services were used "in order that they may become useful domestics."[40]

It has already been noted that Newfoundland's programs for relief of the pauper population were frequently implemented on a more casual and private basis than relief in the other colonies. A poorhouse was not completed until fifteen years after its plans were presented before the Crown in 1846. Meanwhile the Benevolent Irish Society, the St. John's Dorcas Society, the Society for Improving the Condition of the Poor, and St. Vincent de Paul Society, did what they could to ameliorate conditions, which in all frankness, must be said to have surpassed any of the other colonies, in their wretchedness and misery. In short there was little evidence of a significant use of advocacy for the less fortunate apart from the efforts of a "few public servants and private citizens."[41]

In 1834 an act was passed for the maintenance of Bastard children to be followed some years later by one for Infant Paupers which allowed $350 for the boarding out of thirty-one crippled, orphaned, and pauper children. No similar legislation was passed until the children's clauses in the 1931 Public Welfare Act. However, given the repeated ravages of tuberculosis and diphtheria which decimated infant populations perhaps the colonial government relied upon these as a grim final solution to the problems of child dependence. Newfoundland's reputation last century as a demographic disaster area was infamous.[42]

As early appreciation for the need of specialized facilities was articulated by the Benevolent Irish Society (BIS), founded in St. John's in 1806. A committee of charity from the outset observed that it must "attend carefully to the claims of children of parents whose vices and misfortunes prevent their supporting their offspring" and it agreed that such children must be placed out "to good masters." By 1823 however the BIS realized that in a colony so distressed as Newfoundland even this was easier said than done and suggested that an orphan asylum be erected to alleviate their "unhappy condition." The society, which never received crown aid nor was granted incorporation because of its exclusive Irish membership, lacked the necessary funds to support such an institution. Therefore a curious situation arose. The BIS had an orphan asylum but no orphans, although approximately four hundred children attended day schools in the building.[43] The cellars of the St. John's orphan asylum were used for general relief supplies and its rooms used for meetings. The asylum was used in 1902 for charity balls but not for orphans! *The Patriot and Terra Nova Herald* in 1859 stated that "for forty years the Society has pledged to open an orphan asylum."[44] A similar situation occurred in Prince Edward Island in 1856 when an orphan school but not an asylum was approved by the legislature and consisted of a room for daily instruction, whereas in New Brunswick in 1838 a school was equipped in the almshouse.[45]

It was not until 1854 that specialized facilities were available for Newfoundland's destitute children when the first catholic orphanage at the Convent of Mercy opened its doors. A year later the Church of England Widows' and Orphans' Asylum was founded to counteract the legacy of cholera which left so many widows and orphans in its wake. By the end of the century catholic children had several other orphanages including Belvidere, Villa Nova, as well as Mt. Cashel Boys' Industrial school while protestant girls were provided for by the Methodist Orphanage founded in 1888.[46]

The Saint John POH was founded in 1854 after a public meeting called by the Protestant clergy and partly in response to the circumstances these gentlemen observed children were subject to in the prison and the poorhouse, and partly as a response to the orphans resulting from the asiatic cholera. The original shelter was destroyed in the 1877 fire and the children taken at Canadian Pacific Railway expense to Boston to stay in The Home for Little Wanderers.[47] The POH, while receiving children regardless of religion, included half-orphans, orphans, and the deserted or destitute offspring of the indigent, inebriate, or those confined to asylums or penitentiaries, nevertheless prohibited children who were "diseased, of physical blemish, or unsound mind."[48] Frequently then these were the children who were destined to be confined as public charges in the almshouses.

With its own schoolroom ensuring complete segregation from the outside world and the rules supervising strictly the visits from parents or relatives, whose undesirable influences were viewed with suspicion as if the surrender of their children was inevitably the consequence of moral flaw rather than of poverty and desperation, the orphan asylum not only scrupulously protected its children from the general pauper and criminal populations but also from the perceived influences of unsatisfactory family life. For those involved in child rescue there was no doubt that institutional life was superior to that of lower class homes. The 1867 annual report observed that the home, with only nineteen children (seventeen had been "adopted" and placed that year) operated "in the routine of a large family [and] there is not much interest beyond its own walls." The following report described the home as "an embryo asylum" which it remained only doubling its numbers by 1910 until it amalgamated in 1922 with the Provincial Memorial Home to prevent duplication of facilities and ensure more economical management.[49]

Just as the clauses of the Poor Law persisted in New Brunswick so did the congregate nature of the POH. In decades where elsewhere "depopulation" was occurring with fostering becoming more the order of the day, this particular institution in fact increased in population so that even as late as 1970 it still sheltered 122 children despite the adverse criticisms in the 1961 CWC Survey. This, the third CWC Survey conducted between 1928 and 1961, observed that the type of child the POH cared for should not be in an institution but either in a surrogate home or kept within its own family.[50]

Although certainly segregated into, and dependent upon, an institutional setting for their protection, most New Brunswick dependent children last century were far from adequately cared for, according to changing contemporary patterns. One institution provided an exception to the general rule. This was the Wiggins Home, founded "for the benefit of destitute male orphans and destitute male fatherless children" [of mariners], which was incorporated in 1867. "An ornament to the city," the citizens of Saint John regarded it as an architectural beauty and greatly admired its bathrooms, water closets, basins with hot and cold running water, and its central heating system. The boys were not bound out until fifteen years of age, later than the custom in other institutions. In 1884 this limit was raised to seventeen years so that the boys would not "lose the good effects of their training." The boys' education was exceptional and consisted of a curriculum that included grammar, geography, history, arithmetic, quadratic equations, writing, and the study of the first six books of Euclid. In keeping with the philosophy of all child rescue institutions the boys were trained into useful occupations as well and spent two days a week at soldering, telegraphy, carpentry sewing and patching, wood splitting, knitting, and mattress and pillow picking. The home was always relatively small, select, generously endowed under the conditions of Stephen Wiggins' will, and was a singular congenial setting representing the family model under house parents.[51]

IV

The asylum, by our standards, was far from a satisfactory environment for dependent children but if judged according to the municipal houses operating under local authorities, then the asylum attempted at least to simulate a degree of warmth and domesticity, and to create a quasi-family atmosphere. The female governance of these institutions did in fact modify the starkness of the poor house and the unremitting drudgery of the house of industry. Moreover, given their relatively small populations, ranging from forty or fifty in the more modest endeavours of Halifax and Charlottetown to two hundred or so in Saint John POH at its height, the asylums did not resemble the depersonal, non-domestic and inappropriate architecture found in many of the huge orphan asylums of Great Britain and the more crowded ones in Toronto or Winnipeg. An approximation of family atmosphere is, however, not the same as the realization of it and in the area of "serial contamination" orphan asylums come to positively endanger the very lives they purported to protect.

In several ways the orphan asylum epitomized the first three criteria of the concept of childhood postulated by the authors. The inmates were segregated within specialized premises and protected in an assiduously cultivated environment from the intrusions of the outside world. These intrusions were perceived by managers and caretakers as having both a moral and physical dimension. The separation of children from guardians or a surviving parent was spelled out in agreements whereby the children were signed over in total custody and wardship to the orphanage with parents denied any rights over their treatment or indentures, this being qualified only if they kept up fee payments in those institutions which received fee paying clients. The reason given for this extreme action was that children must be protected from the contaminations of inadequate, irreligious, or immoral family influences. The first report of the Halifax Industrial and Ragged Schools Society, 1864, best summarizes the attitude.

> Political economists may preach on the natural rights of parents, and the dangerous abuse of charity, but are they to allow parents to sacrifice their offspring to their vices — to offer them in the fire to Moloch? They cannot stand by without attempting to rescue them.[52]

Visiting privileges were, therefore, vigilantly controlled and confined to a few hours a week. When outbreaks of disease occurred either within the home or in the outside community even these privileges were withdrawn so that the children were further isolated, sometimes for months at a time in cases of extended or serial quarantine.[53] For example, the Church of England orphan asylum in St. John's in 1860, was quarantined on and off for a half year due to whooping cough, scarlet fever, and measles. In 1897, this asylum boasted of two hospital wards but still had six deaths that year notwithstanding that it was "better equipped for treatment of children's diseases than any other institution in the Island."[54] An examination of the other institutions merely suggest that the comparison was relative!

Conscious efforts to protect and segregate their charges most certainly led to a profound emotional residue in the vulnerable psychés of children already burdened by a sense of abandonment, rejection, or bereavement, for young minds cannot be expected to comprehend on a rational level the social and economic constraints which forced many parents and relatives to seek out institutional custody of their children either on a temporary basis or for permanent refuge. Moreover, to be isolated on admission until a clean bill of health was granted, or to be treated in isolation for head lice, pink-eye, ringworm, or the "itch," must have aggravated the trauma of separation from familiar surroundings or kinfolk and exaggerated a child's sense of loss.

The reluctance of most homes to allow their children to mix freely with the outside world was based on more than the dire consequences of introducing even minor diseases into their close confines. The ladies' committees that supervised the domestic economy and decided on admission and demission came to believe that their institutions were superior to uncontrolled working class family life. To permit indiscriminate association at school and in play was to throw away all their hard won advantages. Not only were the homes selective in whom they admitted but the attempts at creating a well ordered asylum within a disordered world offered a special moral environment for the proper rescue of the children selected.

This unnatural protection was compounded by the fact that most homes, at the outset at least, and in several cases well into their histories (such as the Saint John POH) further segregated the children by having their own classrooms and schools. It is interesting to note that once school systems compelled medical inspection and provided vaccinations the various orphanages relented and sent their children into the public schools. Before this, however, it was ensured by exaggerated segregation practices that the outside world of family and peer groups would not interfere with the internal domestic arrangements of the homes. Consequently the homes turned in on themselves and saw their regimen as the most desirable of environments using the analogy of the "family" notwithstanding the inevitable distortion of family values despite the best will in the world on the part of the caretakers.

In 1889 the St. John's press sensationalized the capital as "A City in Danger . . . The Angel of Death Still on the Wing" when the citizenry was alarmed by an outbreak of typhoid in Villa Nova Orphanage at Manuels. Although the epidemic was contained and its source traced to stagnant water, 127 boys contracted the dread disease and Father Norris the superintendent died along with four boys. It was said that he had "overlooked the proper internal arrangements in his fervour to extend the home" but the moralizing tone of this comment must be discountenanced when one recalls the lack of public interest in the orphanage and the lack of public aid, as well as the depressed and unhealthy conditions common to the Island as a whole.[55]

Scarlet fever, cholera, typhoid, diphtheria, poliomyelitis, scrofula, rickets and bronchitis all appear with depressing regularity in the history of the orphan asylums. The records are replete with items such as that from Saint John POH in 1887 which said that "our little Stewy . . . the pet of the household died of whooping cough."[56] The children in the St. John's homes were conspicuously susceptible to the ravages of tuberculosis as indeed was the whole population of the Island itself. The homes in their bid to protect child life in fact were unable to protect them from the problems of children's diseases. Therefore, they actually became seedbeds of disease — unwholesome congregate systems — ill prepared to counteract the problems of serial contamination. In 1875, the Protestant Infants' Home of Halifax had purchased "cheap thin cotton" to make baby "shrouds." Two years later scarlet fever hit Nova Scotia, and, deaths were so common at the home that the ladies' committee was compelled to ask the commissioners of the poor if they might use the Poors' house hearse to save the expense of cab hire for baby funerals. As late as 1899 the death rate at this institution was 26%.[57] The infants' homes were undoubtedly the most vulnerable to debilitation and disease, morbidity and mortality.

Conclusion

When the Newfoundland Widows' Aid and Orphans' Friend Society issued its 1881 report, it observed that its girls dressed in gay red cloaks and its boys in handsome sailor suits presented a "delightful contrast" between them and charity children of the past. The contrast consisted also "between themselves and what they might have been but for the saving culture of this noble institution."

On several counts this remark is a salutary reminder of the dilemma of nineteenth century child rescue which have been illustrated throughout the paper. Prior to the nineteenth dependent children in anglophone British North America had been accorded little specialized care in few facilities. In societies that provided minimal aid for those in want, children were relieved along with their parents and friends. Beginning in the nineteenth century, religiously motivated men and women organized themselves into societies to relieve cases of acute and chronic distress. Of all the classes succored, dependent children offered the greatest scope for maritime philanthropy. Destitute old men and women were forlorn objects of pity; destitute children were objects of pity and promise. Carefully selected and separated from the contamination of a sinful world that often included their parents, the children could be rescued from and made secure against the sins and failing that had brought their families low. The new children's institutions had effectively separated their inmates from a disordered society and given them a wholesome quasi-family environment. Separated from their families and friends, the children were kept from social intercourse with neighbourhood children lest such contacts undermine the work of the institutions.

While they rescued their dependent children by protecting and separating from adult society and thus ensuring them a "childhood," the managers of the institutions were compelled at the same time to make them socially useful. To make them useful required that they be taught to work and made to contribute in the process to their upkeep. The work they did in and out of the homes confirmed their inferior social and economic status. On one hand they were ensured a partial childhood and on the other they were prepared to be exploited. The "noble institution" rescued them as children for exploitation as youths and adults.

Notes

[1]These criteria are explicated by Schnell in "Childhood as Ideology," *British Journal of Educational Studies* 27 (February 1979): 7-8. They have been used in a survey, "Childhood and Charity in Nineteenth Century British North America," *Histoire sociale/Social History* 15 (Mai - May 1982): 157-179.

[2]Report of the State of the Orphan House (circa. 1752) CO 217, Vol. 18; Governors of Nova Scotia to Lords of Trade, Belcher 3/11/1761; RG 1, Sect. 4, 37; Dalhousie and Perot Returns, RG 26, Series C, Vol. 3; *Journal of House of Assembly* (1832), p. 59, Provincial Archives of Nova Scotia (PANS). Also see G.E. Hart, "Early Private Relief in Nova Scotia," (1953), RG 25, Series C, Vol. 9,1, PANS, and Margeurite H.L. Grant, "Historical Background of the Nova Scotia Hospital . . .," *Nova Scotia Medical Bulletin* (May 1937): 250-258. Minute Book of the

Poor and Work House (1869-1880), No. 2363/8, Provincial Archives of Prince Edward Island (PAPEI).

³Almost identical terminology was retained in the Revised Statutes of 1952, Chapter 221, "Support of the Poor Act." Discussed in the Canadian Welfare Council (CWC) Survey of New Brunswick, 1949, pp. 12, 63, MG 28 I 10, Vol. 135, Public Archives of Canada (PAC). See also Kierstead papers, UA RG 63, Boxes 1, 2, University of New Brunswick.

⁴Stuart R. Godfrey, "Introduction of Social Legislation in Newfoundland," a paper read to the Newfoundland Historical Society, 19/4/1979, pp. 3-9, and Barbara Smith, "The Historical Development of Child Welfare Legislation in Newfoundland, 1832-1949," B.S.W. Thesis (1971), Centre for Newfoundland Studies, Memorial University (MU). Also see H.M. Mosdell, "When Was That? A Chronological Dictionary of Important Events in Newfoundland Down to and Including the Year 1922," Provincial Archives of Newfoundland, (PANF).

⁵Discussed by Margaret E. Anstey, directory of the Children's Aid Society (CAS) of Saint John, in "Memo: Re Organization of Child and Family Welfare," Charlottetown (August 1931), MG 28 I 10, Vol. 19, PAC.

⁶B. Mulcahy, Secretary of Office of Charities Committee, Poors' Asylum, to Hon. Commissioner of Works and Mines, Halifax, 21/6/1898, RG 25, Series C, Vol. 5, PANS; and Report of Inspector, G.L. Sinclair to Hon. C.E. Church, Commissioner of Public Works and Mines, in "Public Charities," Legislature of Nova Scotia (1900), p. 38, McGill University Archives (MUA).

⁷Sinclair to Church, pp. 23, 43.

⁸F.A. Hall to Hon. Geo E.P. Morris, Premier, 10/4/1911, in Poor Asylum (1910-11), GN 2/5 17H, PANF.

⁹Sinclair to Church, pp. 21, 32; Halifax Poor House Affairs Report (1851), AK HV/79c, PANS.

¹⁰M.F. Howley, *Ecclesiastical History of Newfoundland* (Belleville, Ontario: MIKA Publishing Co., 1979), pp. 228, 276-277.

¹¹Sinclair to Church, p. 32.

¹²William Hattie, Health Officer, "Report on Public Charities, Nova Scotia, 1914," pp. 8, 33, 50, MUA. *The Acadian Recorder*, 26/12/1882, reported children enjoying the Christmas fare in the Halifax Poors' Asylum.

¹³Canadian Welfare Council Survey Report (1949), p. 12.

¹⁴Canadian Council of Child Welfare Survey Report (1928-29), MG 30 E 256, Vol. 36, PAC.

¹⁵Charlotte Whitton to Isobel Harvey, Superintendent of Neglected Children, 27/3/1943, MG 30 E 256, Vol. 4, PAC.

¹⁶Poor House and Farm Journal (Feb. 1885 - Nov. 1907), RG 35, Series King County, Cornwallis, PANS. The *Halifax Evening Express*, 27/3/1875, reports infant deaths in the Halifax Poors' Asylum.

¹⁷Saint John Almshouse (1853-1963), Provincial Archives of New Brunswick (PANB).

¹⁸Minutes 4/2/1873, 28/1/1875, March and April 1875; First Minute Book (12/1/1875 to 1890), Halifax Infants' Home, MG 20, 177: 1, and 2, PANS.

¹⁹Record Book Halifax Poors' Asylum, 7/3/1843, PANS.

²⁰Superintendent's Report, 28/4/1896, RG 25, Series C, Vol. 4, PANS.

²¹Discussed by authors in "The Rise and Fall of Protestant Orphans' Homes as Woman's Domain," *ATLANTIS* (Spring 1982): 21-35.

[22]*Daily Examiner* (Charlottetown), 25/7/1883.

[23]Poor House and Farm Journal, King County, Cornwallis, 15/2/1845. Reports for 1847, 1848, 1850, 1853, record total children and total deaths. See also "List of Apprentices Bound Out from 1/1/1832 to 1847," HVP79 (1847). K. Williams, "Poor Relief and Medicine in Nova Scotia," refers to prevalent maltreatment of apprentices, *Nova Scotia Historical Society*, Vol. 24, p. 40, PANS.

[24]14/2/1814, Hubbard Papers, Shelf 28, LD3 859579, New Brunswick Museum (NBM).

[25]17/8/1837, Forrester Family, NBM.

[26]5/6/1815, Delesdernier Family, NBM.

[27]*Journal of the House of Assembly* (JHA), New Brunswick (1857), pp. 136 and Appendix "Provincial Institutions" DXLIX-DLXI, PANB. In these same years, children were in the Halifax Bridewell since in April 1855 an application to indenture was made to a thirteen year old girl. Proceedings of Committee of House of Refuge (1853-57), MG 20 214, PANS.

[28]JHA (1857), DLVII-DLVIII; Boys' Industrial Home, *Annual Reports*, (1920-48), Brunswick Department of Health, NBM.

[29]30/5/1860 and 23/5/1860, Public Library of Newfoundland (PLNF). First Report Protestant Industrial School, Halifax, p. 4, in Reports (1864-1928), HVH13, PANS.

[30]Church of England Widows' and Orphans' Asylum, Anglican Archives, St. John's.

[31]J.R. Smallwood, *The Book of Newfoundland* (St. John's: Newfoundland Book Publishers, 1937), discusses many early societies. The Factory Committee meeting of 14/11/1835 is reported in *The Royal Gazette and Newfoundland Advertiser*, 24/11/1835, PLNF. J.W. Withers, "St. John's A Century Ago from Vol. I of the Royal Gazette" (1907), discusses smallpox ravaging the land in 1807 and the burden it placed on The Society for Improving . . . the Poor, PANF. The Reports 31/7/1808 - 31/7/1808 — 31/7/1809, and 1811, as well as the St. Vincent de Paul Society report in *The Patriot*, 19/12/1859, are in PANF.

[32]First Report Halifax Industrial School (1865), p. 5, MG 1, Vol. 3792 (R.V. Harris Collection); Halifax Poor Man's Friend Society Reports (1820-24) AK HS H13, and Minutes, MG 3, 180:2 (1820-27), PANS. See George E. Hart, "The Halifax Poor Man's Friend Society 1820-27: An Early Social Experiment," *Canadian Historical Review*, 24 (June 1953): 109-123. The climbing boys are discussed in *Journal of House of Assembly* (1844), Appendix 25, pp. 45-47, 53, and *Morning Chronicle*, 18/7/1867, *Presbyterian Witness*, 1/2/1862, *Christian Messenger*, 28/5/1862, 21/10/1863, and *Morning Journal*, 6/6/1862.

[33]*Thirty-fifth Report of Director of Child Welfare, Nova Scotia*, 30/11/1947 (Halifax: King's Printer, 1948), pp. 8-9. Ernest Blois, first director from 1912 to 1947, had been a teacher and superintendent at the Industrial School. First Report Halifax Protestant Industrial School (1865), p. 8. Records of Nova Scotia Society for Prevention of Cruelty to Animals, Vols. 513-515, MG 20, PANS.

[34]Reports of St. Paul's Almshouse of Industry for Girls (1868-1895), HV JA 2P, Reports of Halifax Protestant Orphans' Home (1857-1948) AK HV P94, and *Morning Journal*, 20/12/1861, PANS.

[35]The phenomenon of transforming previously independent children into "dependent" children has been discussed by P.T. Rooke, "The 'Child-Institutional-

ized' in Canada, Britain and the U.S.A.: A Trans-Atlantic Perspective," *The Journal of Educational Thought* 11 (August 1977): 156-171.

[36]Typescript on Orphan Children, n.d., Kelso Papers, MG 30, C 97, Vol. 8, PAC.

[37]See Joy Parr, *Labouring Children* (London: Croom-Helm/Montreal: McGill-Queens University Press, 1980), and discussed by the authors in "The 'King's Children' in English Canada: A Psychohistorical Study of Rejection, Abandonment and Colonial Response (1869-1930)," *The Journal of Psychohistory* 8 (Spring 1981): 387-420. Another aspect has been discussed by the authors in "Making the Way More Comfortable: Charlotte Whitton's Child Welfare Career," *The Journal of Canadian Studies* (forthcoming).

[38]See the pioneering studies on this, Neil Sutherland, *Children in English Canada* (Toronto: University of Toronto Press, 1976) and Andrew Jones and Leonard Rutman, *In the Children's Aid: J.J. Kelso and Child Welfare in Ontario* (Toronto: University of Toronto Press, 1981).

[39]First Report Halifax POH, PANS.

[40]Reports (1857-1871), especially 1859 Report, PANS.

[41]Godfrey, "Introduction of Social Legislation. . .," p. 20.

[42]Smith, "The Historical Development. . .," p. 4. Joyce Nevitt, *White Caps and Black Bands: Nursing in Newfoundland to 1934* (St. John's: Jesperson Press, 1978). Even in 1917 the eight year average of infant mortality in Newfoundland was still 189 per 1,000 according to figures in Armine Nutting Gosling, *William Gilbert Gosling: A Tribute* (New York: The Guild Press, 1935). While mayor of St. John's, Gosling promoted the Child Welfare Association.

[43]*Centenary Souvenir Book of the Basilica of St. John the Baptist* (1855-1955); general correspondence relating to Benevolent Irish Society and *Centenary Volume of Benevolent Irish Society* (1806-1906), pp. 41-42, 176, Smallwood, *The Book of Newfoundland*, pp. 171-185, and *Christian Brothers' Jubilee* (1876-1926), PANF.

[44]*The Patriot and Terra Nova Herald* (Newfoundland), 28/2/1859, PANF.

[45]Saint John Almshouse (1838), PANB; and John M. Starr, Inspector of Schools, 25/2/1856, PAPEI.

[46]Smallwood, pp. 303-304; Howley, pp. 377, 370. Records of Widows' and Orphans' Asylum (1855), Anglican Archives (AANF); and Records of Methodist Orphanage (1888), United Church Archives, St. John's.

[47]Max G. Barter, Superintendent, "New Brunswick Protestant Orphans' Home," 5/3/1965, and Annual Reports (1867-1914), R 362.732 PRO, NBM. [48]Canadian Welfare Council Survey Report (1949), p. 109.

[49]Saint John Protestant Orphan Asylum Reports (1867-1914); Barter, "New Brunswick Protestant Orphans' Home"; *The Observer* (Maitland, N.B.), 5/4/1973, NBM.

[50]*Evening Times-Globe,* 20/5/1970. Report of the New Bruswick Task Force on Social Development, Vol. 1, (Sept. 1971), Saint John City Library.

[51]Minute Book, 1/6/1891-28/1/1901/, Wiggins Home, Saint John. The Act of Incorporation, 10/6/1867, and further acts, 1/4/1884, 21/4/1884; and *Daily Telegraph*, 16/3/1874, NBM.

[52]First Report Halifax Industrial School (1865), PANS.

[53]The authors have discussed this matter in an unpublished manuscript, "Death, Diet and Disease: Aspects of 'Serial' Contamination in British North American Orphanages, 1850-1930."

[54]Widows' and Orphans' Asylum Reports (1860) and (1897), AANF.

[55]Villa Nova, Manuels, Newfoundland; *Evening Telegram*, 22/7/1889, and letter from "Health" to Editor, 5/8/1889, PLNF.

[56]Widows' and Orphans' Asylum Report (1860), AANF.

[57]Halifax Infants' Home Reports, Minutes 7/9/1875, 5/3/1877, 3/2/1890, MG 20 177:1-2; *Morning Chronicle*, 196/1899, PANS.

[58]Widows' and Orphans' Asylum Report (1881), AANF.

Perspectives on Illegitimacy: The Changing Role of the Sisters of Misericordia in Edmonton, 1900-1906

Leslie Savage

Historians of childhood are familiar with the abundant evidence of the exposure, abandonment, sale, enslavement, beating, mutilation and killing of child life in past times.[1] The softening of attitudes towards children since the fifteenth century has been heralded as a major social and ideological change, one that has contributed very significantly to the structuring of modern family and social life.[2] When the Order of the Sisters of Misericordia was founded in Montreal (1848), its aim was to rescue unwed mothers from dishonour, to relieve them from penury and to restore them to a virtuous life in which no further lapse from conventional morality would occur. Linked to this goal, and giving institutional expression to the modern concern for the preservation of child life, is the Misericordia's focus on the rescue of the illegitimate born and unborn from the threat of death by abortion, infanticide, neglect or abandonment.[3] The dual concern for child rescue, in the literal sense, and female reform, directed the work of the Order during its first fifty years. By 1898 the Misericordia maternity refuges in Montreal, New York and Ottawa had provided for over fourteen thousand unwed mothers and their children, in institutions specifically dedicated to and organized for that purpose.[4]

When in 1900, however, four Sisters of the Misericordia established a mission of the community in Edmonton, the central focus of their work rapidly changed from child rescue and female reform to general medical service and hospital nursing. This text argues that the evolution of the role of the Edmonton Misericordia was a response to the different socio-economic conditions and moral attitudes of early twentieth century Edmonton as opposed to nineteenth century Montreal. Thematically, it is a study of the ways in which the threat to illegitimate infant life posed by the outcast status of unwed mothers has varied over time and geography in Canada, and of how the institutional change of one female religious community has reflected shifting Canadian patterns of popular ideology and custom.

In order to foster an appreciation of the change in the institutional focus of the Edmonton Misericordia, it is necessary to outline briefly the origins of the order in Quebec and the tradition of Roman Catholic religious benevolence to distressed women and abandoned children thereby represented. The major part of the discussion, however, is given to the portrayal of the Edmonton milieu into which the Misericordia Sisters came in 1900, and the circumstances of the Misericordia in that setting between 1900 and 1906.

105

The history of illegitimacy in British North America is in its infancy, and may remain forever stunted owing to a lack of documentary evidence. For European communities, the quantitative analysis of parish records[5] has allowed historical family reconstruction in a manner that is unlikely to be replicated, at least for an Anglo-Canadian population that was religiously heterogeneous and in some areas highly transient.[6] Professor Peter Ward's study of unwed maternity in three nineteenth century Ontario parishes relies on civil court depositions, specifically the Affidavits of Affiliation filed by unwed mothers in support of maintenance claims against the putative fathers of their children, to show that attitudes to unwed maternity were less condemnatory than has commonly been supposed.[7] Such affidavits, provided for by law in Alberta after 1903, are not available for the Edmonton population, having been destroyed along with all civil court case files up to 1949.[8] Published law reports, census reports, parish baptismal records of the St. Joachim Roman Catholic Church in Edmonton, the files of the Attorney General and the monthly *Chronicles* or newsletters of the Edmonton Misericordia, as well as secondary materials, are the sources on which the following discussion is based. It is noteworthy that up to the 1920's there appear to have been no case histories of patients or unwed mothers kept by the Misericordia Sisters in Edmonton; nor is there evidence to suggest that hospital procedure, policy direction or financial administration, were carried out in a formal routine manner.[9]

The Origins of Foundling Hospitals and Female Refuges

The beginnings of the work of the Misericordia Sisters can be traced to the efforts of the early Christian Fathers to eradicate the infanticidal practices of pagan antiquity. In the provisions made for destitute, abandoned, exposed and neglected children in early Christian and medieval Europe, arrangements made in the name of Christian *caritas* and the heavenly salvation of both the donors and the recipients of charity, can be glimpsed the distant origins of the modern rescue and reform of unwed mothers and illegitimate children.[10] Infanticide, in direct or indirect form, is generally recognized by historians to have been directed at the illegitimate above all. It is, however, only since the seventeenth century that the unborn illegitimate have been the focus of charitable concern in the form of relief and assistance to, and rehabilitation for, unmarried and destitute pregnant women.[11]

The Christian Fathers who challenged the social structure of the Romanized Mediterranean world opposed infanticide. The Christian Covenant of baptism indicates an affiliation to God through Jesus Christ that takes precedence over all worldly relationships, even familial ones, so that parents, being only guardians of their children in this world, do not have the right to dispose of their children as they see fit.[12] Constantine affirmed that God creates souls for life, not death, which, along with the belief that only baptism can accord remission from original sin, increased the determination of Christians to rescue exposed and abandoned children, whose souls were otherwise forever imperilled. The faithful were exhorted to bring their unwanted children, or those whose care was beyond their means, to the church steps, rather that kill or expose them.[13] It was, however, several centuries before the establishment of the first known foundling hospital, by Dateus of Milan in 787.[14] The history of foundling hospitals throughout the Middle Ages and early modern period reflects, however, identical concerns with those of the early Christian fathers: the rescue of children from death, their baptism and rearing by surrogate mothers.[15] More often than not it appears that refuges for foundlings and abandoned children were part of the more generalized form of charitable care for the mendicant, the elderly, the ill and the incapacitated that was exercised by religious orders in hospices such as the French *hôtels-dieux.*

Two aspects of the convent tradition made the religious orders particularly appropriate for the care of destitute children and eventually of unmarried mothers. From earliest times the religious orders were associated with the mendicant tradition in Christendom, and saw charitable works as a natural extension of their own vows of poverty. Secondly, as has been discussed by Hélène Bergues, the influence of the Penitential theologians, from the sixth century on, was crucial in establishing a disciplined system of penance and absolution in religious life.[16] This from early times allowed women in distress as a result of illicit pregnancy to seek refuge in convents, there to repent and seek heavenly forgiveness, as well as to safely deliver the child. The link between this tradition and the Misericordia is clearly seen in the name given to unwed mothers, who in Montreal were called the penitents.[17] Up until the seventeenth century in France, however, it appears that the care of both foundlings and unwed mothers was not widely differentiated from general religious charity that provided relief to all classes of individuals unable to provide for themselves.

It was with the establishment of the General Hospital of Paris by Louis XIV in 1656 that the notion of rehabilitation was introduced into institutionalized social assistance. Historians have amply documented the dramatic rise in illegitimacy rates in France during the seventeenth century.[18] Illegitimate children formed the largest single element of a swelling mendicant population who were jobless and homeless. In response to the plight of this increasingly rowdy group, the French Crown created the General Hospital of Paris with the objective of "obliging the worthy poor to work and the others to let themselves be maintained under a severe discipline."[19] At first all inmates were indiscriminately housed; soon it was observed, however, that to put hardened criminals in the same hostel as victims of misfortune corrupted the latter but did nothing to improve the former, so different classes of inmates were separated in various institutions. For women, housed in the Salpêtrière, the difference between the worthy and unworthy hinged not only on the degree of debauchery but also on the hope for improvement or correction. The seventeenth century institutionalization of destitute unwed mothers in this convent (run by the Sisters of Charity under Vincent de Paul) section of the General Hospital of Paris is a direct predecessor of the dispensing of charity to unmarried mothers in French Canada, and embodied an effort to rehabilitate the women inmates to a virtuous life as well as to provide for their physical needs for the duration of their pregnancies and confinement. By the time France began to send settlers to colonize the St. Lawrence outposts, then, the tradition of female reform in French religious convent communities had been established.

Religious Charity in Quebec, 1690 - 1800

In law and religion, Quebec society incorporated many elements of the ancien régime, even after the demise of the royal administration in France and North America. The *Coûtume de Paris* formed the basis of Quebec civil law even in the 1860's when the Quebec Civil Code was promulgated.[20] The church as well encouraged an adherence to old world standards. Almost from the beginning of colonial rule, Quebec ecclesiasts rejected the modernisms of the Post-Tridentine French Catholic Church and remained ardent ultramontanists. In 1659 the Vicariate Apostolic in Quebec was made a diocese, shifting ecclesiastical authority from the French Church to the Vatican. The British conquest in 1760 confirmed the break with the liberality of the French Church.[21] Particularly in regulations governing marriage and family life, the traditions and official attitudes of the ancien régime appear to have prevailed, although not consistently nor in all far-flung rural parishes of the colony. Indicative of this conservatism is for example the degree to which "l'incapacité de la femme" and "la puissance maritale" of the Quebec husband both preserved "the ancient rule of customary law regarding *le douaire* as it was manifest in the *Coûtume de Paris*,"[22] and again in the legal circumstances of foundling children, who, as in France under the monarchical régime had no status in law and who were therefore automatically subject to the guardianship of the person or institution who undertook their care.

The care of foundlings, as other indigents, from the beginning of the colonial regime devolved upon the church with assistance from the colonial administration. Historians of social life in New France have found evidence of social assistance, adoption, fostering and binding out of foundlings and orphans.[23] The history of care for unwed mothers is less developed; the evidence that does exist, however, links such care in the colony to the precedent of the General Hospital of Paris, with similar concerns for the protection of unborn infant life as a motive in female protection and for the separation of redeemable women from the hopelessly debauched.[24] Thus as well as inheriting from France a patriarchal family structure, Quebec also was subject to the tradition of religious charity in the provision of social assistance to unwed mothers and their children. It was not, however, until the nineteenth century that the specialization of these initiatives in child saving and female reform attained its institutional zenith.

The Misericordia in Late Nineteenth Century Montreal

From early colonial times, social assistance to unwed mothers and children was closely connected to religious salvation and convent charity, but it was social conditions in nineteenth century Montreal that gave particular urgency to the Misericordia Mission.

These conditions have been well documented by historians. During the 1850's the population of Montreal climbed from 57,000 to over 92,000.[25] Urban migrations in the 1830's and massive Irish immigration in the 1840's had led an influx of the dispossessed, destitute and desperate to seek their livelihood in the city. Overcrowded tenement suburbs resulted. During the 1850's Montrealers were plagued by fires that left tens of thousands homeless, by national tension, rioting and cholera epidemics.[26] By the late 1850's, however, the factories along the Lachine Canal, the building of the Victoria Bridge and the Montreal waterworks, meant the "opening of new frontiers of opportunity" and also "brought new relationships to the social classes of Montreal." At this time began the mobilization of the labour force into a capitalist industrial economy; by the end of the century the economic structure was dependent to a large extent on the cheap labour of working women.[27] Scholars note that domestic service and factory work were the main occupations for women in the Montreal work-force. One quarter of all working people in 1825 were female domestic servants. By 1881 almost 16 per cent of Montreal's female population worked in manufacturing industries. Apart from low status, abysmal working conditions, sexual harassment and for domestic servants loneliness, the most significant feature of women's work in nineteenth century Montreal was, as in other industrializing cities at that time, low pay.[28] In factories one-half to one-third of the man's wage for comparable work was the normal female's salary. More than one salary was often required by a working class family in order to make ends meet, and women's wages were geared to assist, rather than to support, a family.[29] For working-class women in the districts that surrounded the factories of Montreal, low wages went hand-in-hand with an unstable labour market, inadequate and crowded housing, poor nutrition, illness, high mortality rates and a "fragmented" family life.[30]

Despite the importance of women in the urban work force, the reigning ideology concerning the role of women upheld the most desirable position for women as that of wife and mother. The French-Canadian woman was to be, above all else, "une bonne mère."[31] The primary attribute of a "good mother" in a society where the titular head of the family is male is that she provide herself with a husband. A mother who failed to do so was associated with a life of debauchery even when it was recognized that she might have erred only once, or strayed by accident from the accepted route to motherhood.

It is difficult to know the circumstances and fates of women who did conceive and bear children out of wedlock. Of those who came to the Misericordia between 1885 and 1900, almost one-third were less than twenty years old, forty percent were in their early twenties and twelve percent were over thirty. Fifty percent were domestic servants, thirteen percent were factory workers.[32] The desperation they may have faced can only be suggested by advertisements such as: "wanted, a Female Servant of good character, who understands Cooking and the Drudgery of the House. A woman having a child will not answer."[33] The isolation, through family fragmentation, of many young people in nineteenth century Montreal, has been shown to be a reality of urban social life, so that many of the most likely candidates for unwed motherhood, that is, domestic servants, may have been without family resources to fall back on in times of emergency.[34] That many such women were compelled through circumstance, ignorance, despair or malevolence to abandon their newborn infants is attested to by the records of the Sisters of Charity (The Grey Nuns) of Montreal who until the Misericordia established its own orphanage in 1889[35] were accustomed to receive not only the illegitimate infants born at the Misericordia but also those found abandoned in the streets of the city. In 1866 there were six hundred and fifty-two foundlings delivered to the various orphanages of the Sisters; of these three were dead on arrival; seven were frozen; over four hundred were almost naked; eighteen had had no postnatal care whatever; thirteen were wounded; forty-six were syphilitic and eight were drugged with opium. Most were ill; most were verminous. In the year of Canadian Confederation, public health authorities talked openly of the "plague of infanticide" that beleaguered the city.[36] This was twenty years after the founding of the Misericordia, at a point in time when the number of penitents received annually by the Misericordia averaged two hundred and fifty.[37] It is not unreasonable to speculate that in the 1840's when the Misericordia was founded the situation was equally bad or worse.

The circumstances in which the Order of the Sisters of Misericordia was founded, first as a congregation in the Hospice Ste. Pélagie in 1846, then as the Order of the Sisters of Misericordia in 1848, have been documented elsewhere.[38] What is important to note, in order to further the understanding of the evolution of the Misericordia role in Edmonton, is the institutional organization of the Montreal Misericordia and its concentration on the rehabilitation of unwed mothers.

The aims of the Order as expressed in its Rule pertained on the one hand to the conduct of the women professing their vows, on the other to the behaviour expected of the penitents. The former stipulated a communal life where all property and resources were shared equally; where the Superior was elected, and where the process of decision-making was democratic. Poverty and obedience were the rule and chastity not only the rule but intended as a prime source of inspiration to the girls and women who resided in the hospice. It was a communal organization in which there existed, however, an elected hierarchical order empowered to mete out discipline.[39]

A foremost goal of the Misericordia was the rehabilitation of unwed mothers. Behavioural reform was to accompany spiritual renewal. The penitents were "to bear in mind that they have entered this house in order to learn to know, to love and to serve God, and begin an entirely new life."[40] The Sisters were instructed to make them understand that "their honour as well as their happiness . . . depend on their not being obliged to return to the maternity," an admonition that reflects a secular concern with the prevention of repeated illegitimate pregnancies,[41] just as the admonitions for spiritual and physical mercy reflect concern for the relief of suffering. The Rule of the Order was quite explicit about the achievement of this goal. The Fourth Rule of Chapter One, for instance, counsels the Sisters that in their dealing with the penitents they "must avoid carefully speaking, formally or implicitly, about the sin that is the cause of . . . dishonour; for the shame that they would entail would be capable of preventing all the good that one hopes to do by other means."[42] Instructions such as these, embodied in the *Règlements pour les personnes qui se sont offertes à Dieu pour conduire l'oeuvre de l'hospice de Ste. Pélagie érigé à Montréal*, leave no doubt that the intention of the Order was reformatory as well as redemptive. The Sisters hoped that the penitent would achieve absolution of sin and also, equally important, a practical return to conventional morality. A reconstruction of the daily routine of the inhabitants of the Misericordia reveals that separation from the outside world, isolation from the past and from family and friends, acceptance of the defined order, compliance with the rites of religious life and dependence on the sisters, acted to protect the unwed mother from the hostility of society that did not tolerate sexual nonconformity in women. In so doing it served to "save the honour of families" at the same time as to "diminish the dreadful crime of infanticide."[43] The educative function of the unwed mother's sojourn with the sisters has been described elsewhere in terms of a process of separation, isolation, dependence and protection. These features have been described by Rooke and Schnell[44] as the distinctive characteristics of an ideology of childhood that began to be recognized and accepted in nineteenth century Canada. Returned to a symbolic state of childhood, then, the unwed mother could relearn the lessons of sexual behaviour and family mores that prevailed in nineteenth century Quebec. When failure to meet the ideal of feminine virtue resulted in unwed pregnancy, the response in France and New France, under the *ancien régime*, had been restraint in a refuge little differentiated from a prison, in which however the notion of separation of the virtuous from the bawdy was incorporated. By mid-nineteenth century restraint had fully shifted to rehabilitation through a focus on re-education. The unwed mother would, through a process of separation attended by protection, supervision, dependence and a disallowance of parental responsibility, undergo a re-socialization aimed at her incorporation into the accepted order of feminity. Spiritual redemption followed repentence, confession and communion. Temporal salvation however was a question of changed attitudes and behaviour. The aim was not to remove the stigma of unwed motherhood, but in the context of the prevailing code of sexual morality, to invoke repentence and reformation through the interweaving of good example, remorse, submission and faith.

The Misericordia Sisters in Edmonton: Institutional Change

In May, 1900, four sisters of the Misericordia — St. Francois de Sales, St. Frances Cabrini, St. Frédéric and St. Edmond — and a nurse, Jane Kennedy,[45] arrived in Edmonton by train, with the intent of providing care for unwed mothers in Edmonton as they had done in Montreal. As the Edmonton mission evolved, however, Misericordia Hospital shifted its primary focus from service to unwed mothers to general nursing and medical care, with one branch of the hospital maintained for unwed mothers. This shift in emphasis in the role of the Misericordia can best be understood in the light of two changes: firstly, the change in locale of the Misericordia from Montreal to Alberta; and secondly, the change in the nature of the Edmonton milieu from a frontier town in 1900 to a modern, if small, city by 1910.

The greatest problem during the initial stages of the Edmonton mission was a lack of money. Anxiety about finances permeates the first few years of the *Chronicles*,[46] a preoccupation understandable in the light of the self-sufficiency expected of the mission. It had been agreed that the Oblate Fathers and the ecclesiastical corporation would help the Sisters get started with a gift of land and a loan of $10,000,[47] but that the mission would have to be independent. It is doubtful that the loan was granted until the construction of the new hospital was begun in 1905. Many charitable endeavours received government assistance at this time, both in Montreal and in the Northwest. The work of "enfants trouvés" had, under the French régime in Quebec one-hundred and thirty years earlier, been subsidized to some extent by the state, but modern aid was slow to materialize. By 1898, the Misericordia in Montreal had received, during fifty years of service, $4,800 in government help, out of total expenditures of some $337,000.[49] In the Northwest Territories public aid to hospitals was regulated by legislation. By 1900 both the Edmonton General Hospital and the Saint Albert Hospital were receiving government subsidies according to patient per day scale that differentiated between patients who paid all, part, or none of the regular fee. Ten cents per day was paid for every patient registered; an extra forty cents daily for every "partially free patient," and another forty cents per day on top of that for every "free patient."[50] But the Misericordia was not eligible for those grants until it was incorporated in 1904.

There is no record in the *Chronicles* of funds received from the Mother House, as it was a primary condition of outlying missions that they should generate funds to cover their expenses. Laundry, shirt-making, shoemaking, carpentry and knitting had been among the early money-making activities of the Montreal Order, and some of these were taken up in Edmonton. The most frequently mentioned endeavour in the *Chronicles* , though, is the collection of alms, or "l'oeuvre des quêtes."[51] In this the Sisters became very proficient. They set about raising funds in an organized manner, travelling to towns as far away as Calgary, where there was little sympathy for their cause, and Medicine Hat, where both Catholics and Protestants contributed generously.[53]

The other method of raising money to pay the expenses of the mission was the charging of fees to patients. The Sisters' preoccupation with these levies, in the newsletterss, reinforces the impression of general anxiety about economics that pervades the *Chronicles* during the first years. "We received a pensionnaire today at $2.00 per day; we were proud of this, but the joy was shortlived. . . ."[53] As late as March, 1904, when Dr. Forin, an Edmonton medical practitioner, sent a patient at $2.00 a day it merited a "Dieu le bénit", for money was still in short supply. Although the mission was perfectly willing and even eager to accept non-paying clients as long as they truly had no means of support, the Sisters went so far as hiring a lawyer, on March 26, 1901, to help them collect from the husband of an ex-patient who, they knew, was perfectly capable of paying but had neglected to pay the bill.[54]

As well as the problems caused by the domestic economics, there was another difficulty, more elusive as to its identification and its explanation. This was the fact that, although the tiny quarters of the Sisters often seemed overcrowded, there was no instantaneous recognition among the population of Edmonton that here, at last, was a much-needed refuge for homeless and destitute unmarried mothers. All sorts of patients, visitors and guests, both paying and impecunious, came to stay with the Sisters, but to the consternation of the latter, not many of these were unwed mothers. Although a few single girls came to last out their confinements, the majority of the patients were married women. There were mixed feelings about these clients. On the one hand they usually paid their fees; on the other, the "pensionnaires" were often accompanied from afar by their husbands, some of whom turned up to take meals with their wives, and others by their children, who had to be looked after as well. From the beginning, too, the Sisters' mission served as an orphanage.[55] The *Chronicles* register a certain perplexity about the surfeit of "dames pensionnaires" and "enfants" contrasted to the relative infrequency of "penitentes." On 21 December 1903, for example, a Sister wrote that "a poor protestant woman came to place with us a child of one month; she seemed ashamed to admit that he belongs to her fifteen-year old daughter. Asked why she did not send the daughter to us she replied that "she did not know about our house — cré-tu que je te cré! — I assure you there is no lack of these unfortunate girls . . . if they all came here the house would soon be filled up."[56] The interjection — "Do you think I can believe you"? — belies the Sister's scepticism about what she regarded as a poor excuse. The fact that not many illegitimate babies were born at the Misericordia during the first few years did not please the Sisters. Table 1 indicates the small size of the operation and the low incidence of births at the hospital.

Of six illegitimate births in St. Joachim in 1901, only two unwed mothers came to the Misericordia; in 1902 four of six, and 1903 five of seven.[58] These represent only the baptised Roman Catholic illegitimate births (See Table 2); there is no way to know how many illegitimacies occurred where the child was not baptised. This shows an increasing use of the Misericordia but one which must be measured against the growth in the overall population, which was rapid during these years. Clearly the Sisters were operating under conditions very different to those in Montreal. These differences cannot be understood merely in the light of a smaller population base, for illegitimacies in St. Joachim parish were in excess of the number of Misericordia births. Other factors must be considered in order to understand why the Sisters were not successful in attracting more unwed mothers to their refuge.

To understand the change in institutional strategy of the Misericordia and the reasons for it, it is necessary to appreciate a number of factors pertaining to socio-economic and cultural conditions in Edmonton and surrounding areas, circa 1900.

Table 1

Residents, Baptisms and Illegitimacies at the Misericordia[57]
1900 - 1905

	1901	1902	1903	1904	1905
Residents (December)	14	27	23	23	37
Penitents (December)	4	4	3	2	3
Baptisms (all year)	3	5	8	12	7
Illegitimate Baptisms (all year)	2	4	5	8	6

Table 2

Illegitimate Births as a Percentage of Infant Baptisms[59]
1899 - 1904

1899	1900	1901	1902	1903	1904
7.1%	17.8%	9.7%	7.8%	10.9%	10.9%

The demography of the Northwest Territories and Alberta is an important factor in the history of the Misericordia in Edmonton. The 1901 Census gives the population of Alberta as 65,876, although some doubts exist about the consistency and accuracy of enumeration returns at that time.[60] Between 1900 and 1906, however, it is certain that the primary demographic reality in the Territories was rapid population growth accompanied by an equally dramatic change in the ethnic composition of the population. By 1906 the new Province of Alberta counted 185,400 people of at least fifteen national and linguistic identities, and the ethnic distribution of the population had shifted from a predominance of Native peoples in 1885 to a majority (56 per cent) of non-Canadian-born.[61]

In 1885, among both the European and Métis populations, the predominant language was French and the principal religion was Roman Catholicism.[62] French Canadians outnumbered both the Scots and the English. Of the Métis enumerated in the 1885 Census, 94 per cent were Francophone. Roman Catholics were twice as numerous as all denominations of Protestants. By 1900, however, the influx of Anglophone immigration had well begun, and from that time on the Francophone population declined in proportion to English speaking residents.

For French-speaking Catholics, despite hopes to the contrary, it was a matter of consolidating the initiatives already taken in settling the west, rather than expanding their population base. Whereas the population of Edmonton climbed from 2,626 in 1901 to 11,167 in 1906, that of Francophone Saint Albert stayed relatively stable, increasing only slightly from 472 to 543.[63] In Saint Boniface the Archbishop, Mgr. Langevin said in 1898 that he needed more settlers to consolidate the position of the Franco-Catholics in the Red River and Assiniboine districts, as well as on the banks of the Saskatchewan, in Edmonton and Prince Albert. Franco-Catholic leaders in both the east and the west shared the belief that French Canadians belonged in an agricultural society, and that taking up homesteads in Western Canada was preferable to moving away to factory towns in New England.[64] Ironically, as noted by Painchaud, the perception that a westward Francophone emigration would undermine the viability of Franco-Catholic culture in North America by splitting its geographic base[65] caused Catholic westerners to struggle even more vigorously to establish centres in the Northwest. Despite their efforts, however, *la francophonie* in the west continued to lose ground to other European groups. Certainly the diminishing Franco-Catholic influence in the west was one reason for both the coming of the Misericordia and for its failure to attract a larger number of penitents than it did.

Another aspect of demography that relates directly to the question of unwed maternity is the ratio of men to women. The scarcity of single women compared to the number of single men is characteristic of Alberta at this time. Although the overall ratio of single women to single men improved slightly from 15:24 in 1901 to 16;24 in 1906, the ratio of women of marriageable and reproductive age, fifteen to forty-four years old, to men of the same age, diminished significantly from 18:24 in 1901 to 14:24 in 1906.[66]

The relative numbers of men and women made marriage a strong probability even for unmarried mothers. Statistically, eighty-three per cent of women over nineteen in Alberta in 1901 were married; of those twenty-five years and over, the records show that one hundred per cent were married.[67] Indeed the Misericordia had difficulty keeping nurses, who invariable left to marry after a few years in Edmonton, as did a number of the novices. A woman on the Northwest frontier was unlikely to stay single long. In a country of young men the marriage prospects for women are enhanced, and the potential for illegitimacy, and stigma attached thereto reduced, especially where agriculture is the primary occupation and a wife of essential value as a help-mate.

Another factor bearing on illegitimacy was the question of whether or not a single woman could have afforded to support herself and a child, in the economic climate of the Northwest. As early as 1885, agriculture was the main occupation of the 'European' people of Alberta, with 1584 farmers, ranchers, dairymen or cowboys, in a population of 15,533. In contrast, 689 people were employed in commerce and the professions, 421 in industry and 185 in domestic service. By 1900 the number of industrial establishments had almost doubled over sixteen years from sixty in 1885 to 105 in 1901 whereas the population had increased about five times.[68] Because agricultural workers can be paid in services and goods, it is difficult to specify exact values for their labour. Women's agricultural work moreover is often performed by family members who are not paid at all. But industrial employment and wages indicate in approximate terms at least the level of pay for female labour. Table 3 indicates comparative salaries and numbers of employed; it is based on all industrial employees in Alberta in 1901 and those employed in five cotton mills only in Montreal.

The relative affluence of labouring Albertans compared to Montrealers at this time is clear from a comparison of the average annual male wage earnings.

For a Montreal mill family to earn the same as one man might earn in Alberta, would require that both husband and wife, as well as seventeen children, labour in the factory. If the wages of a husband could easily support a family in Alberta, there may have been greater incentive than if otherwise for women to have married, and given the shortage of females, more likelihood for them to have done so. For women who did earn their own wages, work in rural districts was likely limited to domestic service, but in the city it included a variety of jobs such as shop-assistant, law clerk, telephone operator, shirt-making, laundress and domestic servant.[70] The latter earned fifteen to thirty dollars monthly, twice the wages paid in Toronto.[71] Salaries were such that the Young Women's Christian Association could charge $4.00 per week for a room and two meals daily.[72] Before the Association's rooming house had even opened there were seven applications. It seems that single women could and did support themselves, although often just as stop-gap before marriage, in Edmonton at the turn of the century. On the other hand, of one hundred fifty boarding spaces in Edmonton in 1907, only four indicated they would accept single women. What economies could have allowed, social pressure may have discouraged.

Regulations governing marriage, family relations and the care of abandoned or neglected children in Alberta, prior to 1905, were based on both

Table 3

Industrial Wages, Montreal and Alberta in 1901[69]

Employees by Sex and Age	Five Cotton Mills Montreal	All of Alberta
Males employed	3,156	138
Average annual wage	$414	$2,843
Women employed	2,416	17
Average annual wage	$230	$344
Children employed	1,123	25
Average annual wage	$125	$155

English precedent and on the Canadian legal code as interpreted by local magistrates.[73] As the area became more densely populated, however, the Legislative Assembly of the Territories saw fit to pass Ordinances regulating various aspects of social life on a more regional basis. By 1898, duly ordained ministers and clergymen of any church were authorized to perform marriages. This attempt to regularize marital proceedings can be assumed to have met with success in populated areas of European settlement, but on the fringes of these communities, where Native and Métis customs prevailed, it is questionable how quickly official marriages replaced the older forms of consensual union that had been current in fur-trade society.

Sylvia Van Kirk has made clear that the definition of what constituted legal marriage was in question during the pre-settlement era.[74] In these early days the longevity and perceived legitimacy of the country marriage depended on the will of the husband, who in the early days of the trade could either turn off his country wife when retiring from the employ of the trading company, or continue to recognize the marriage either by settling in Canada or taking his wife back to the British Isles. The outcome was a matter of considerable importance to the country-born, the children of fur-trade society. In the event of the birth of half-siblings to a new wife, the possibility of a contested patrimony could and sometimes did arise, with varying outcomes in the courts[75] and with continuing ambiguity as to the definition of what constituted a legal marriage.

If the legal ambiguities of marriage persisted up to the pre-confederation period in Alberta, so did social attitudes towards the various intersecting configurations of reproduction and marital conformity. Reported court cases provide evidence as to conflicting notions of acceptable morality. Magistrates often upheld the letter and spirit of the marriage ordinance but just as frequently made rulings that indicated some tolerance for sexual nonconformity at least on the part of the women.[76]

The ambiguity over the official nature of marriage was an important influence on the operations of the Misericordia. The stigma of illegitimacy rests on a careful and precise articulation of what constitutes a sanctioned marriage. Without such definition, the question of legitimate birth cannot encompass the degree of importance that it otherwise assumes. When marriage is a private arrangement between two consenting partners, as appears to have been the case in Native societies, rather than an official celebration incurring the participation, in person or proxy, of the families of the couple, the church and the state, the status of children born to the marriage, in terms of their "lawfulness" or "unlawfulness" is not an issue.

Consistent with the effort to impose regulated standards of marriage on the population were official efforts to provide in law for children born outside of those regulations. For the Territories, the 1903 Ordinance for the Support of Illegitimate Children specifies that affidavits could be filed "while the mother was pregnant or within six months after the birth of the child, . . . declaring that the person afterwards charged in the action is really the father of the child," and deposited in the office of the Clerk of the Supreme Court for the judicial district in which she resides.[77] The text of the Ordinance is such that the intent of the legislation is ambiguous. It is unclear whether it was meant to prevent unwed mothers claiming paternal support (as no action was to be sustained *unless* the affidavit had been filed) or to give them recourse to such support. In any case, as no affidavits have been found for the Territories, other evidence must be considered for Western Canada. Apart from the official view embodied in law, however, what can be said about the offspring of illicit unions in turn of the century Alberta, save that they often did not inherit? Were they welcomed and nurtured as future help-mates and companions in a sparsely populated rural economy? Was their illegitimate status simply irrelevant? Or did the stigma of their birth cause rejection, psychological or physical, and manifest itself in a range of mechanisms including infanticide as well as disinheritance, as it had done at some times and in some circumstances in European civilization for centuries past?

Evidence is hard to come by. Court records provide some glimpses of social attitudes towards sexual nonconformity and towards the victims of infanticide. In two clearcut cases of child murder by the unmarried mothers of newborn infants, the local magistrates refused to press charges on the grounds that the women had already suffered enough from their predicaments. In one case, Elizabeth C., employed as a domestic servant at the Phillips' Ranch, tried to conceal her pregnancy, but unsuccessfully so, according to a neighbor's testimony at the inquest.[78] When she went into labour both the farmer and his wife were away for the day. Alone, Lizzie gave birth to a child that was later found by Mrs. Phillips, still in its birthing caul and dead, in a box under the bed. Another case involved a second domestic, this time an Anna M., the sole servant at the Camrose Inn.[79] Her child's delivery too was unattended in spite of the sure knowledge of bystanders that she was pregnant and in labour, as they later admitted to the magistrate. A boarder found the child in the hotel's outdoor privy. An autopsy later proved that the mother's claim to a stillborn infant was false. It was clear to the magistrate that Anna had, in desperation or ignorance, disposed of her infant with little or no attempt to give it any life-giving care. Anna, like Lizzie C., appears to have lived in sea of silent disapproval that condemned her to a lonely pregnancy and solitary labour for which she was utterly unprepared and unable to deal with. No sooner were the dead infants discovered then the police were called in. No-one offered to assist these women, or call a doctor in time to have prevented the infant's death, a fact which may have moved the sympathy of the magistrates. In neither one case nor the other were charges laid against the women. While the magistrates' exoneration of the mothers indicates a commendable tolerance of their plight, it demonstrates at the same time an attitude to the infants that is casual if not indifferent. And this is the same indifference to children born as bastards that is at the heart of the stigmatization of unwed maternity and illegitimacy: an indifference born of a social will to regulate the sexual activity of women through the stigmatization of illegitimate births. Here we have not an example of the Christian conformity to social norms in marital affairs that was endorsed and taught by the Misericordia, but instead a manifestation of a much more ancient form of social ordering, the legitimation of infanticide by governing authorities when the infant in question was born out of wedlock. This masquerades as sympathy for the desperate plight of the unwed mother. Such attitudes are likely to have been detrimental to the efforts of the Misericordia to rehabilitate unwed mothers in the Northwest. For just as a relatively relaxed attitude to unwed maternity would have meant that little incentive existed for women to flee from their families to bear an illegitimate child, the quasi-condoning of infanticide may have reduced considerably the life-span of a forever unknowable number of newborn in remote and isolated homesteads and camps.

The 1903 Ordinance for the Support of Illegitimate Children theoretically provided recourse for unmarried mothers to obtain financial help from putative fathers. At the same time the Ordinance Respecting the Action for Seduction (1903)[80] provided a jail term for men who corrupted the morals of "previously chaste" women, even though such a sentence would obviously have made difficult the financial assistance required by the child and mother. As in the reported cases of infanticide, judgements rendered by local magistrates in seduction cases appear to have afforded women considerable tolerance and sympathy.

In September, 1902, for example, one Lougheed of Medicine Hat appealed his sentence of one year in prison for having seduced under the promise of marriage one Kate McCutcheon. Kate had been judged to be "of previously chaste character" in spite of the fact that "the illicit connection was renewed about once a week, each time under a separate and distinct promise of marriage, from June 1901 to December 24, 1902." Moreover the judge ruled that reasonably speaking, "this young woman's faith in the accused should have been shaken long before the occurrence in question," from which had resulted a pregnancy. He noted that it was "rather difficult to believe that this particular promise of September, 1902, repeated for the sixtieth or seventieth time under the very same circumstances, was really and truly the inducement to which she allowed herself to yield on that day." Nevertheless the court excused the girl's conduct, and sustained Lougheed's conviction.[81]

Another case of upholding the "previously chaste character" of a seduced female is that of Lillie Hunt, who had been seen in compromising position with another man and had accompanied the accused to a hotel, registered as Mr. and Mrs. and had prostituted herself to him for money. The judge found in Lillie's favour, however, ruling that in spite of the foregoing evidence she had not been proven to be of previously unchaste character.[82]

The interpretation of legislation by regional magistrates can be read as indicative of the way a certain community is likely to regard an issue. The court records in Alberta reflect a variety of attitudes. Given the profound cultural diversity of the people, their small number, the balance of sex distribution weighted heavily in favour of men, the regionality of legislative interpretation, the difficulty of the established churches in providing adequate religious support, and the lack of tradition in the question of regulated marriage, it is not surprising that frontier attitudes were rife with ambivalence. The absence of a consolidated outlook in questions of marriage and the legitimacy of children meant that illegitimacy as stigma had a less profound grip on the mentality of the people than was the case in Montreal. For the Misericordia Sisters, this meant that relatively few unwed mothers experienced the social rejection, or fear of it, that made them, in Montreal, seek refuge in the convent hospital.

Yet another factor that made the Misericordia solution to the problem of illegitimacy less than popular, among a segment of the population at least, was the attitude of the missionaries, both male and female, to Métis women, particularly those they saw as unconforming to the Church's moral code. Bishop Grandin's opinion that Métis women in general lacked self-control was echoed by the Misericordia Sisters, who were intolerant of what they saw as dangerously immoral behaviour among all women, but thought Métis women particularly prone to depravity. The image of the "pauvre brebeuf égarée," the little lost lamb who needed only to be shown the way to salvation, was the predominant theme, in the Montreal Misericordia, in the treatment of unwed mothers by 1900. This image, however, was inconsistent with the independent behaviour of the frontier women who, having been delivered of their infants at the Misericordia and having left them there in the Sisters' care, frequently turned up later to reclaim them, bringing along or sending in their stead husbands, lawyers, and lovers to plead their cases. The Métis mother of "little Mary," for instance, who had been three years with the Sisters, turned up in June, 1904, to take away her daughter, making a dreadful scene and eventually succeeding in leading away the crying child.[83] Mme. R., a Métisse, drove the Sisters "to distraction", between December, 1900, and June, 1901, with scenes in which she tried to reclaim Agnes, her daughter. Eventually the Sisters conceded, but dressed the child in her original ragged clothing to send her off. The demeanour of the the mother did nothing to reassure them about the future happiness or well-being, let alone proper education, of the child; nor did the alternate appearance of past and present "husbands," one of whom was Agnes' father who paid for her keep. Mme. A. sent the lawyer Mr. MacDonald to argue for the release of her daughter; but the Sisters had Père Leduc "whose worth equals three good lawyers" to settle the matter — although, and here the record obviously omits part of the story — in the mother's favour.[84] Not only did Métis mothers appear from time to time to disturb the equilibrium of the convent orphanage, but on one occasion at least a grandmother as well made her presence felt by trying to reclaim her daughter, who three months earlier in December 1900, had been delivered of little

Veronique,[85] and was reluctant to leave the mission. The grandmother eventually had to apologize for her ungraceful conduct, but not until she had quite unsettled the Sisters in charge. These women scarcely present a picture of dependent femininity in need of protection. Métis women sometimes did not stay at the convent because they were unwilling to make the required sacrifices.[86] Obviously, other options must have been open to them. In a society where women's company was in high demand, where marriage traditions were flexible, Christian views tenuously imposed, the disinclination of unwed mothers to be truly penitent, that is repentant, is not surprising. It was, however, a matter of scandal for the newly arrived Misericordia Sisters, who were quite open, in the newsletters, about their feelings as to unrepentant sinners. One woman from St. Albert was scathingly described as "an absolute trollop . . . all got up in silk from boots to bonnet . . . entirely in the grip of her own caprice."[87] In spite of the need for paying patients, she was not permitted to stay. In the Northwest such women, who in Montreal might have been absorbed into the large and more anonymous Misericordia institution, were unable to withstand the close scrutiny of the Misericordia. On the other hand, the Sisters' attitude to these women seems to be consistent with the outlook of female reformers in Ontario at this time, which was that all wayward women, regardless of race or religion, are debauched and depraved.[88]

While it would be misleading to overemphasize this hostility of the Sisters towards Métis women, their attitude highlights the attempts of "le Canada civilisé" to impose on the vast Northwestern half of the country the marital and family values that English, Scots and French legislators, social leaders, politicians and entrepreneurs had, by 1900, successfully established in Eastern Canada. Nineteenth century Canadians recognized that it is through the family, in the early years of a child's life, that the patterns of social life are set.[89] If the expansionist aims of either Anglophone or Francophone visionaries[90] were to be realized, it was crucial to instill in the people moral values attaching to family life that were replicas of those in the East. The coming of the Misericordia to Edmonton can be seen in the light of such hopes. But poised against this effort to acclimatize the prairies and the Northwest to Eastern values were many obstacles. One was the general shortage of women; another, the shortage of priests;[91] another, the pre-existence of less formal marriage customs. To the missionaries, these factors were symbolic of a real or imaginary element of sexual abandonment that loomed as part of the wilderness they were trying to bring under control. The Métisses were reminders of the precarious position of white society in the Northwest.

The relative lack of interest of Albertan unwed mothers in having institutional convent care during their confinement meant a waning of the Misericordia's role in service to penitents, relative to their Montreal activity. The growth of Edmonton between 1900 and 1910, and the urgent need for expanded health services, provided the opportunity for the Edmonton Sisters to move in a different direction, into general nursing and hospital care.

It should be noted that although some other Misericordia missions were originally established as general maternity hospitals, the Mother House in Montreal did not undergo a transition similar to that of the Edmonton Order, whose institutional change of direction was not the result of a horizontal shift throughout the breadth of the Order's operations, or of policy change of administered from the top. It was rather a specific reaction to local conditions in Alberta.

J.M.S. Careless has placed the beginning of urban development in Edmonton and Calgary in the 1880's,[92] asserting that both cities were from the start "involved in the steam-and-steel technology and transport" and that "railway technology . . . integrated the new western cities into a continent-wide metropolitan pattern."[93] In 1906 Edmonton had only two wholesale firms; by 1911, almost fifty.[94] Between 1904 and 1914, land annexations by Edmonton almost tripled the area of the city.[95] By this time Edmonton owned and operated its own water service, sewage system, electric light and telephone systems, and boasted thirteen banks, twenty-two hotels, two daily, five weekly and three monthly newspapers, four saw mills, two flour mills, a brewery, a wood mill and woodware factory, three steam laundries, two brick-yards and a seven-storey packing and storage plant.[96] Careless maintains that by 1914 Edmonton was, a modern city if a small one, judged by criteria such as patterned residential districts, physical layout of streets and parks, social awareness and amenities and occupational patterning.[97]

The absence of provisions for social assistance,[98] in the first few years of the century, however, created a situation in which religious orders, regardless of their ostensible purpose, were automatically seconded to the care of those unable to look after themselves. In the lack of alternate specialized institutions in the Northwest at this time, the Misericordia took on the character of a general asylum for the helpless and hopeless, as well as that of a hospital. Clergymen from as far as Calgary placed orphans with the Sisters, as did Rev. P. Fitzpatrick, for instance, on October 7, 1903. Another orphan was left by some people from Banff.[99] A number of children were placed for a fee in the hospital, often in cases of marital disputes which caused considerable difficulties for the Sisters, who found themselves in the position of marriage counsellors.[100] Girls as young as thirteen were sent as novices to receive instruction from the Sisters. In one case an old man, whose board was paid by the municipal authorities of Strathcona, came to live at the hospital.[101] In another, an idiot girl with a child was brought to them, thinking she had come to "l'hôpital de l'éternité" in order to die there.[102]

The informal, familial style of the Edmonton Misericordia undoubtedly encouraged its use as a hospital by the general populace. Not only was it customary for doctors attending patients throughout the night to breakfast at the Misericordia,[103] but when maternity patients, or ex-patients from out of town arrived either to stay or to visit, the hospital served as sort of a hotel for them and their husbands and children. With the arrival of more and more non-maternity patients, including males in need of medical attention, the heightened prospect of both fee-paying patients and the possibility of receiving government subsidies, the Misericordia Sisters found that by 1906 they were operating a general, rather than a maternity hospital, with thirty non-maternity cases, not counting the children in the sick bay. All the rooms in the house were over-flowing. The hospital had lost the domestic ambiance of the old refuge. As a Sister wrote; "What a commotion we have in the house at present; we are barely able to respond to or look after visitors and strangers who come to us; in truth we are beginning to know what it is to operate a general hospital."[104] In March 1906 the Sisters moved to their newly constructed *Hôpital.*

Table 4 demonstrates the growth of the generalized side of the Misericordia, and the orphanage component, as well as the waning of attention devoted to unwed mothers.

While the number of unwed mothers stayed fairly constant, the general nursing patients increased from zero to forty-seven between 1907 to 1914, and the Sisters from five to fourteen. The addition of five nurses for the children in 1914 reflects an increasing concern for the specialized infant care necessary as the Misericordia sustained ongoing responsibility for the children born at

Table 4

Misericordia Residents as of December 30th of each year[105]
1901 - 1906 and 1915

	1901	1902	1903	1904	1905	1906	1915
Sisters	5	6	5	5	6	10	14
Nurses	1	2	2	3	2	8	17
Novices	-	3	-	5	3	-	-
Unwed mothers	4	4	3	2	3	-	4
Children	3	11	12	7	17	7	23
Patients	-	-	-	1	3	24	47
Nursemaids	-	-	-	-	-	-	5
Servants	1	1	1	1	1	5	3
Total	14	27	23	24	35	54	113

the hospital to unwed mothers. While the primary activity in terms of numbers became general medical care, still the care of infants and unmarried pregnant women remained a high priority in other ways.[106]

In the early years, this emphasis on children replaced, in some measure, the educative role that was truncated as the Order's work with unwed mothers diminished in relation to the overall operation.

Increasingly, from 1906 on, the emphasis was on Catholic socialization. The orphanage built in 1911, a wing of the hospital, by 1920 had space for sixty-five children. From the earliest years, the Sisters had emphasized the necessity of a Catholic upbringing above all else, and not infrequently had become embroiled in custody battles in order to secure the religious education of the child.

Between December, 1900, and June, 1901, for example, the Sisters were drawn into a custody struggle in which a father of three children had placed them at the Misericordia because they had been ill-cared for by the mother, who was "living in concubinage with another man and thus had no rights over her children."[107] The mother made repeated efforts to regain her children, coming to the convent time and time again, sending others in her stead, employing a lawyer, and creating long and noisome scenes. At one point in May the Sisters were forced to agree to allow Mme. R. to take the little girl (the two boys having been sent to the Grey Nuns' orphanage), because they had no court order to keep her, but it seems that in the end this did not work out, for in September, 1907, the father returned with $23.00 payment for the child's keep.[108] There is no doubt that the Sisters sided throughout with the father. The *Chronicles* for December 25 in that year contain a note about a child who is in danger of losing her faith because she is living with a Protestant step-mother — the inference being that she would be better off living with the Sisters. On another occasion a woman who had already brought her infant grandson to the Sisters returned with the child's mother, a girl of fifteen; she was Protestant but was taken in on the hope that she would convert. A lawyer was engaged to draw up papers for her to sign, giving the Sisters custody of the child so that they could "make of him a little Christian without fear of being troubled later" by the mother.[109] The same was the case a few months later when "a poor unfortunate woman from Regina" signed over custody of her child so that the Sisters could educate him as they saw fit, that is, as a Catholic. While these attitudes are perhaps obvious ones for the Sisters to have demonstrated, it is interesting that they did not by any means refuse non-Catholics. Instead they saw the assistance offered to Protestants as a means of furthering the Franco-Catholicism of the Northwest, hoping, if not to convert the mother, at least to baptize and educate the child. The Sisters were at first apprehensive about the future of a child who could be reclaimed at any time by a parent who had once abandoned him, and was in their view likely to repeat the procedure. In the provisions they made for the custody of orphans and illegitimate children the Sisters learned they must follow a legal format that required parents or guardians to formally relinquish what the courts considered the "natural" rights and duties of parents. This reluctance to surrender children to their parents was shared by child care institutions elsewhere, notably, as Rooke and Schnell have demonstrated, in the Protestant Orphans' Homes of Ontario.[110]

As indicated by Table 4, however, this emphasis on children was secondary to the role of the Misericordia in general hospital nursing after 1906. The Misericordia was the third general hospital in Edmonton. In 1895 the Grey Nuns of Montreal had built their General Hospital. Shortly after the Misericordia opened as a Maternity Hospital, Edmonton's Public Hospital opened, furnished by the Masonic Lodge, the Odd Fellows, the Forresters and the Women's Christian Temperance Union.[111] By October, 1905, the Misericordia Hospital construction was well under way.[112] By 1908 there were also a Sanitarium Hospital and an Isolation hospital in Edmonton.[113] Not until 1912, seven years after the Misericordia Sisters were under way with their general hospital attention, did a Protestant hostel for unwed mothers open, the Beulah Home. The first report of the director reflected a noticeably modern approach: "our girls", wrote Miss Chatham, "are not degenerates, they need all our help, and often can be started on a new life and for that reason we want to keep them separate from delinquents of the street as far as possible."[114] The Misericordia did not, however, relinquish entirely its special care for unwed mothers. It was in fact as a result of a dispute with the Government of Alberta over admissions policies to the Pineview Home, the contemporary wing of the new Misericordia Hospital devoted to unmarried mothers, that the Sisters sold the hospital to the Government and thus left the Province.[115]

In the history of the Sisters of Misericordia in Edmonton, two broad themes can be discerned. The first is the attempt by religious, cultural and political leaders to impose the values of Christian Europe, filtered through eastern Canadian society, on the Northwest frontier. In particular, social leaders tried to replicate the moral attitudes which posited in illegitimacy a good deal of stigma. The second theme is that there were inherent in local conditions certain factors that resisted such an imposition.

In spite of the isolated cases of infanticide, the evidence does not point to widespread abandonment or infanticide by unwed mothers in Alberta. A high incidence of illegitimacy such as there was in St. Joachim parish, coupled with a low incidence of recourse by unwed mothers to the refuge run by that Sisters, indicates that attitudes towards unwed maternity were not intolerant, and that a good percentage of unwed mothers probably remained at home to give birth to and rear their children. The fact that even before the arrival of the Misericordia, in 1899, the illegitimacy ratio was over seven per cent of all baptisms, and that the first year they were in Edmonton, when only two illegitimate births took place at the hospice, the rate was an astonishing seventeen per cent of all baptisms, indicates that it was not as a result of the Misericordia and the potential of their presence to draw women from other parts of the

Province to Edmonton, that caused the high ratio of illegitimate births. The high illegitimacy ratio in St. Joachim predates the arrival of the Misericordia.

The coming of the Misericordia to the Northwest was a part of the attempt by Franco-Catholic religious groups to order family life on the frontier through providing a resource of assistance and rehabilitation to women who conceived children out of wedlock. The fact that the Misericordia quickly shifted its focus away from unwed mothers is an indication of the inappropriateness of the rehabilitative model as applied to unwed mothers in the culturally diverse and rapidly expanding western population of 1900. The ability of the Misericordia to adapt so quickly to new circumstances attests to the flexible nature of the Misericordia Order, and also furthers the appreciation of the voluntaristic, communitarian institutional model. Most importantly, however, the example of the Misericordia, considered in two different Canadian contexts, points the way to an increased understanding of the way in which an institution devoted to child rescue and female reform re-ordered its priorities so as to survive as a vital community in a new environment where the moral standards and social attitudes no longer echoed the European pattern that had been transferred to Eastern Canada. For in its shift away from a primary concentration on child rescue and female reform, the Misericordia endorsed an attitude that clearly prevailed in Edmonton: unwed maternity was perhaps still a disgrace, but not such a heinous one as to require the separation of the mother from family and friends and her disappearance behind convent walls. The rescue of unborn illegitimate children from the threat of infanticide could henceforth conceivably be carried out not in secrecy by a private and discrete religious organization, but publicly and with an increasing degree of government intervention.

Nowhere in the first twelve years of the Misericordia *Chronicles* written in Edmonton is there an indication that the change in role from child rescue and female reform to general hospital service was the result of policies articulated by either the Montreal Mother House, the Oblate Fathers who were the spiritual and often temporal advisors of the Edmonton Sisters, or of the Edmonton Superiors. In the Edmonton mission the rehabilitative program as it was followed by penitents in Montreal was impossible, for the informal, domestic and familial atmosphere of the refuge rendered impracticable the strict separation of unwed mothers from both peers and Sisters, as well as the institutional life of prayer, contemplation and work as it was known in the Montreal Order. Once the hospital was built in 1906, the focus shifted to general nursing. the change in role was the result of changing conditions, social behaviour and moral attitudes in society, to which the Sisters responded. Given the very long tradition in western society of the cloistering of unwed mothers in religious institutions in order to assure the baptism of their offspring and to encourage their future observance of the rules of conventional sexual morality, this shift is nothing short of remarkable; for it indicates the degree of redundancy in modern times of the requirement that illegitimate children must be actively rescued from abuse, abandonment or murder.

Notes

[1]See for example the following: Isaac Abt and Fielding Garrison, *History of Pediatrics* (Philadelphia and London: W.B. Saunders, 1965); David Bakan, *Slaughter of the Innocents* (Toronto: Jossey-Bass, 1971); Lloyd deMause, ed., *The History of Childhood* (London: Souvenir Press, 1976); Louis Lallemand, *Histoire des Enfants abandonnés et délaissés* (Paris: Picard, 1885); William L. Langer, "Infanticide: A Historical Survey," *History of Childhood Quarterly* 1 (1973-74): 354-387; W.E.H. Lecky, *History of European Morals* (New York: Braziller, 1955); John T. Noonan, *Contraception: A History of Its Treatment by the Catholic Theologians and Canonists* (Cambridge: Harvard University Press, 1965); Hélène Bergues, *La Prévention des Naissances dans la Famille* (Paris: Presses Universitaires de France, 1960).

[2]Philippe Ariés, *Centuries of Childhood: A Social History of Family Life*, trans. Robert Baldick (New York: Alfred A. Knopf, Vintage Books, 1962), pp. 403-404.

[3]Mother Superior Marie Perras (Mère Marie de la Miséricorde), Correspondence to Stanislaus Drapeau, 1870, quoted in Thérèse Gingras, s.m., "Aux Sources Premières" (Archives of the Sisters of Misericordia, 1979), p. 24: "The work is to receive unwed mothers, thereby saving the honour of their families, and above all eliminating the dreadful crime of infanticide."

[4]Sister Sainte-Mechtilde, "La Fille-Mère et ses problèmes sociaux," (Ph.D. dissertation, University of Montreal, 1934), p. 173.

[5]Karla Oosterveen, Richard M. Smith and Susan Stewart, "Family Reconstitution and the study of bastardy: evidence from certain English parishes"; Jean Meyer, "Illegitimates and foundlings in pre-Industrial France"; Etienne van de Walle, "Illegitimacy in France during the nineteenth century"; Ann-Sofie Kâlvemark, "Illegitimacy and marriage in three Swedish parishes in the nineteenth century," in Peter Laslett *et al*, eds., *Bastardy and Its Comparative History* (Cambridge:Harvard University Press, 1980).

[6]Michael B. Katz, *The People of Hamilton, Canada West: Family and Class in the Mid-Nineteenth* (Cambridge: Harvard University Press, 1975), indicates that transience was a common feature of life in southern Ontario in the decade 1851 - 1861, a fact which makes family reconstitution not impossible, as Katz has shown, but difficult enough to preclude the likelihood of numerous such studies being completed in the future. W. Peter Ward, in his study, "Unwed Motherhood in Nineteenth Century English Canada," has discussed the further difficulty of assessing illegitimacy rates in communities where parishes of different denominations overlapped. See *Canadian Historical Association Historical Papers* (1981): 34 - 56. For a comprehensive discussion of the difficulties attending the historical study of illegitimacy and the three most common metrics used to interpret quantitative data, see John Knodel and Steven Hochstadt, "Urban and Rural Illegitimacy in Imperial Germany," in Laslett *et al*, pp. 284-312.

[7]Ward, "Unwed Motherhood," p. 55.

[8]Personal communication, Department of the Attorney General, Government of Alberta, July, 1982.

[9]*Chronicles* of the Sisters of Misericordia, Edmonton, 1900-1920 *passim.*

[10]See for instance Alan Macfarlane, "Illegitimacy and illegitimates in English history," in Laslett *et al*, pp. 77-78.

[11]During the seventeenth century education and rehabilitation began to be recognized in France as socially useful when applied to wayward women. See notes 18 and 19, and also Jacques Donzelot, *The Policing of Families*, trans. Robert Hurley with a foreword by Gilles Deleuze (New York: Random House, Pantheon Books, 1979), p. 23, who suggests that "a study needs to be made concerning the parallel histories of convents for the preservation and correction of young girls, supervised brothels for prostitutes and foundling hospitals. These three institutions arose and declined within approximately the same time span. In the seventeenth century, convents were induced by the Counter-Reformation to take in unmarried women in order to train them for missionary, relief and educative work. At the same time, Vincent de Paul set out to centralize the disposition of abandoned children. . . .The repression of prostitutes also dates from this period."

[12]Matt. 23:9. "Call no man your father upon the earth; for one is your Father, which is in heaven."

[13]Abt and Garrison, p. 42 and p. 56. See also H. Leclercq, "Alumni," *Dictionnaire d'archéologie chrétienne et de liturgie*, p. 1302, and Bergues, p. 164.

[14]Abt and Garrison, p. 58.

[15]C. Billot, "Les Enfants abandonnés à Chartres à la fin du moyen age," *Annales de Démographie historique* (1975): 167-186. See also Bergues, p. 166 and Lallemand, p. 125.

[16]Bergues, p. 195.

[17]Gingras, pp. 1-28 *passim.*

[18]See Chapters by van de Walle and Meyer in Peter Laslett *et al.*, eds., *Bastardy*; Edward Shorter, *The Making of the Modern Family* (New York: Basic Books, 1975), p. 80; T. Hareven and R. Wheaton, *Family and Sexuality in French History* (Philadelphia: University of Pennsylvania Press, 1980), particularly the chapter by Jean-Louis Flandrin, "Repression and Change in the Sexual Life of Young People in Medieval and Early Modern Times"; and also Bergues, p. 169; and Lallemand, p. 159; Shelby T. McCloy, *Government Assistance in Eighteenth Century France* (Durham, N.C.: Duke University Press, 1946), p. 212; and Camille Bloch, *L'Assitance et l'état en France à la veille de la revolution* (Paris: Alphonse Picard, 1908) pp. 103-104.

[19]Bloch, p. 48.

[20]Louis Antier, *La Survivance de la Seconde Coûtume de Paris: Le Droit Civil du Bas Canada* (Rouen: Ph.D. dissertation, University of Paris, 1923), pp. 7-15.

[21]Cornelius Jaenen, *The Role of the Church in New France* (Toronto: McGraw-Hill Ryerson, 1976), p. 20.

[22]Antier, p. 85.

[23]Jaenen, pp. 111-112. See also Peter N. Moogk, "Les Petits Sauvages: The Children of Eighteenth Century New France," in Joy Parr, ed., *Childhood and Family in Canadian History* (Toronto: McClelland and Stewart, 1982), p. 27; E.-Z. Massicote, "Le Travail des enfants à Montreél, au XVII siècle," *Bulletin des*

Recherches historiques 22 (1916): 57 and Massicote, "Comment on disposait des enfants du roi," *Bulletin des Recherches historiques* 37 (1931): 53.

[24]For a general discussion of metropolitan transfer see Yves F. Zoltvany, *The French Tradition in North America* (New York: Harper and Row, 1969). Examples of female restraint in circumstances that followed to some degree the pattern of the General Hospital of Paris can be seen in E.-Z. Massicote, "Premières Prisons des Femmes à Montréal," *Bulletin des Recherches historiques* 46 (1940): 40-43; Massicote, "Le Refuge des Filles Repenties à Montréal," *Bulletin des Recherches historiques* 46 (1940): 373-377; and Sister Suzanne Collette, s.g.m., "L'Oeuvre des Enfants trouvés," (Ph.D. dissertation, University of Montreal, 1948) p. 24.

[25]J.I. Cooper, "The Social Structure of Montreal in the 1850's," *Canadian Historical Association Report* (June 1956), p. 63.

[26]*Ibid.*, p. 63.

[27]Marie Lavigne and Jennifer Stoddart, "Women's Work in Montreal at the beginning of the century" in Marylee Stephenson, ed., *Women in Canada* (Don Mills: General Publishing, 1977), p. 129.

[28]Genevieve Leslie, "Domestic Service in Canada 1880-1920," and Alice Klein and Wayne Roberts, "Besieged Innocence: The 'Problem' and Problems of Working Women — Toronto 1896-1914," in *Women at Work 1850-1930*, Janice Acton, Bonnie Shepard and Penny Goldsmith, eds., (Toronto: Canadian Women's Educational Press, 1974).

[29]Lavigne and Stoddart, p. 135.

[30]Bettina Bradbury, "The Fragmented Family: Life Cycle, Poverty and Death among Mid-Nineteenth Century Montreal Families," paper delivered to the Canadian Historical Association Annual Meeting, June 1980. See also D. Suzanne Cross, "The Neglected Majority: The Changing role of Women in Nineteenth Century Montreal," in Susan Mann Trofimenkoff and Alison Prentice, eds., *The Neglected Majority: Essays in Canadian Women's History* (Toronto: McClelland and Stewart, 1977), and Marta Danylewycz, "Through Women's Eyes: The Family in Late Nineteenth Century Quebec," paper delivered to the Canadian Historical Association Annual Meeting, June 1980.

[31]Madame Dandurand, "Moeurs Canadiennes-francaises" in *Les Femmes du Canada: Leurs Vies et leurs oeuvres* (published for the Paris Exhibition of 1900, n.p.), p. 31. See also Ruth H. Bloch, "American Feminine Ideals in Transition: The Rise of the Moral Mother," *Feminist Studies* 4 (1978): 111. The relationship between feminine ideals in nineteenth century Quebec and in Anglo-North America needs to be studied.

[32]Sister Sainte-Mechtilde, s.m., p. 10.

[33]*The Montreal Herald*, November 30, 1816, quoted in Lawrence M. Wilson, *This Was Montreal in 1814, 1815, 1816 and 1817* (Montreal: Chateau de Ramezay, 1960), p. 18.

[34]Bradbury, pp. 4-5.

[35]Father A. Fournet, *Mother de da Nativité and the Origin of the Community of the Sisters of Miséricorde* (Montreal: Printing Office of the Institution for Deaf Mutes, 1898), p. 214.

[36]Sister Suzanne Collette, s.g.m., p. 24.

[37]Sister Sainte-Mechtilde, s.m., p. 173.

[38]Fournet, pp. 43-76. See also L'abbé E.-J. Auclair, *Histoire des Soeurs de Miséricorde de Montreal* (Montreal: Printing Office of the Institution for Deaf Mutes,

1928) and Paul-Henri Barabé, o.m.i., *Un Siècle de Miséricorde* (Ottawa: Editions de l'Université, 1948).

[39]Fournet, pp. 22-23.

[40]The Rule of the Misericordia *(Règlements pour les personnes qui se sont offertes à Dieu pour conduire l'oeuvre de l'hospice de Ste.-Pelagie érigé à Montreal,)* quoted in Gingras, p. 21, trans. Leslie Savage.

[41]Bishop Bourget to the Sisters of the Misericordia, quoted by Fournet, p. 182.

[42]*Rule*, quoted in Gingras, p. 21.

[43]See Note 3.

[44]See R.L. Schnell, "Ideology of Childhood: A Reinterpretation of the Common School," *British Journal of Educational Studies* 27 (February, 1979): 7-27; and Patricia T. Rooke, "The Child Institutionalized in Canada, Britain and the United States: A Trans-Atlantic Perspective," *The Journal of Educational Thought* 11 (1977): 156-171. For a description of the rehabilitation of childhood characteristics see Leslie Savage, "Infanticide, Illegitimacy and the Origins and Evolution of the Role of the Misericordia," (M.Ed. Thesis, University of Alberta, 1982).

[45]*Chronicles*, June 1900, Archives of the Misericordia, Lachine, Quebec.

[46]*Ibid.*, Throughout.

[47]Auclair, p. 228.

[48]Massicote, "Travail des Enfants," and "Comment on disposait des enfants."

[49]Auclair, pp. 220-221.

[50]*Consolidated Ordinances of the North West Territories*, 1898, Ch. 20. Also, *Journals of E. Legal*, October 21, 1899, where the subsidy is given as $.35 per day per patient; Oblate Papers, D-1-60, Provincial Archives of Alberta, Edmonton.

[51]*Chronicles*, throughout.

[52]*Ibid.*

[53]*Ibid.*, December 24, 1900.

[54]*Ibid.*, March, 1901.

[55]*Ibid.*, throughout 1901.

[56]*Ibid.*, December 21, 1903.

[57]*Ibid.*, the December letters, 1900-1905, list the number of residents at the end of each year. Some of the figures were provided by Sister Cecile, the Archivist at the Archdiocese of Edmonton. It seems that the original registry books, if any existed, have been destroyed.

[58]Paroisse St. Joachim, *Record of Baptisms 1899-1908*. These were inconsistently maintained after 1905, but appear to be complete for the years 1899 - 1904. The Misericordia was located in this parish.

[59]*Ibid.*

[60]The 1885 Census of the North West Territories, for example, lists the population of Edmonton in that year as 5,613, of whom 3,000 were Indian and 1,000 were Metis, approximately. But the 1906 Census lists the 1901 population of Edmonton as 2,626. Whether the 1901 enumerators ignored the native population or whether by that time the Indians and Metis had disappeared, either through death or dispersion, from Edmonton, is not clear. *Report of the Census of the North West Territories*, 1885 (Ottawa: Maclean, Roger, 1886) pp. 14-15.

[61]*Census of Population and Agriculture of the Northwest Provinces, 1906* (Ottawa: S. Dawson, 1907), p. xiv, Table 6. 6-7 Edward VII., A. 1907.

[62]*Report of the Census of the North West Territories, 1885* lists as living in Edmonton: Indians: 3017; Francophone Metis: 940; French: 82; total Francophone

population: 1522; total Anglophone population: 16, divided between 310 English, 217 Irish, 462 Scots, 3 Welshmen and 64 English-speaking Metis. Table IV, pp. 14-15.

[63]*Census of Canada*, 1906, Table IX, "Population of Cities, Towns and Incorporated Villages in 1906 and 1901 as classed in 1906.

[64]Robert Painchaud, "French-Canadian Historiography and Franco-Catholic Settlement in Western Canada, 1870-1915," *Canadian Hisorical Review* 59 (December, 1978): 45-462, p.56.

[65]*Ibid.*

[66]*Census of Pop. and Agriculture*, pp. xii and xiii.

[67]*Ibid.*

[68]*Ibid.*, and also *North West Territories Census for 1885*, p. 70.

[69]*Census of Canada 1901*, (Ottawa: Dawson, 1905), Vol. III, Table VIII, pp. 114-123.

[70]Young Women's Christian Association, *Minute Book*, 1907, PAA 68.301 1/1-14.

[71]H.C. Klassen, "Life in Frontier Calgary," in A.W. Rasporich, *Western Canada Past and Present* (Calgary: McClelland and Stewart West, 1975), p. 46.

[72]Y.W.C.A. *Minute Book*, 1907.

[73]The magistrates' names, in Alberta, for the period 1899 to 1914, indicate the predominantly Celtic or Anglo-Saxon heritage of these influential men: Newlands, Scott, Harvey, Wetmore, Sifton, Stuart, are examples. (*Territorial Law Reports*, various, 1899-1914.)

[74]Sylvia Van Kirk, *"Many Tender Ties," Women in Fur-Trade Society in Western Canada, 1670-1870* (Winnipeg: Watson & Dwyer, 1980), Chapter Nine.

[75]*Ibid.*

[76]The term 'sexual nonconformity' is of course a relative one.

[77]*Consolided Ordinances of the North West Territories*, 1903, Ch. 9, Section 3.

[78]Files of the Attorney General of Alberta, PAA, 66.166, Box 35.518.544. 1907.

[79]Files of the Attorney General of Alberta, PAA, 66.166, Box 47.782.856. 1906.

[80]*Consolidated Ordinances of the North West Territories*, 1903, Chapter 8.

[81]King v. Lougheed, 6 T.L.R., p. 77, 1902.

[82]Rex v. Rioux, 8 A.L.R., pp. 47-51, 1914.

[83]*Chronicles*, June, 1904.

[84]*Ibid.*

[85]*Ibid.*, March 26, 1901.

[86]*Ibid.*, December 23, 1900.

[87]*Ibid.*, January 5, 1906.

[89]Alexandre Brunet, *La Famille et ses traditions* (Montreal: Eusebe Senecal, 1881), p. 158: "Sitot que vos enfants auront la moindre intelligence, faites-leur savoir qu'ils ont un père qui est au ciel, qui les regarde toujours . . .; car les impressions recues, dès le bas age, des enseignements des parents ne s'effacent plus dans le cours de la vie." ("As soon as your children develop the first signs of a reasoning intelligence, teach them that they have a Father who is in heaven, who watches over them always . . .; for the impressions that are received, from the very earliest age, from the teachings of parents, will never be erased throughout the rest of their lives.")

[90]Painchaud,56.

[91]The shortage of priests and clergymen in the North West is clearly demonstrated in the reported case of King v. Sheran, 4 T.L.R. pp. 86-88. Sheran had

married, *per verba de presenti*, Mary Brown, an Indian woman. His brother-in-law testified that "Nicholas Sheran told me on several occasions that he intended to marry her whenever a clergyman came along. His sister, my wife, used to remonstrate with him for living with this woman in the way he was doing. He was a Roman Catholic. There was no resident Catholic clergyman in the neighbourhood during the time they lived together. Catholics had no means of marrying at that time unless a priest happened to come along. When I was married I met a travelling priest at Macleod and drove him down to the coal banks for the purpose of marrying my wife to me." At the time, Father Lebret also testified before the court, saying that "The rule of the Church is that no Catholic shall present himself for marriage before a clergyman of any other denomination; that if a Catholic . . . is so married . . . he grievously infringes the rules of his Church . . . and that there are no circumstances under which a Catholic man and woman would be justified in going before a Protestant clergyman for the purpose of marriage." In spite of these difficulties Sheran's marriage was declared irregular, and his two sons by Mary Brown were ruled to be illegitimate; Sheran's sister thus inherited his estate, rather than the sons; Mary Brown made no claim.

[92]J.M.S. Careless, "Aspects of Urban Life in the West," in A.W. Rasporich and H.C. Klassen, eds., *Prairie Perspectives 2* (Toronto: Holt, Rinehart and Winston, 1973), p. 25.

[93]*Ibid.*, p. 38.

[94]*Ibid.*, p. 25.

[95]*Ibid.*, p. 36.

[96]*City of Edmonton Directory for 1908*, p. 35.

[97]Careless, p. 38.

[98]In Farrell v. Wilton, 3 T.L.R., p. 232, the Court ruling devolved upon the absence of any organized forms of social assistance.

[99]*Chronicles*, October 24, 1903.

[100]*Ibid.*, June 22, 1904.

[101]*Ibid.*, February 6, 1903.

[102]*Ibid.*, September 6, 1900.

[103]*Ibid.*, November 7, 1903.

[104]*Ibid.*, July 4, 1906.

[105]*Ibid.*, December 30, 1901, and every year until 1906, and 1914.

[106]The concern for unwed mothers and their children led in 1963 to the establishment of the Pineview Home, which remained under the auspices of the Order of the Sisters of Misericordia until 1969.

[107]*Chronicles*, December 17, 1900.

[108]*Ibid.*, September 10, 1907.

[109]*Ibid.*, January 12, 1904.

[110]*Edmonton Bulletin*, December 10, 1900.

[111]*Le Courier de L'Ouest*, October 14, 1905.

[112]*City of Edmonton Directory*, 1908.

[113]Beulah Home Papers, PAA, 71.47/1.

[114]*Edmonton Journal*, April 21, 1976 and September 27, 1969.

Physical Perfection for Spiritual Welfare:
Health Care for the Urban Child, 1900-1939

Norah Lewis

> The child is the asset of the State, and all conditions should be arranged as far as possible to get the best results from that child. It [child welfare] is a business transaction, and results are what we are looking for in all business transactions. We do not want inferior products turned out that may or may not answer the purpose, but as perfect a thing as can be produced; something to be proud of; something with stability and quality, that can be used for the purpose of development and advancement and for protection, if need be, of the State to which it belongs.[1]

This statement by Dr. Isabel Arthur of Nelson to the 1917 meeting of British Columbia's Health Officers expressed an attitude many social reformers articulated during the past century. Motivated by political, economic, and humanitarian considerations, these reformers devoted considerable time and energy to improving the quality of life for children.[2] Between 1880 and 1920, better methods of disease control, better techniques in health care, and greater understanding of the developmental processes and the needs of children, meant that children born during the early decades of this century had a greater chance of surviving to adulthood than had children of any previous generation.[3]

Health professionals and child care advisors argued that science provided greater efficiency in both industry and the school system, therefore science should be just as efficient in improving child care rearing techniques and the quality of family life.[4] Furthermore, advisors believed that once new scientific methods of child care were demonstrated to parents, the value of these new techniques were so rational and so obvious that parents would immediately adopt the new measures.[5]

Cognizant of new developments in health care, advisors laboured tirelessly to utilize efficiently and economically the new principles of health care in order to improve children's health, to retard the spread of infectious diseases, and to prevent the development of further physical defects. In addition, they worked to educate both children (future parents) and parents in the scientific approach to child health care. Advisors generally believed parents to be incompetent, and thus incapable of providing proper nourishment for children's bodies and minds without both instruction and advice.[6] To accomplish these goals, advisors adopted two distinct but interrelated methods. First, in order to improve the physical health of children, advisors developed health care programs that functioned both within the school system and through community health care facilities. These programs monitored children's health from birth to school leaving age, through routine examinations to detect illnesses and physical defects.[7] Second, children were viewed as instruments and schools as agencies through which to educate parents to practice better nutrition and hygiene, better home management, and a 'higher' moral standard.[8] Advisors not only encouraged but also expected children to carry the message of health care home to their parents. Public Health Nurse Eileen Carruthers described the process as adult education by second-hand methods.[9] In addition, advisors attempted to educate parents in child care techniques during routine home visits, by public lectures, through home nursing classes, at well baby and preschool clinics, and through the media.[10] Their goal was to leave no children uneducated nor parents uninformed about the scientific principles of child care. Although advisors directed their efforts toward improving the health care of all children, this study focuses on programs and services provided to children in urban settings. A study of the period 1900 to 1939 demonstrates that children in British Columbia's urban centres had access to a growing number of programs specifically designed to meet their health care needs.

I

As immigrants from all parts of the world made their way into the new province of British Columbia, urban centres grew and expanded. Towns grew up around the mines and smelters of the Kootenays; fruit farming initiated in the Kootenays spread to the Okanagan; fish canneries and pulp and paper mills flourished along the coast from the Naas to the Fraser Rivers; whaling stations operated from the West Coast of Vancouver and Queen Charlotte Islands.[11] As a port of entry and the terminus of the Canadian Pacific Railway, a large number of the newcomers flooded into Vancouver and many settled in the city, thereby taxing Vancouver's facilities to the limit.[12] Over a fifty year period, for example, the Vancouver school system developed from one room with sixteen pupils in 1873 to 31 schools with 12,990 pupils in 1913, and by 1938 Vancouver's sixty-eight schools had an enrollment of 38,519 students.[13] Since the school board's building program could not keep abreast of rapidly increasing demands for school facilities, children frequently attended classrooms that were badly lit, poorly ventilated, unsanitary, and occasionally vermin infested.[14]

The influx of immigrants also taxed the city's housing facilities as well as the school system, and many of the city's children lived in two room tenements, small cabins, rooms above or at the rear of stores, or in rooming houses. Often these accommodations lacked bathing facilities. School health workers reported that some cabin dwellers who were fortunate enough to have bathrooms charged their neighbours one dollar for three baths. Nor were parents permitted two-for-the-price- of-one, if children bathed together. Little wonder many children suffered the effects of uncleanliness with impetigo, scabies, pediculosis, ring worm, eye infections, and discharging ears. Nor is it surprising children suffered outbreaks and epidemics of measles, mumps, whooping cough, diphtheria, scarlet fever, and even small pox. Children were also exposed to cases of untreated tuberculosis. Deformities of the body, decaying teeth, and enlarged tonsils went untreated if not undetected. In 1908, R.P. McLennan, chairman of the management committee of the Vancouver Board of School Trustees, claimed that, in most cases, the four new safe, well-lit, and properly ventilated schools opened that year provided children with safer keeping and purer air than experienced in their own homes.[15]

Smaller cities also faced problems coping with their growing school populations. Each winter, cities such as Nanaimo, Victoria, and New Westminster, faced overcrowding in their schools, the result of an annual influx of students from surrounding areas. Between 1900 and 1939, the enrollment in Victoria schools increased from 2,898 to 4,991 pupils, in Nanaimo school enrollment increased from 1,268 to 1,882 pupils, and in New Westminster school enrollment increased from 1,221 to 3,869 students.[16] None of the province's urban school districts, however, faced the rapid population growth experienced by Vancouver.

Both health professionals and educators expressed concern about the poor physical health of school children. Beginning in 1900, physical drill was recommended as a regular part of the school program. Advisors fully expected the program to produce immediate improvement in children's physiques and to develop school pride. J.J. Woods, secretary of the Vancouver Board of School Trustees, reported that by the end of the first year the new program "has already shown its need and usefulness in our fire drills".[17] But advisors expected more from the exercise program than expertise in fire drills, and such classes were only the beginning of a series of programs designed to improve the physical health of school children. In fact, during the next four decades, health programs grew and expanded to provide not only for children's physical care, but also for their mental health and moral development.

Why did advisors focus health care on school children? First, school children were a highly visible group with which to work. Furthermore, educators agreed that working with healthy children was more satisfying than working with children who suffered with diseases and disabilities. In 1912, Dr. C.J. Fagan, provincial health officer from 1899 to 1914, reported, "Today it is the accepted principle that the educationist and the hygienist must work hand in hand."[18]

But a second and more important reason for focusing on health care for school children was articulated by Summerland physician F.W. Andrews, who pointed out in 1916 that the regular systematic medical inspection of school children was a branch of preventive medicine.[19] Through regular medical inspections, physical defects were detected and corrected before permanant damage resulted. Sight or hearing loss could be prevented if eye or ear infections were treated before irrepairable damage occured. Advisors believed the detection and correction of defects to be an investment for the future, and they justified the provision of medical inspection programs as a sound financial investment. In 1908, R.P. McLennan reported, "The more care the community takes of the children, the more use and less burden they will be in later life."[20] Fifteen years later, J.S. Gordon, inspector of schools for Vancouver from 1912 to 1933, argued, "School economists may decry the additional expenditure and call the work a frill, but the man of vision will see in it a wise investment that will pay dividends in due season."[21]

Discoveries in bacteriology indicated that vaccination, immunization, and quarantine procedures prevented, or at least controlled, the spread of infectious and contagious diseases. Schools were obvious points of contact for many victims of communicable diseases; therefore, a third reason for focusing on school children was that children could be vaccinated and immunized before they contacted a disease, and infected children could be located early and quarantined before the disease spread to other individuals.[22]

The fourth reason, and one supported by a large number of advisors of the era, was eugenics, a popular theory of the time, and the desire to establish a superior race by ensuring those individuals constituting 'the race' be kept under medical observation and educated along 'right lines'.[23] In 1912, F.W. Brydone-Jack, Vancouver's school medical officer from 1910 to 1918, reported, "The aim of medical inspection is to elevate the physical and mental condition of the race by carefully guarding the children."[24] Dr. Isabel Arthur stated, "Do we get the fit from the unfit?"[25] Therefore, she argued, any individuals considering marriage should be required to produce a certificate of good health signed by a capable and conscientious physician, before being permitted to marry and reproduce.

The fifth and final argument used by advisors to support school medical inspections was their belief that many apathetic and incompetent parents failed to have their children's defects corrected; therefore, the state was obligated to report children's defects to parents and to emphasize the necessity of early treatment.[26] Advisors found, for example, that some parents neglected to isolate children infected with contagious or infectious diseases.

Advisors firmly believed a healthy body led to a healthy mind. In 1909, E. Lazelle Anderson, a Vancouver school medical officer, encouraged by the success of the relatively new medical inspection program in Vancouver schools, pointed out that through such a program "all the pupils might be brought to a high standard of physical and mental development".[27] Provincial Health Officer Henry Esson Young voiced the same ideal in 1920 and again in 1935 when he stated that, "Physical perfection must and does go hand in hand with spiritual welfare."[28] The difficulty confronted by health workers was to convince parents that without healthy bodies they could not expect their children to have healthy minds.

By initiating a school medical inspection program in 1907, the Vancouver School Board followed the lead of New York City and a number of cities in Great Britain, and led most urban areas of Canada.[29] The Victoria School Board initiated its medical inspection program a year later, and the passage of the "School Health Inspection Act" of 1910 required the annual medical inspection of all school children in the province.[30] But as early as 1904, Vancouver teachers began the systematic testing of children's eyesight.[31] Alarmed at the number of school children suffering eye infections and defective vision, Vancouver teachers requested instruction in eye testing procedures. During the first year of the eye testing program, teachers tested the eyesight of 3,386 children. Of that number, 576 had defective eyesight, and thirty-five were directed to local physician Dr. Glen Campbell for further treatment.[32] Testing school children's eyesight continued for the next two years. W.P. Argue, inspector of Vancouver schools from 1903 to 1912, reported that until eye testing took place, many parents were unaware that their children had defective vision.[33]

In 1907, Dr. Georgina Urquhart, appointed full-time school medical officer from 1907 to 1912, began a systematic school medical program designed to treat what she considered to be the most pressing needs. Urquhart's efforts met with some success. McLennan reported that during the second year of the program, the incidence of skin diseases was one-third and of uncleanliness one-half that of the first year of the program. Urquhart, however, complained about the irresponsibility of parents who failed to keep their children clean or the infectious ones home.[34]

Health workers across the province adopted the medical examination procedures first established by Vancouver's school medical officers. The school medical officers examined all school children at least once a year for cleanliness, communicable diseases, skin disorders, and pediculosis. At the same time, their weight and height were measured, hearing and sight tested, tonsils, adenoids, teeth and respiratory systems checked, and any physical defects such as flat feet, paralysis of limbs, or curvature of the spine noted. School medical officers notified parents of children suffering from diseases or physical defects, and instructed them to take their children to their family physicians or dentists for treatment. They recommended to teachers any modifications to be made in school programs for children suffering from defects.[35] Brydone-Jack reported that, "We devote an average of fourteen minutes to each child for a physical examination, but when a child has a suspicious (medical) history we take a longer time."[36]

As school medical programs developed and expanded, school nurses assisted and supplemented the work of the school medical officers. Vancouver appointed the first school nurse in the province, Elizabeth Breeze, in 1910, and other school districts quickly followed.[37] School nurses assisted school medical officers when they examined children. They sent notices of physical defects and diseases to parents, and instructed parents to have the children treated by their family physicians or dentists. Nurses followed up notices with home visits to ensure parents understood the need for treatment of diseases or defects. As time and energy permitted, they examined all school children on a regular schedule. They also gave short health talks to children, and instructed them in toothbrush and handkerchief drill.[38]

Home visits constituted a routine part of school nurses' duties. At that time, nurses encouraged parents to have their children's defects corrected, instructed parents on home ventilation, selection of proper clothing, infant care, children's sleeping habits, nutrition, and hygiene. By 1912, Breeze considered home visits the most important feature of her work, but she also indicated that the school nurses' visits were not always welcome.[39] J.S. Gordon justified the intrusion by nurses into home life by pointing out "Much has been done by the nurses in the education of parents in many homes, thereby ensuring more hygenic conditions for children at home as well as in school."[40] During 1911, Breeze and her co-workers made 905 home visits, and two years later the members of the school nursing team made 3,809 visits as well as making 47,260 examinations during the school term. Through the course of their home visits, school nurses frequently found families who not only required medical attention, but also lacked essentials such as food, clothing, and fuel. Nurses supplied emergency care for such cases from funds provided by concerned local philanthropical groups, and then referred the family to one of the city's charitable organizations. In other instances, they obtained free medical treatment or free eyeglasses for poor children.[41]

As the school population grew, so did the duties of school health workers. In 1918, for example, after special training, Vancouver nurses screened children before they saw the medical health officer. By the 1934-35 school term, Vancouver's school medical officer inspected all children before they entered the school system for the first time, all students in grades 4, 7, and 10, and all students involved in high school athletic programs. By the following year, medical inspections of grades 4 and 10 became part of the school nurses duties (table 1).

Victoria's school health workers did not have to cope with as large a school population as Vancouver. As late as 1939, the Victoria school medical officer still examined all beginners, all students in grades 1, 3, 4, 8, 10, and 12, and those involved in school athletic teams. Undoubtedly, the expansion of the school medical program throughout urban areas resulted from the indefatigueable work of the school nursing staff.[42]

II

Table 1

Vancouver School Medical Inspection Program
1911 to 1939

Year	Enrolled Vancouver School	Physical Inspection by School Health Offices	Reporting to School Board Clinic	Reported Communicable Diseases	Reported Inspections by School Nurses	Home Visits by School Nurses
1910	9,081	21,217	—	—	21,212	574
1911	11,385	6,879	2,202	366	42,260	905
1912	12,393	9,965	1,820	809	56,688	1,181
1913	12,990	12,182	1,340	596	66,592	3,809
1914	13,312	10,182	1,791	732	59,970	3,225
1915	13,182	11,789	1,175	749	64,056	3,174
1916	13,805	12,315	1,763	1,724	53,880	2,990
1917	15,069	12,469	1,616	954	61,546	3,184
1918	15,849	10,394	1,729	2,375	52,231	2,947
1919	16,500	12,436	1,768	—	52,752	4,588
1920	18,000	14,282	—	498	72,380	3,685
1921	18,590	12,404	—	756	87,529	4,040
1922	19,485	12,489	611	544	100,302	6,690
1923	19,064	5,076	1,035	1,821	—	—
1924	20,283	5,762	2,967	2,964	—	—
1925	20,845	5,175	8,000	1,739	113,157	5,740
1926	21,053	5,717	1,709	2,807	117,880	—
1927	21,735	5,832	1,153	4,737	127,142	7,488
1928	36,809	5,162	408	1,817	122,263	—
1929	37,222	12,858	555	3,758	207,865	10,287
1930	38,515	14,347	544	1,987	227,780	8,538
1931	38,627	—	—	—	—	—
1932	39,866	12,548	789	4,267	208,654	8,290
1933	39,163	10,581	894	1,787	134,890	5,730
1934	39,463	8,141	879	1,792	173,093	—
1935	39,328	9,248	900	1,621	—	—
1936	39,418	7,661	647	11,344	228,250	8,959
1937	39,120	12,510	148	2,473	173,093	13,409
1938	38,519	12,592	—	—	—	—
1939	37,492	12,596	125	1,446	135,159	14,059

Sources: Vancouver Board of Health *Reports,* 1910 to 1939; Vancouver Board of School Trustees, *Reports,* 1910 to 1939. Lack of numbers indicates absence of information. In 1928 Point Grey and South Vancouver Districts amalgamated with Vancouver and in 1937 the Greater Vancouver Health Unit formed. In 1936, 347 cases of rubella, 2,090 cases of mumps and 2,125 cases of measles were reported.

As health workers conducted regular medical inspections, they became aware of both the diversity and the extent of health problems that afflicted school children, and although they systematically notified parents of their children's defects, notification did not ensure either treatment or correction. Many parents could not, and others would not, provide the medical or dental care required by their children. If physical defects remained uncorrected, however, the medical inspection program served a very limited purpose indeed. To ensure needed medical treatment was carried out, in 1912 the Vancouver School Board opened a free clinic where health workers routinely tested and treated school children for minor ailments. The clinic proved an unqualified success, and during the first year of operation, 1,895 children were examined and treated during and after school hours.[43]

The clinic, however, provided no treatment for the most serious and extensive defect found among school children — decaying and carious teeth. In 1909, the school medical officer reported that only ten per cent of Vancouver's school children showed any evidence of dental care, and that at least sixty percent showed a total neglect of their teeth.[44] In an effort to teach children to preserve their teeth, the school medical officer arranged for members of the Vancouver Dental Association to go about the city's schools giving lectures illustrated with magic lantern slides on dental care.[45] But lectures and lantern slides did not solve financial difficulties of many families whose children needed dental care, therefore in 1913, the Vancouver School Board established a part-time free dental clinic to treat serious cases.[46] But as medical inspections became more thorough and free dental care became available, health workers reported all dental defects rather than just major cavities. In 1915, for example, health workers reported that ninety percent of Vancouver's school children had dental defects. During that year the Vancouver School dentists supplied 1,220 fillings, 263 root fillings, 292 treatments, and 439 extractions.[47] Twenty-four years later, 5,273 Vancouver school children took advantage of the school dental clinic, even through dental treatment was restricted to children in the first six grades.[48]

The dental clinic provided care only to families whose income fell below a specified income, thereby denying free treatment to a large number of low income families whose income exceeded the maximum amount allowed. In 1916, Vancouver School Dentist J. Milton Jones recommended the establishment of a self-sustaining dental clinic, the cost of which was to be paid by the patients on a reduced scale of fees. The board initiated this plan in 1920.[49]

Other school districts also established dental clinics. Victoria opened its clinic in April, 1920, and New Westminster followed during the 1926-27 term.[50] Once opened, the clinics were well utilized. In 1932-33, the New Westminster dental staff made a survey of the dental needs of New Westminster school children, and found a 150 percent increase over the previous year in the number of children eligible for dental treatment. The inspector of schools explained that the increase resulted from the current economic depression, and the work of the clinic becoming better known among parents in the community.[51]

Advisors used a second method to promote dental care among school children. As school nurses made their rounds, they conducted toothbrush drills and made dental inspections to ensure children brushed their teeth in order to maintain the dental work that had been completed at the clinics.[52]

Health workers justified the expenditure for dental care as a sound financial investment. In 1935, New Westminster's (unnamed) dental surgeon reported that he believed sixteen percent of school absentees in that city resulted from dental defects. Absenteeism, he argued, led to academic retardation, therefore, "Preventative dentistry when reviewed from this angle alone became a forceful feature in the economics of school education.[53]

Although eye testing began in 1904, eye infections and defective eyesight among children continued to concern advisors throughout the next four decades. Charitable organizations financed eye treatment and provided free eye glasses for needy children until 1917, when the Vancouver School Board assumed the responsibility.[54] Eye care continued to be an essential on-going service, and in 1938, with the increase in Vancouver's school population and the financial distress created by the depression, the school board, assisted by donations from the Parent Teachers Federation and the City Social Service Department, provided 355 pairs of glasses and paid for the repair of another sixty-one pairs.[55]

Eye glasses, however, did not solve the problems for all children with defective vision. In 1911, Brydone-Jack reported the need for a special class for children with seriously defective eyesight.[56] Five years later, the Vancouver School Board opened the first school for blind children in the province. The first class consisted of five blind students, three from Victoria and two from Vancouver. Mrs. T. Burke, the class' first teacher, was also blind. Because blindness was a problem not limited to urban centres, the Provincial Department of Education assumed responsibility for the School For The Blind in 1921, and the school served as an educational institution for blind children from across the province.[57]

To assist other children with visual impairment, the Vancouver School Board opened sight saving classes at General Gordon School in 1928. Two teachers trained in California in work with the visually impaired were employed to instruct the classes. The classes did not lack candidates, and by 1939 Dr. Harold White, School Medical Officer from 1922 to 1942, reported three such classes operating in the Vancouver school system.[58] Other urban school districts do not report the establishment of classes for the visually impaired, but the absence of such classes may indicate other centres lacked sufficient numbers of visually impaired children to warrant organizing special classes. In all likelihood, blind children enrolled directly in the School For The Blind and not in regular city school classes.

Vancouver's first school for the deaf (and dumb), organized in 1914, had an initial enrollment of eight students. J.S. Gordon described the instructor, Mabel Bigney, as a "lady well qualified both in her training and her personal qualities" to work with deaf children.[59] During 1915, enrollment increased to thirteen students under the instruction of two teachers trained in teaching the deaf. As with the School For The Blind, the need for training the deaf extended beyond the boundaries of Vancouver; therefore, in 1921, the Provincial Department of Education assumed responsibility for the school.[60] For those children in Vancouver and Victoria who suffered only partial hearing loss, lip reading classes commenced in 1938 as part of their regular school program.[61]

Other treatments were used to treat other types of defects. Physical exercises, designed to stir the blood, to stimulate the brain, and to expand the lungs, constituted a regular part of the school program. Brydone-Jack pointed out that physical exercises corrected bad posture, and that bad posture compressed the chest and the lungs, which in turn caused congestion of the eyeballs, thereby leading to excessive eyestrain, weak eyes, and frequently caused one shoulder to be higher than the other.[62] School authorities in all cities within the province sanctioned instruction in physical exercises and participation in school sports programs.[63]

Instruction in sports was not confined to the in-school programs, but extended to the playgrounds and parks. In 1908, the Board of School Trustees recommended that playground supervisors be appointed to all Vancouver school grounds. All school grounds were equipped with simple outdoor equipment.[64] Between 1909 and 1914, the city's playgrounds and parks were well used both during and after school hours. During the 1911-12 school term, for example, 44,252 children used the playgrounds at Fairview, Mount Pleasant, and Grandview schools.[65] Ten playground supervisors, four of whom were women, supervised city playgrounds during the summer of 1914, but playground usage declined that summer as the threat of war in Europe made paper selling a profitable activity for many boys who would have otherwise utilized the playgrounds. In the face of budget cuts during the year, the school board designated playground supervision a luxury program and removed it from the budget.[66]

In 1910, the Province of British Columbia accepted the terms and conditions laid out under the Strathcona Trust for the encouragement of formalized physical training and military drill in schools.[67] In order to qualify for financial assistance under the terms of the grant, school districts, normal schools, and the Provincial Department of Education organized training classes for teachers in physical exercises and military drill. In addition, summer training classes met at Vancouver, Vernon, Victoria, and Nelson. Vancouver and Victoria school boards provided evening classes to train and qualify teachers to teach physical training in their classrooms. In 1925, J.H. Putman and G.H. Weir reported classroom physical training programs ranged from poor to excellent and they argued for more efficient training programs for teachers.[68]

The establishment of cadet corps in high schools paralleled the development of physical training programs. Cadet corps organized in Victoria and Vancouver as early as 1903 offered military drill and rifle training to boys. Militia officers, non-commissioned officers, and former army personnel served as instructors. In Victoria, Sergeant Major A. Mulcahy and in Vancouver Sergeant Major H.C. Bundy served as drill instructors. Bundy was described as "a man with an excellent record for both military and naval service."[69] C.K. Haverstock served as instructor to the New Westminster cadet corps which was formed in 1913.[70]

What was the purpose of cadet training? Some educational authorities considered cadet training a form of physical fitness and discipline, a preparation for manhood. But other educators, who viewed with concern the growing political unrest in Europe, agreed with J.S. Gordon that British youth should be trained to be a lover of peace as well as a tower of strength in war.[71] Margaret Strong, inspector of schools for New Westminster, argued that the formation of cadet corps in that city was "a profitable investment and one which our city will appreciate."[72] Strong believed cadet training was excellent citizenship training.

Educators urged all high school and older elementary school boys to participate in military drill, but participation in rifle drill involved a smaller group of volunteers. The 101 Vancouver High School Cadet Corps that toured Australia in 1912 demonstrated competence in both foot and arms drill in order to qualify for the tour.[73] The outbreak of war in 1914 enhanced the popularity of cadet corps, and by 1915 Bundy reported that in Vancouver alone twenty-two corps in five battalions competed in the annual drill and shooting competitions for cups and medals donated by local citizens. Cadet corps continued in Victoria schools throughout the 1930's, but were discontinued in Vancouver high schools in 1933, when the school board decided to "sever connections with the Department of Militia and Defence."[74] A rise in anti-militarism among Vancouver educators and members of the public caused the corps to be disbanded, but with the outbreak of war in 1939 the British Columbia Department of Education re-instated compulsory cadet training and foot and arms drills became a regular part of high school life for males.[75]

Advisors claimed that physical exercises and military drill produced excellent results with physically normal children, but as early as 1911, Bundy reported that other children required special exercises and instruction "to cure or to improve existing defects".[76] The first attempt at special exercises occured in 1923, when the Vancouver School Board employed a full time physical exercise instructor qualified in the type of remedial work designed to correct abnormalities caused by poor posture, poor seating, and poor footwear. During the first year of the program, 1,236 children received treatment, and Dr. White expressed delight with the results of the program.[77] By 1930, the program expanded to correct more serious disabilities such as spine and chest deformities, paralysis of the extremities, and flat feet. During that year, 1,025 children received medical treatment. Of that number, 455 suffered from poor posture, 729 from fallen arches, fourteen with scoliosis, seventeen with paralysis, nine with deformed chests and one with a sprained elbow. The school medical officer prescribed exercises and the school nurse supervised their implementation.[78] Parents attended the first lesson and observed their children so they could continue the program at home. In 1937, Elizabeth Breeze reported encouraging results from special exercises, but she did not indicate the number of children involved nor the number completing the series of exercises.[79] Although these specialized exercises probably alleviated physical defects to some degree, a few children regarded exercise time as a pleasant break from classroom routine.

One major cause of health problems among children was malnutrition. In 1916, Provincial School Nurse Blanche Swan noted,

> The percentage of malnutrition has increased perceptibly, the increase being mainly confined to the cities, and is probably explained by the financial stringency which has been so keenly felt, especially in Western Canada, and which has necessitated the practice of strictist economy by all classes, economy, which unfortunately is not always wisely placed.[80]

During 1920, under the direction of the school medical officer, all Vancouver school children were tested against the height, weight, and age scale established by Thos. D. Wood, Professor of Education at Columbia University (1910-1913). Of the 14,282 school children examined, 3,584 (25.1 percent) rated ten percent or more below normal weight or height as indicated by Wood's tables. The previous year, one-half the receiving class at Strathcona School alone suffered from malnutrition.[81] The lack of proper nourishment lowered children's resistance to disease, skin disorders, and led to general apathy toward school. In an effort to meet the needs of malnourished children, a milk distribution program was initiated in Vancouver schools in 1919. During the first year of the program, 177 children received free milk paid for by a local chapter of the Independent Daughters of the Empire (IODE) and the Parent Teacher Federation. Victoria's children fared no better, and in 1919, School Nurse Muriel Grimmer arranged free milk for undernourished children.[82] Free milk distribution continued until at least 1927. School records fail to indicate when this service discontinued. Whether for milk, dental care, or any number of health programs, advisors believed the energy and money spent in providing medical inspection-health care programs was money wisely invested.

III

Infectious and contagious diseases, including the common cold, concerned advisors. Outbreaks of smallpox, diphtheria, scarlet fever, whooping cough, and mumps could and often did reach epidemic proportions in both urban and rural areas of the province. All school health workers followed the same general treatment procedure: infected children were excluded from the classroom; their entire families, classmates, and playmates were inspected and reinspected until all danger of the disease passed. Brydone-Jack reported that between 1903 and 1913, 10,430 children were exposed to smallpox, diphtheria, or scarlet fever, and that only 2,889 of that number were immunized.[83] He stated that educational authorities should demand each child entering the school system provide proof of vaccination, "and only in cases where parents go before a magistrate and swear that they have conscientious objections should exemption be granted".[84] Brydone-Jack's fears of a smallpox epidemic were not unrealistic. J.S. Gordon reported that during the 1924-25 school year, time lost by smallpox cases and their contacts totalled 1,310 school days, or an average of sixty children for each school day.[85]

Advisors attempted to educate parents to the desirability of having children vaccinated. Beginning in 1907, the Vancouver Board of Health provided free vaccine to the school medical officer, but by 1917, of the 12,469 school children examined, only 2,243 had been vaccinated.[86] During the smallpox scares of 1920-21 and 1925, the Vancouver School Board again attempted to have all school children vaccinated, either through the school clinic or by family physicians. Of the 18,590 children enrolled in Vancouver schools during 1921, 10,553 received vaccinations and 1,403 children failed to comply with the vaccination order. Additionally, 789 children did not require vaccination because they were considered unsusceptible, and 5,814 children registered as conscientious objectors.[87] A March 10, 1925, "Order-in-Council" made vaccination obligatory for all individuals not registered as conscientious objectors, and by September of that year, only 324 of Vancouver's 19,759 school children failed to comply with the regulation.[88] In their *Survey of the School System*, Putman and Weir, however, noted the excessive class time lost by children excluded from school because they were not vaccinated.[89] An outbreak of a particularly virulent type of smallpox in 1932 resulted in sixteen deaths among fifty-six cases, and led to 8000 children being vaccinated within a four day period.[90] To the relief of health workers, between 1929 and 1939 the number of cases of smallpox among Vancouver school children declined from seventy-five reported cases to no reported cases.[91]

Vaccination proved a highly emotional issue among some members of the community. Objectors believed no disease was prevented by loading the body with what they described as putrid filth from a sick cow. During the 1925 debate surrounding obligatory vaccination, the editor of *The Vancouver Sun* raged, "Vaccination is discredited. It is illogical. It is dirty. It is one of the most damnable injuries one person ever tried to inflict upon another."[92] Health authorities attempted to reassure the public about the controlled conditions under which vaccine was produced and tested, but letters to the editor of *The Vancouver Sun* clearly indicated they failed to convince all members of the public.[93] But school health officials had the final word, and Harold White reported in 1939 that eighty-four percent of Richmond school children had been vaccinated against smallpox and sixty-eight percent had been immunized against diphtheria.[94]

Diphtheria, another recurring contagious disease, responded well to immunization, and the availability of diphtheria toxoid in 1923 provided health workers with a new tool in their fight to reduce the incidence of the disease.[95] In 1926, Vancouver's school medical officer recommended and attempted to execute an extensive immunization program, but the effects of the program did not bring an immediate decrease in the number of cases. Rather, the number of reported cases of diphtheria increased from seventy-four in 1926 to 187 in 1929.[96]

Between 1929 and 1934, 30,000 Vancouver children were immunized, and by 1938 no cases of diphtheria occurred among Vancouver children, although seventeen occured in other areas in the province.[97] Toxoid immunization against diphtheria also met with opposition from many parents, although not as vigourously as that waged against vaccination. As late as 1938, Dr. J.R. McIntosh, Vancouver's medical officer, stated in a report carried in *The Vancouver Province* that "Young children do not feel the slightest effects of toxoid immunization under the age of 12."[98] Three Vancouver physicians took MacIntosh to task, and publically declared in a letter to the editor of the same paper that any poison introduced into the body through the use of toxoids had detrimental effects in a child's body and led to increased cases of heart disorders among children under ten years of age. They failed, however, to substantiate their claims with either research or statistical evidence.[99]

Health professionals in both urban and rural areas believed their immunization and vaccination programs effected a decrease in the incidence of smallpox and diphtheria. Although the decrease in the number of cases appeared to substantiate their claims, George Rosen, professor of public health education at Columbia University, expressed another opinion. Rosen argued that from 1870 onwards, a number of infectious diseases, including smallpox and diphtheria, began to wane in both virility and frequency.[100] If this is true, the total effect of immunization cannot be clearly evaluated, but what can be clearly demonstrated is that by 1939 fewer cases and fewer deaths occured from these diseases than ever before.

Although medical advisors recognized the highly contagious nature of smallpox and diphtheria, they did not or would not recognize the highly contagious nature of tuberculosis. Despite the fact that Robert Koch, a German physician, had identified the tubercule bacillus and that subsequent research established the highly infectious nature of the disease,[101] it was not until 1912 that open cases of pulmonary tuberculosis were banned from the Vancouver school system. Unfortunately, annual medical inspections located only advanced cases of tuberculosis, and incipient cases went undetected.[102]

School nurses reported that over crowded housing, malnutrition, lack of sunshine and fresh air, as well as close proximity to active cases of tuberculosis, made children highly susceptible to the disease. To overcome these problems, health workers advocated tubercular and pre-tubercular children be removed from regular classrooms and placed in open air classrooms where they received rest and nourishment. In 1912, two open air classrooms opened at the Vancouver Children's Aid Centre. In addition, the construction of windows in the new classrooms at West Kitsilano School permitted these classrooms to be easily converted into open air classrooms.[103] Five years later, the local Rotary Club provided open air facilities for tubercular children in their newly opened health centre on Cambie Street.[104] The school board had no open air school of its own until the 1925-26 school term, when it opened a three room open air school at the Charles Dickens School. Seventy-five poorly nourished, anemic, and sickly children quickly transferred to the school, where White claimed they thrived on fresh air, hot balanced mid-day meals, rest, breathing exercises, and organized play. In April, 1934, H.N. Mac-Corkindale, Inspector of Schools, reported the open air school closed because of necessary budget cuts. The children then moved to the preventorium operated for convalescent and tuberculosis contact children by the Vancouver Rotary Club.[105]

The need for open air facilities was not limited to Vancouver. In 1919, Victoria's school nurse, Muriel Grimmer, collected the names of physically debilitated children attending Victoria schools, and, at the urging of Grimmer, Captain Ian St. Clair, physical director of Victoria schools, and Dr. H.E. Young, the school board moved to provide open air classrooms for unhealthy school children.[106]

Not until 1923, with the formation of the Provincial Division of Tuberculosis Control, did health workers diligently seek out and treat active cases of tuberculosis, check patients contacts, maintain follow-up work on former patients, and educate members of the medical profession and the general public on the treatment and prevention of tuberculosis.[107] As school children received their annual medical inspections, suspected cases of tuberculosis were X-rayed to provide definitive evidence of the presence or absence of the disease. In 1935-36, health workers in several urban areas of the province including Vancouver and Prince Rupert used tuberculin tests to detect the disease among school children.[108] Any infected individual was treated at one of the Tuberculosis clinics in Vancouver, Victoria, Tranqulle, or the Queen Alexandra Solarium at Malahat Beach on Vancouver Island.[109]

By the late 1930's, only children entering the Vancouver school system for the first time, all high school students, and any suspected cases were given tuberculin tests.[110] Those children giving a positive reaction to the test and all teachers were X-rayed. In 1939, White reported that no advanced cases of tuberculosis and only four minimally advanced cases existed among school children in the Vancouver Metropolitian Health Unit. Although pleased with the results, health workers did not relax their campaign against tuberculosis.[111]

People living in Vancouver, Peace River, the Okanagan, Lillooet, Vanderhoof, and other goiter prone belts of the province are subject to endemic goitre. As a preventive measure, in 1926 Vancouver and Ladysmith health workers began the regular administration of iodine tablets to school children. With parent's permission and the payment of ten cents, each child received one iodine pill a week during the school term.[112] In 1932, the provincial health officer urged iodine be regularly administered to all school children living in goitre prone belts.[113] No record was kept of the number of iodine pills distributed, but between 1930 and 1936 the percentage of cases of endemic goitre among Vancouver school children decreased from 3.9 percent to 1.1 percent. In 1937, Dr. White reported 7,349 Vancouver school children received iodine pills through the school medical system.[114] The distribution of iodine pills continued until the 1940's, when iodine became a standard additive to table salt.

IV

At the same time that school boards moved to provide programs for physically defective children, they also developed programs for subnormal or mentally defective children. The Vancouver School Board initiated its first class for subnormal children in 1910, with a specially trained teacher in charge. The venture proved so successful that by June, 1911, a second class was organized.[115] Recognizing the need for an educational program for subnormal children, the Victoria school trustees investigated the Seattle School for Defective Children, and as a result opened a classroom for mentally defective children in 1913. But Victoria's Inspector of Schools Edward Paul believed subnormal children required more extensive care, and he urged the provincial government to provide an institution for mentally subnormal children rather than place such children in day schools in the city. Seventeen years later, A. Josephine Dauphinee, Vancouver's Supervisor of Special Classes, hailed the conversion of New Westminster's old mental hospital to a training school as a suitable facility for 'unstable and low-grade' children.[116]

A major development in the treatment of subnormal or exceptional school children occurred in February, 1918, when the Vancouver School Board appointed a full-time psychologist to make a special study of retarded and slow children within the school system, and to organize special classes for those "found to be incapable of receiving much benefit from the instruction given in ordinary classes".[117] In her first eleven months, Clinical Psychologist Martha Lindley and her two assistants examined over 400 children, of whom 116 underwent further observation. Lindley placed ninety-five children in special classes.[118] During the next four years, through a testing and selection program, Lindley organized twenty-two special classes with an enrollment of 427 pupils.[119] She first removed retarded children from the classroom because they provided a "drag upon the average and superior pupils".[120] She then surveyed the school system for children she believed to be incapable of further academic advancement. The children were tested, screened, and those deemed slow segregated into classes suited to their needs and mental capacities. Lindley also screened students with speech defects before turning them over to a speech teacher for corrective treatment. She insisted that the patriotic duty of the clinic staff was to seek out, evaluate, and provide necessary classes for crippled children unable to attend regular classrooms. Lindley stated that it was good business to look after children who were potential paupers, criminals, or public charges of any kind. "For this reason I feel justified in asking for an extension of our work as far as possible."[121] Lindley was supported in her work by J.S. Gordon, who also believed the establishment of special classes represented a good financial investment. Children so trained would not become an economic liability to the community.[122]

The policy of the Vancouver School Board in regard to subnormal children was not unusual for the time, although Vancouver appears to have been in the forefront in the development of such programs. Gordon proudly reported that during the 1918-19 school term, two prominent Canadians, Dr. C.K. Clarke and Dr. C.M. Hincks, both members of the Canadian National Committee on Mental Health, visited Vancouver and reported, "That in this work [with the subnormal] Vancouver is leading all Canada."[123] Six years later, Putman and Weir commended the work of the school board on its humanitarian instincts and the success of its programs for the subnormal, but they criticized the excessive cost of the program. To make the program more cost efficient, Putman and Weir recommended that the nineteen existing classes meet in three or four central areas, rather than scattered throughout the city's schools. This system would reduce the number of classes, increase class enrollment, and reduce the number of classroom teachers required to operate the program, thereby releasing money for the employment of special instructors in home economics and manual training. But the school board did not implement Putman and Weir's recommendations. In 1939, special classes operated in sixteen elementary and two high schools. In addition, a special class, formed in 1936 for foreign born non-English speaking students met at Seymour School.[124]

By the 1930's, intelligence and achievement tests had arrived. Vancouver, Victoria, and New Westminster schools reported extensive use of tests such as the Stanford-Binet Intelligence and the Detroit First-Grade Intelligence tests, the Thorndike-McCall Reading Test and standardized tests in English, Latin, chemistry, biology, physics, and arithmetic as the main basis for classification and promotion of school children.[125] In 1936, G.H. Deane, Victoria's inspector of schools, reported that as teachers used achievement and standardized tests, they realized "the value of mental measurement in diagnosing individual cases and prescribing the right treatment".[126] As a result of such testing, children were labeled, rightly or wrongly, early in their school life, and test results rather than their potential determined their school program.

V

Improving children's physical health was the first thrust of the school health program; improving children's knowledge of personal hygiene and principles of health care was the second. J.S. Gordon valued health education in Vancouver schools not just for disease prevention, "but in the education of children, parents, and the public along hygienic lines".[127] In a pamphlet distributed in 1926 by the Provincial Board of Health, Mrs. C.A. Lucas, Superintendent of the Saanich Health Centre, pointed out that teaching health education to school children was a patriotic duty. She argued that health education prepared school children, the citizen of the future, to demand proper health care for themselves and their communities. Because few students attended high school, Lucas contended that children in the seventh and eighth grades should have a good working knowledge of the fundamentals of good health and methods of disease prevention.[128]

As early as 1894, anatomy, physiology, and hygiene formed part of the high school program, but lessons focused on learning parts of the body and their uses and not on health care principles.[129] At its inception in 1901, the Vancouver Normal School included lessons in physiology and hygiene in the nature study courses.[130] Dr. H.E. Young, Minister of Education, 1907 to 1915, initiated the move towards health education when he requested teachers post a set of health rules in their classrooms, teach a series of short lessons on each health rule, and encourage children to observe the rules.[131] In the same year, British Columbia's Council for Public Instruction provided free copies of Stowell's *Essentials in Health* for use in high schools. Four years later, the same agency provided *How to be Healthy* for use by high school students.[132]

Not until the 1925-26 school term did health education become a prescribed course in British Columbia public schools.[133] To equip teachers to instruct health education classes, the 1925 provincial summer school for teachers offered a course entitled, "Hygiene and Child Health," taught by Vancouver's head school nurse, Elizabeth Breeze. In 1927-28, health education classes became a regular feature of the normal school training program.[134]

The 1925-26 health education program for public schools focused on teaching students to establish good personal health habits, to develop positive attitudes toward personal hygiene and health care, and to develop a sense of responsibility for others. Through the first eight grades, the health program focused on nutrition, cleanliness of self and surroundings, and control of infectious and contagious diseases. Grades one to six learned the need for proper rest, sleep, fresh air, and exercise. Children were expected to apply their knowledge of health care principles to remedy unhealthy conditions in their homes and communities.[135]

The revised health program of 1928-29 not only instructed children in health care and personal safety, but also attempted

> To lead parents and other adults through the health education program for children to better habits and attitudes, so that the school may become an effective agency for the social aspects of health education in the family, school, and community.[136]

Ideally, curriculum editors expected improved health of individual children and adults to promote national health and race betterment. Traffic safety received special attention in the 1928-29 curriculum revision because of the increased number of trucks and cars within the province.

Classroom teachers of grades one to five conducted daily health inspections for their classes and focused their health lessons on those habits neglected by their students. The 1928-29 curriculum guide in health education outlined in graphic detail the proper way to unfold, blow into, and refold a handkerchief, and the most efficient way to use a toothbrush. By 1929, classroom teachers and not school nurses taught health education classes, conducted handkerchief and toothbrush drills, and made daily cleanliness inspections.[137]

Educational authorities believed compulsory health education classes an essential component of the school program. In 1931, Victoria's Inspector of Schools G.H. Deane, warned,

> It's [compulsory health education] to lead students to form intellectually correct habits of health, and the achievement of this will be determined by the interest and appeal aroused by the teaching. This objective will be defeated by prescribing a too ambitious course of study, and particularly by making the subject an examination one.[138]

Yet by June, 1936, Vancouver high school students in grades 9, 10, and 11 wrote final examinations in health education. Although the program was intended to teach healthful living, children were tested for book knowledge.[139]

The revision of the public school curriculum in 1936 gave health education a new focus when mental, emotional, moral, and social health were added to physical health and safety education. Ten years before children learned the basic rules for good physical health in 1936, children learned the rules for good mental health.[140]

In 1928, Joy Elmer Morgan, editor of *The Journal of the National Educational Association*, wrote in *The B.C. Teacher*, that "Health including both the mental and the physical is a foundation of character growth."[141] Nine years later, Norman F. Black, editor of *The B.C. Teacher*, urged his fellow teachers to include health education — both physical and mental-within their classroom programs. Instruction in health was essential for children to develop both healthy bodies and minds.[142] Teachers like F.W. Wallace at John Oliver High School in Vancouver observed that the success of school health programs manifested results in the personal application of health principles by students and in their efforts to establish healthful home and communities. At its best, health education developed social consciences among school children and led to improved health for all members of the community.[143]

Not all British Columbia teachers believed the school health program met the needs of the province's future citizens. In 1936, teacher Dorothy Johnson castigated educators for their lack of practicality. Why teach health lessons in school when conditions within the school building, the home, and the community made it impossible for children to apply the lessons?[144]

Students did not receive all their health instructions in health classes, rather, health workers and educators organized special programs designed to teach children specific skills or to encourage the practical application of health principles. Alarmed at the number of working parents who left their infants in the care of young girls, during the 1911-12 school term Vancouver nurses initiated a series of talks on the care and dressing of infants and simple home nursing techniques.[145] Brydone-Jack attributed many of the summer deaths of the city's infants to ignorance by those in charge of infant care. By such classes, he pointed out, "We will be preparing the girls to meet some of the responsibilities of life in a more intelligent manner."[146]

Little Mother's Leagues formed in four Vancouver schools in January, 1917 constituted a child care program available for girls between the ages of ten and fourteen years. School nurses gave nineteen talks, teaching the league members how to feed, clothe, bath, and train a baby.[147] Nurse Lucas explained, "The general care of the baby itself was included, not only his physical care as we ordinarily understand it, but instruction as to how to avoid the formation of bad habits, and particularly concerning the necessity of protecting the baby from communicable diseases.[148]

Upon completing the classes and passing a written examination, the girls received badges and certificates. During the first year of the league's operation, 400 Vancouver girls enrolled and 150 received certificates. By 1920, Little Mother's Leagues met in six Vancouver schools, but only 202 girls took the course and 136 received certificates for completing the program.[149] During the 1920's and the 1930's, as Junior Red Cross classroom branches became more numerous and domestic science classes were revised to include a child care component, and as responsibility for health education shifted from nurses to classroom teacher, Little Mother's Leagues were discontinued.

The Junior Red Cross movement commenced in 1914 as a means for children to participate in the war-time humanitarian work of the Red Cross Society. At the 1919 Cannes Conference of International Red Cross Societies, the conference resolved to retain the Junior Red Cross as a children's peacetime organization devoted to the promotion of good health and humanitarian ideals, good citizenship, and international friendship.[150] The Junior Red Cross program, already established in other areas of Canada, was endorsed for school children by the British Columbia Department of Education in 1922.[151]

Junior Red Cross branches were classroom based clubs operating under the direction of classroom teachers. For a ten cent membership fee, each child received a membership card on which was printed ten health rules and a copy of the Junior Red Cross Magazine. The health rules stressed the need for a nutritious diet, fresh air, sleep, exercise, good posture, elimination, cleanliness of teeth, body, hands, fingernails, and the way to prevent the spread of diseases by covering coughs, sneezes, and sniffles. Club activities encouraged members to develop a wholesome interest in personal physical development by following specific health rules and hygienic practices. The *Junior Red Cross Magazine*, colourful posters for classroom walls, playlets and classroom dramas, reinforced the clubs' health teachings.[152] Although branches operated under the direction of classroom teachers, public health and school nurses addressed them on health topics or awarded achievement badges to those who diligently followed the rules of health.[153]

Was the Junior Red Cross an effective organization? The essential element to the success or failure of the organization was the classroom teacher. When teachers were interested, voluntary participation by teachers encouraged an 'esprit de corps'. Jean Browne, the national secretary of the Junior Red Cross, believed the branches stimulated children to practice better health habits. Ruth Nibeck, B.C. organizer for the Junior Red Cross, believed the branches taught citizenship and concern for others in addition to stimulating children to better health practices.[154]

The Junior Red Cross grew and flourished in British Columbia between 1922 and 1939. By 1936, there were 14,000 members in British Columbia, 5,500 of whom were in Vancouver schools.[155] New Westminster's inspector of schools reported that during the 1930-31 school term, the Junior Red Cross had been effective in both elementary and junior high schools in his city. By 1939-40, the provincial membership reached 30,999 students, representing 25.7 percent of the province's school population, and forty-four of these branches were in high schools.[156]

VI

Although children were considered legitimate instruments through which to educate parents in better physical care, they were not considered suitable messengers to enlighten parents about those "Social-health problems which directly or indirectly have grown out of sex instincts."[157] Controversy centred about who should teach sex education, and whether children should be given sex education at all. At the 1914 meeting of provincial health officers, Dr.

E.C. Hunter, of South Vancouver, noted that several (unnamed) worthy citizens advocated teaching sex hygiene in school. Hunter outlined two possible methods. First, he suggested instructing parents in methods of broaching the subject with their children. Second, he suggested school health workers instruct school children in sex hygiene.[158] Brydone-Jack expressed the view of a number of medical officers when he reported that the Vancouver Medical Association believed sex education, especially for elementary aged children, should be done by parents, after parents had been educated in proper teaching techniques through public lectures.[159] Eleven years later, Putman and Weir recognized the need for sex education, but acknowledged "that the present state of public opinion makes it impossible to study this subject in the public schools".[160] The membership of the Canadian Social Hygiene Council (and other members of the public) believed sex education to be the sole responsibility of parents, and that the schools merely supplement sex education by teaching nature studies and 'kindred subjects'.[161] Parents who felt unequal to the task could seek information through pamphlets, books, or encourage the organization of 'programmes of enlightenment' through organizations such as the Parent Teacher Federation.[162] Laura Jamison, Judge of the Burnaby Juvenile Court, and members of the Canadian Social Hygiene Council urged parents to read authors such as Maude Royden, Edward Carpenter, and Havelock Ellis, who placed sex on a 'high plain'.[163] To help parents achieve this 'high plain' the British Columbia Board of Health reissued five pamphlets prepared by the National League of Health, Maternity, and Child Welfare, London, England, entitled "Some Thoughts for Wives and Mothers and Some Teachings to be Given to Children by Parents Who Find it Difficult to Put Their Thoughts into Words".[164] Although these materials were designed to teach children to 'think rightly' about their wonderful bodies, they contained more information about the birds and the bees than about human sexuality.

If sex education constituted part of the school program, Mrs. C.A. Lucas stated, sex must be taught by specially trained persons, and not by the classroom teacher.[165] Harold White took a pragmatic approach to the teaching of sex; he and Nurse M. Campbell taught the subject to Vancouver high school students. Although White did not report his annual talks on hygiene and sex to high school boys nor Nurse Campbell's talks to high school girls until 1926, former Kitsilano students Frank Hardwick and Ruth Sutton recall that the talks of 1923 and 1924 focused on personal hygiene and physical development. Any reference to sex or human sexuality were couched in extremely oblique terms indeed.[166]

As schools assumed more responsibility for health education, they also assumed more responsibility for moral and ethical education. In an 1918 address to the first annual meeting of the British Columbia Child Welfare Association, William Burns, Principal of the Vancouver Normal School, contended that the ultimate aim of education (and the duty of the school) was character formation and development of correct habits.[167] A year later, Victoria physician, Dr. Ernest Hall, argued that schools must assume those responsibilities the home neglected to fulfill.[168] The movement to teach moral and ethical valued gained momentum during the 1920's and the 1930's, as educators discussed the best way to train children to take their places in a democratic society.[169] In 1929, John Ewing, of the Vancouver Normal School, stated that he believed morals should be taught in classrooms, and that children's moral character could be developed by both direct and indirect teaching.[170] A year later, Mr. T.R. Hall, inspector of schools in the Kelowna District, charged the October convention of the Okanagan Valley teachers that they had an important role to play in teaching ethics and morals.[171] Two Vancouver teachers supported Hall's view. In 1935, in an article in *The B.C. Teacher*, Chas. C. Watson, a teacher at Point Grey High School, discussed in detail the aims and methods used to achieve character development within the specialized and controlled environment of schools.[172] Earlier in the same year, an article by another Vancouver teacher, E.H. Fishback, appeared in the same magazine. Fishback listed nine procedures for teachers to follow when teaching moral education at the junior high school level. Character development, he asserted, "should be the major factor in the minds of those who have charge of the formal education of the rising generation.[173]

Few voices were raised in protest to moral education in schools. In 1919, Mrs. J. Muir, president of the British Columbia Parent Teachers Association, noted and condemned the tendency of the school to assume parent's responsibility for children's physical, mental, and spiritual well-being without consulting parents.[174] Miss M. Harwood, a Summerland teacher, deplored the attempt to replace good parenting by passing the major task of character building to the school and other institutions.[175] Concern of another kind was voiced by Premier T.D. Pattullo in his April, 1935, address to the British Columbia Teacher's Convention. Pattullo claimed that parents tended to neglect their responsibilities and to expect the school to teach things that should be taught in the home.[176] In a 1933 address to a Prince Rupert Parent Teachers meeting, Rev. W.D. Grant Hollingworth pointed out that there were two institutions which dealt with children — the home and the school. The home and the church were responsible for "inculcating into the mind of the child those ideals of Christian living which can and should motivate all behaviour, . . ."[177] But Hollingworth conceded that as children spent more time in school than in church, it was "In the school they really learn to live by living."[178] Reflecting the philosophy of American educator John Dewey, Hollingworth stated it was the duty of the school to give the child "what it needs to know in order to develop into a well-rounded, happy, efficient, citizen".[179] Increasingly, advisors regarded education as the panacea for society's problems and they firmly believed the community and even the world would be a better place when children learned to take care of their bodies, develop their minds, and form good upright moral characters.[180] If diseases such as smallpox and diphtheria could be prevented or at least controlled through education and the application of scientific principles, then social diseases such as poverty, indolence, apathy, and sexual immorality could also be prevented or at least controlled by the same methods.

VII

By the late 1930's, advisors provided health education for urban children by four different approaches: during medical inspections and routine physical examinations; through lectures given by school medical officers to parent teacher meetings; through health care agencies; through the press and radio.[181]

Advisors firmly believed their efforts on behalf of school children were successful. They pointed to special programs staffed by specially trained personnel that met the needs of the blind, the deaf, the intellectually subnormal, the malnourished, and those with physical defects. Advisors believed health care and health education paid dividends by producing a healthier populace than formerly, and they convinced school administrators, community leaders, provincial authorities, and politicians that health care was a sound investment in the future of the community and the province. Educational and health authorities responded with financial assistance and moral support for health care-health educational programs conducted in the classrooms, through special clinics, and through other activities conducted outside regular school programs.

To justify the expenditure of money for health care-health educational programs, advisors pointed to statistical evidence. Between 1915 and 1939, the province's mortality rate for children under twenty years of age declined by 40 percent, from 31.88 percent of total deaths to 12.87 percent.[182] What is impossible to determine, however, is whether better health care alone accounted for the decline, or whether improved health care plus pure milk, clean water, improved medical techniques, and better sanitation contributed to the decline.

In 1937, the British Columbia Board of Health sent questionnaries to all school trustees in the province, soliciting their opinions about school health programs[183] Dr. Young then incorporated these responses into his annual report. Responding trustees unanimously agreed that the province's school children were healthier than they had been before the provision of health services, as evidenced by fewer outbreaks of contagious diseases and absenteeism from schools. Physical defects were corrected earlier in children's lives, and infections were treated before they spread. One board believed "the betterment of health conditions in the school was reflected in the general well being of the community".[184] Another board stated that "Mothers are better educated in the care of children."[185] Young concluded that the public was satisfied with the school health program.

But the methodical care given school children did not always work to their advantage. Children who tested below normal on intelligence tests moved into special classes instructed by teachers trained to work with the subnormal. Removing children deemed intellectually inferior, those with speech defects, and those with physical handicaps from regular classrooms allowed teachers to concentrate on normal and superior children. Children labeled slow or different as early as grade 1 continued through a series of special classes purported to make them self-supporting citizens.[186]

Throughout the 1930's, advisors regarded children as the instruments and schools as the agency through which to educate parents. In January, 1936, Dr. Young reported,

> We have concentrated our public health teaching in the populace using the schools as a basis. It is the best approach to the home, and the counsel given parents is illustrated by the children of the family, as examples of what can be done when rules and regulations of the improvement of the daily life is shown.[187]

At no time did advisors consider the tension such a process could create between parent and child. Advisors firmly believed health bodies led to healthy minds, therefore, by 1939, health care and health education focused not only on the physical care of children, but also on building wholesome attitudes and social consciences that advisors believed would lead to the betterment of life in both home and community.

Notes

I am grateful to Neil Sutherland and George Ledingham for their comments on this paper.

[1]Isabel Arthur, "Child Welfare," British Columbia Board of Health, *Report*, 1918, p. G139 (hereafter BCBH, *Report*).

[2]Neil Sutherland, *Children in English-Canadian Society: Framing the Twentieth-Cetury Consensus* (Toronto: University of Toronto Press, 1976); Ivy Pinchbeck and Margaret Hewitt, *Children in English Society*, Vol. II, *From Eighteenth Century to the Children's Act, 1948* (Toronto: University of Toronto Press, 1973); Anthony Platt, *The Child Savers: The Invention of Delinquency* (Chicago: University of Chicago Press, 1969).

[3]George Rosen, "A Healthier World," *The Nation's Children, The White House Conference on Children and Youth*, Eli Ginzberg (New York: Columbia University Press, 1960), pp. 139-157; see also John Newson and Elizabeth Newson, "The Cultural Aspects of Child Rearing in the English Speaking World," *Rethinking Childhood: Perspectives on Development and Society*, Arleen Skolnick (Berkley: Little, Brown and Co., 1976), pp. 324-343.

[4]Bernard Wishy, *The Child and the Republic*, (Philadelphia: University of Pennsylvania Press, 1968), p. VI; Raymond E. Callahan, *Education and the Cult of*

Efficiency, (Chicago: University of Chicago Press, 1962), p. 23; for discussion of attempts of efficiency in education in British Columbia, see Timothy A. Dunn, "The Rise of Mass Public Schooling in British Columbia, 1900-1929," in J. Donald Wilson and David C. Jones, eds., *Schooling and Society in 20th Century British Columbia* (Calgary: Detselig Enterprises Ltd., 1980), pp. 23-51.

[5]Robert Sears, Eleanor Maccoby, Harry Levin, *Patterns of Child Rearing* (Evanston: Row, Peterson and Co., 1957), pp. 5-7; BCBH, *Report*, 1929, p. A7; see also Neil Sutherland, "Social Policy, 'Deviant Children.' and the Public Health Apparatus in British Columbia Between the Wars," *The Journal of Educational Thought* 14 (1980), pp. 80-90.

[6]A.W. Hunter, "Medical Inspection from the Standpoint of the Parent, the Teacher, and the Physician," BCBH, *Report*, 1914, pp. U66-76; see also Christopher Lasch, *Haven in a Heartless World, The Family Beseiged* (New York: Basic Books, 1977), pp. 3-20.

[7]"Medical Inspection of Schools," BCBH, *Reports*, 1910 to 1939.

[8]"Women's Institute Convention," *Vernon News*, Nov. 6, 1919, p. 11; M.A. Twiddy, "A Child Study Group," *Public Health Nurses' Bulletin 2* (March 1938): 49, (hereafter PHNB); British Columbia Public Schools, *Report*, 1936-37, p. 156 (hereafter BCPS, *Report*).

[9]Eileen Carruthers, "Discussion Groups for Mothers," PHNB 2 (April 1935): 10.

[10]Anne E. Wells, "Principles and Methods of Publicity in Health Education," *Canadian Public Health Journal*, 23 (Sept. 1932): 442-447, (hereafter *CPHJ*).

[11]F.W. Howay, "The Settlement and Progress of British Columbia, 1871-1914," in *Historical Essays on British Columbia*, J. Friesen and H.K. Ralston (Toronto: McClelland and Stewart, 1976), p. 38.

[12]Margaret Ormsby, *British Columbia: A History* (Toronto: Macmillan, 1958), pp. 296-303.

[13]"Life and Growth of Vancouver Schools," *Romance of Vancouver Jubilee Number*, Native Sons of British Columbia, 1936, pp. 33-34; BCPS, *Report*, 1936; *Ibid.*, 1939.

[14]"Life and Growth of Vancouver Schools," pp. 33-34.

[15]BCBH, *Report*, 1912, p. M10; *Ibid.*, 1914, pp. U10-11 U66-77; *Ibid.*, 1918-19, pp. G179-197; Vancouver Board of School Trustees, *Report*, 1908, p. 8; ibid., 1909, p. 40, (hereafter, VBST, *Report*).

[16]BCPS, *Report*, 1900; *Ibid.*, 1939.

[17]*Ibid*, 1900, p. 224; *Ibid.*, 1901, p. 239.

[18]BCBH, *Report*, 1912, p. M3.

[19]F.W. Andrew, "Medical Inspection of School Children," *Women's Institute Quarterly* 11 (October 1916): 9-13; see also BCBH, *Report*, 1914, p. U69.

[20]VBST, *Report*, 1908, p. 20.

[21]BPS, *Report*, 1924, p. T63.

[22]*Ibid.*, p. T10; Rosen, "A Healthier World," pp. 139-140; BCBH, *Report*, 1937, pp. H5-6.

[23]Andrew, "Medical Inspection of School Children," p. 11; for a discussion of the eugenics movement see Carol Bacchi, "Race Regeneration and Social Purity: A Story of the English-Speaking Suffragists," *Histoire sociale/Social History*, 11 (November 1978): 460-474.

[24]VBST, *Report*, 1912, p. 36.

²⁵BCBH, *Report,* 1918, p. G139.

²⁶Andrew, "Medical Inspection of School Children," p. 9; BCBH, *Report,* 1914, pp. U67-69.

²⁷VBST, *Report,* 1909, p. 40

²⁸BCBH, *Report,* 1920, p. A15, *Ibid.,* 1935, p. I15.

²⁹Sutherland, *Children in English-Canadian Society,* pp. 46-47.

³⁰VBST, *Report,* 1907, p. 16; BCPS, *Report,* 1905, p. A57; *Ibid.,* 1909, p. A31; British Columbia , *Statutes* 1910, "School Health Inspection Act."

³¹VBST, *Report,* 1903, p. 17; T.F. Rose states eye inspection began in 1902. *From Shaman to Modern Medicine: A Century of the Healing Arts in British Columbia (Vancouver: Mitchell Press, 1972), p. 103. "Life and Growth of Vancouver Schools," states eye inspections began in 1899.*

³²*BCPS, Report,* 1905, p. A57.

³³VBST, *Report,* 1907, p. 16.

³⁴*Ibid.,* 1908, p. 20.

r³⁵BCPS, *Reports,* 1911, pp. M7-10.

³⁶VBST, *Report,* 1912, p. 32.

³⁷*Ibid.,* 1911, p. 53; Breeze worked as head school nurse from 1910 to 1936, and from 1936 to 1939 directed nursing in the newly organized Vancouver Metropolitan Health Unit.

³⁸Elizabeth Breeze, "School Nursing," *PHNB* 1 (October 1924): 4; Helen Hartley, "Toothbrush and Handkerchief Drill," *Public Health Nurse,* 1918, pp. 1-4.

³⁹BCBH, *Report,* 1911, p. M14; Vancouver Board of Health, *Report,* 1924, p. 24 (hereafter VBH, *Report).*

⁴⁰BCPS, *Report,* 1914, p. A64.

⁴¹VBH, *Report,* 1911, pp. 33, 40-43; *Ibid.,* 1913, p. 24; BCPS, *Report,* 1914, p. A64. During 1912, the Women's Educational Club provided $1,018.70 in aid to needy children.

⁴²BCBH, *Report,* 1914, p. P6; BCPS, *Report,* 1914, p. A66; *Ibid.,* 1935, p. S53; *Ibid.,* 1939, p. H60.

⁴³BCPS, *Reports,* 1912, p. A50; VBST, *Report,* 1912, p. 31.

⁴⁴VBST, *Report,* 1909, p. 40.

⁴⁵BCPS, *Report,* 1912, p. A50.

⁴⁶VBST, *Report,* 1913, p. 18.

⁴⁷*Ibid.,* 1915, pp. 40, 42; *Ibid.,* 1916, p. 42.

⁴⁸BCPS, *Report,* 1937, p. 155; VBH, *Report,* 1939, p. 18.

⁴⁹VBST, *Report,* 1916, p. 43; "School Dental Clinics Doing Good Work but more Urgently Needed," *The Vancouver Sun,* October 3, 1921.

⁵⁰BCPS, *Report,* 1920, p. C43; *Ibid.,* 1937, p. A60.

⁵¹*Ibid.,* 1933, p. M53.

⁵²VBST, *Report,* 1917, pp. 41, 45, Hartley, "Toothbrush and Handkerchief Drills," p. 1.

⁵³BCPS, *Report,* 1935, p. S55.

⁵⁴VBST, *Report,* 1917, p. 14; *Ibid.,* 1918, p. 41.

⁵⁵VBH, *Report,* 1938, p. 17.

⁵⁶VBST, *Report,* 1911, p. 63; *Ibid.,* p. 41.

⁵⁷BCPS, *Report,* 1916, p. A50; *Ibid.,* 1921, p. C42.

⁵⁸VBH, *Report,* 1928, p. 24; *Ibid.,* 1939, p. 16.

⁵⁹BCPS, *Report,* 1915, p. A48.

[60]*Ibid.*, 1916, p. A50; VBST, *Report*, 1921, p. 8.

[61]VBH, *Report*, 1939, p. 17; BCPS, *Report*, 1938, p. H59.

[62]VBST, *Report*, 1911, p. 42.

[63]BCPS, *Report*, 1912, p. A28; *Ibid.*, p. 239; *Ibid.*, 1912, p. A27.

[64]VBST, *Report*, 1908, p. 12; BCPS, *Report*, 1909, p. A29, A36.

[65]VBST, *Report*, 1911, p. 11; BCPS, *Report*, 1912, p. A51.

[66]VBST, *Report*, 1914, p. 18.

[67]"The Strathcona Trust," BCPS, *Report*, 1911, pp. A69-71.

[68]*Ibid.*, *Ibid.*, 1913, p. A68; J.H. Putman and G.M. Weir reported both excellent and poor work in physical training being done under the trust. British Columbia, *Survey of the School System* (Victoria: King's Printer, 1925), p. 395.

[69]A.M. Ross, "The Romance of Vancouver's Schools," in *Schools of Old Vancouver* by James M. Sanderson (Vancouver Historical Society, 1971), p. 17; BCPS, *Report*, 1904, p. A13; *Ibid.*, 1914, p. A66.

[70]BCPS, *Report*, 1914, p. A66; Major T. Jamison-Quirk (ret) Canadian Provost Corps.

[71]*Ibid.*, *Report*, 1905, p. A57; Ross, "The Romance of Vancouver's Schools" p. 17; see also Desmond Morton, "The Cadet Movement in the Moment of Canadian Militarism, 1909-1914," *Journal of Canadian Studies*, XIII (Summer, 1978), pp. 56-68.

[72]BCPS, *Report*, 1914, p. A66.

[73]*Ibid.*, 1913, p. A46; *Ibid.*, 1915, p. A49.

[74]*Ibid.*, 1934, p. N61; VBST, *Report*, 1933, p. 37; *Ibid.*, 1940, p. 51.

[75]BCPS, *Report*, 1940, p. B91; Putman and Weir, *Survey of the School System*, p. 395, Putman and Weir reported some principals objected to school cadet corps on the grounds corps tended towards militarism.

[76]VBST, *Report*, 1913, p. 37.

[77]BCPS, *Report*, 1924, p. F42; VBST, *Report*, 1923, p. 24.

[78]VBST, *Report*, 1930, p. 50; Ruby Simpson and G. Hanna, "Corrective Physical Education," *CPHJ* 23 (March, 1932): 141.

[79]VBST, *Report*, 1937, p. 15.

[80]BCBH, *Report*, 1916, p. 122.

[81]VBH, *Report*, 1920, p. 23; VBST, *Report*, 1919, p. 37; for details for the application of Wood's tables see S. Josephine Baker, *Child Hygiene* (New York: Harper, 1925), pp. 418-421.

[82]VBST, *Report*, 1920, pp. 39, 45; BCPS, *Report*, 1920, C43; VBH, *Report*, 1927, p. 23.

[83]VBST, *Report*, 1913, pp. 34-35.

[84]*Ibid.*, p. 35.

[85]BCPS, *Report*, 1925, p. Q17.

[86]VBST, *Report*, 1917, p. 36.

[87]VBH, *Report*, 1921, p. 21.

[88]*Ibid.*, 1925, p. 24; VBST, *Report*, 1925, pp. 17-18; "Order-in-Council," March 19, 1925.

[89]Putman and Weir, *Survey of the School System*, p. 396.

[90]BCBH, *Report*, 1932, p. Y4; J.W. MacIntosh, "Smallpox in Vancouver, Preliminary Report," *CPHJ* 13 (March, 1932): 144-145.

[91]BCBH, *Report*, 1929-1939.

[92]"The Curse of Vaccination," *The Vancouver Sun*, September 3, 1926; see also H.D. Dyer, "The Trouble and Risks from Modern Attempts to Check the Spread of Infectious Diseases in Schools," BCBH, *Report*, 1914, pp. 656-657.

[93]Letters to the Editor, *The Vancouver Sun*, October 1, 1926; *Ibid.*, October 6, 1926.

[94]VBH, *Report*, 1939, p. 19.

[95]Rosen, *A History of Public Health*, (New York: M.D. Publications, 1958), p. 337.

[96]VBH, *Report*, 1926, p. 24; *Ibid.*, 1930, p. 23; BCBH, *Report*, 1929, p. U23.

[97]VBH, *Report*, 1929, p. 23; *Ibid.*, p. 23; *Ibid .*, 1939, p. 23.

[98]"Toxoid Treatment for Young Babies," *The Vancouver Province*, January 8, 1938, editorial page.

[99]"Cases Against Toxoid," *The Vancouver Province*, January 15, 1938, editorial page. Letter to the editor signed by three Vancouver physicians E.F. Fridleifson, N.F. McConnell, and A.S. Murphy.

[100]Rosen, *A History of Public Health*, pp. 38-39, 384-390.

[101]BCBH, *Report*, 1914, pp. U10-11.

[102]BCPS, *Report*, 1912, p. A50; VBH, *Report*, 1911, p. 63.

[103]VBST, *Report*, 1913, p. 36.

[104]*Ibid.*, 1917, p. 36.

[105]BCPS, *Report*, 1926, p. R44; *Ibid.*, 1934, p. N47.

[106]*Ibid.*, p. A43.

[107]J.T. Marshall, "Development of Public Health in British Columbia," *CPHJ* 25 (Aug. 1935): 366-367.

[108]BCBH, *Report*, p. FF25.

[109]*Ibid.*, 1924, pp. Q15-16; *Ibid.*, 1926, pp. M19-20; *Ibid.*, 1936, pp. M9-10; *Ibid.*, 1939, p. E31; VBH, *Report*, 1938, p. 14.

[110]"T.B. Test in City Schools," *The Vancouver Sun*, Sept. 12, 1938; VBH, *Report*, 1938, p. 16; "Public Health Services in B.C.," *The Colonist*, Oct. 4, 1934.

[111]VBH, *Report*, 1939, p. 15.

[112]"Endemic Goitre," *Bulletin of the British Columbia Board of Health* 2 (June, 1932) p. 73.

[113]*Ibid.*

[114]BCPS, *Report*, 1937, p. 155; VBH, *Report*, 1937, p. 22.

[115]VBST, *Report*, 1910, p. 18.

[116]BCPS, *Report*, 1911, p. A43; *Ibid.*, 1913, p. A53; VBST, *Report*, 1930, p. 79.

[117]BCPS, *Report*, 1918, p. 45.

[118]VBST, *Report*, 1918, p. 45.

[119]BCPS, *Report*, 1923, p. F41.

[120]VBST, *Report*, 1918, p. 45.

[121]*Ibid.*, p. 47.

[122]BCPS, *Report*, 1919, p. A38.

[123]*Ibid.*

[124]Putman and Weir *Survey of the School System*, pp. 391-394; VBST, *Report*, 1936, p. 71; *Ibid.*, 1939, p. 108.

[125]BCPS, *Report*, 1936, p. H90; VBST, *Report*, 1930, p. 44; *Ibid.*, 1935, p. 76; *Ibid.*, 1938, pp. 102-103.

[126]BCPS, *Report*, 1935, p. S53; "Life and Growth of Vancouver Schools," p. 34.

[127]BCPS *Report*, 1921, p. 142.

[128]C.A. Lucas, *Public Health Education in the Schools*, BCBH, 1926, pp. 3-13.

[129]"Historical Resume of Teacher-Training in British Columbia," BCPS, *Report*, 1927, p. 40-41.

[130]*Ibid.*, 1902, pp. V40-41.

[131]*Ibid.*, 1909, pp. A64-71.

[132]*Ibid.*, p. A77; *Ibid.*, 1913-14, p. A15.

[133]*Programme of Studies for Elementary Schools*, 1925 MS26, pp. 16, 24, 32, 39.

[134]BCPS, *Reports*, 1925, pp. M69-70; *Ibid.*, 1928, p. V49.

[135]*British Columbia Programme of Studies for Elementary Schools*, 1925-26.

[136]*Ibid.*, 1928-29, p. 103.

[137]*Ibid.*, pp. 18-19.

[138]BCPS, *Report*, 1931, p. 144.

[139]*Ibid.*, 1936, p. H34.

[140]*Programme of Studies for Elementary Schools*, 1936, pp. 16-17.

[141]Joy Elmer Morgan, "The Sources of Ethical Character," *The B.C. Teacher* 7 (Jan. 1928): 21.

[142]"Do We Mean It?" *The B.C. Teacher* 16 (Jan. 1937): 209-212.

[143]F.W. Wallace, "The Revision of the High School Health Course," *Ibid.* 15 (March 1936): *British Columbia Course of Studies for Junior High Schools*, 1936, p. 23.

[144]Dorothy Johnson, "Health," *The B.C. Teacher* 15 (April 1936): 30-32.

[145]VBST, *Report*, 1911, p. 62; BCPS, *Report*, 1912, p. A50.

[146]VBST, *Report*, 1911, pp. 62-63.

[147]*Ibid.*, 1917, p. 41.

[148]C.A. Lucas, "Little Mother's League Classes as Conducted in Saanich over a Period of five years," *PHNB* 1 (April 1927): 8-10.

[149]VBST, *Report*, 1917, pp. 40-41.

[150]"Recommendations and Resolutions, Committee of Red Cross Societies, 1919," CPHJ 11 (April 1920): 154; BCPS, *Report*, 1918, pp. 15-16.

[151]Jean E. Browne, "The Contribution of Junior Red Cross in Education," *The B.C. Teacher* 10 (Feb. 1931): 47-50.

[152]*Ibid.*, Ruth Witbeck, "Practical Citizenship as Taught at Tecumseh School," *Ibid.*, XVI (June 1936): 322-330.

[153]Elsie Groves Benedict, "The Contribution of the Junior Red Cross to Public Health," *CPHJ* 17 (July 1927): 322-330.

[154]Ruth Witbeck, "Practical Citizenship," p. 19.

[155]BCPS, *Report*, 1937, p. J57.

[156]*Ibid.*, 1940, p. B29.

[157]Laura E. Jamison, "Sex Education in the Child Welfare Program," BCBH, 1936 (a paper read before the Vancouver Child Welfare Conference, 1927).

[158]BCBH, *Report*, 1914, p. U70.

[159]*Ibid.*, p. U71-72.

[160]Putman and Weir, *Survey of the School System*, p. 531.

[161]Jamison, "Sex Education in the Child Welfare Program," pp. 3-7; see also the address of Dr. Ernest Hall in the Child Welfare Association of British Columbia, *Report*, 1918, p. 18.

[162]Jamison, "Sex Education in the Child Welfare Program," pp. 3-7; Lucas, *Public Health in Schools*, p. 7.

[163]For a discussion of books available see Michael Bliss, "Pure Books of Avoided Subjects, Pre-Freudian Sexual Ideas in Canada," in *Studies in Canadian Social History*, ed. Michael Horn and Ronald Sabourin (Toronto: McClelland and Stewart, 1974), pp. 362-346.

[164]"Some Thoughts for Wives and Mothers and Some Teachings to be given to Children by Parents Who Find it Difficult to put Their Thoughts into Words," BCBH, 1936 (by permission of the National League of Health, Maternity, and Child Welfare, London, England).

[165]Lucas, *Public Health Education in Schools*, p. 7.

[166]VBH, *Report*, 1926, p. 24; Former Kitsilano High School graduates Ruth Sutton and Frank Hardwick.

[167]British Columbia Child Welfare Association, *Report*, 1918, p. 4.

[168]*Ibid.*, 1919, p. 5.

[169]J. Elmer Brown, "Modern Educational Objectives," *The B.C. Teacher* 6 (June 1927): 23-29; Morgan, "The Sources of Ethical Character," pp. 20-24. For a discussion of moral development and character education see *Proceedings of the National Conference on Character Education in Relation to Canadian Citizenship*, 1919; David Purpel and Kevin Ryan, *Moral Education . . . It Comes with the Territory* (Berkley: McCuthcon, 1976), pp. 3-10; Wilson Riles, "Role of the School in Moral Development," Proceedings of the 1974 Educational Services Conference, pp. 69-79.

[170]John M. Ewing, "Can Morals Be Taught?" *The B.C. Teacher* 9 (Dec. 1928): 7-11; "The Highest Morality Shall Be Inculcated," *Ibid.* 12 (Feb. 1933): 19-20.

[172]Chas. C. Watson, "The Development of Character: Its Relation to Education," *The B.C. Teacher* 16 (June 1935): 10-15.

[173]E.H. Fishback, "Character Education in the Junior High School," *Ibid.*, (Jan 1935), pp. 11-12.

[174]J. Muir, "Parent's Responsibility," British Columbia Welfare Association, *Report*, 1919, p. 41.

[175]M. Harwood, "How Parents Can Help Teachers," BCBH, 1931, p. 5.

[176]T.D. Pattullo, "Education as a Public Service," *The B.C. Teacher* 16 (May 1935): 4.

[177]"Strong Plea on Behalf of Youth of Prince Rupert, Parent-Teacher Meeting," *Prince Rupert Evening Empire*, Sept. 12, 1933, p. 1.

[178]*Ibid.*, p. 2.

[179]*Ibid.*, p. 2; see also "Sees Real Emergency," *Prince Rupert Daily News*, Sept. 21, 1933, pp. 1-4.

[180]"What Will Happen When the Boy if Father to the Man?" *Vernon News*, Oct. 14, 1925, p. 11.

[181]BCPS, *Report*, 1937, p. 156; VBH, *Report*, 1939, p. 12.

[182]BCBH, *Report*, 1915 to 1939; British Columbia's vital statistics up to 1927 cannot be considered totally accurate, see Herbert French, "The Low Birth Rate of British Columbia — Some Causes and a Remedy," *CPHJ*, XVIII (June 1927), pp. 262 — 266.

[183]BCBH, *Report*, 1937,, pp. H3-8.
[184]*Ibid.*, p. H6.
[185]*Ibid.*, p. H5.
[186]"Life and Growth of Vancouver Schools," p. 34.
[187]BCBH, *Report*, 1935, p. K55.

"Not to Punish But to Reform": Juvenile Delinquency and Children's Protection Act in Alberta, 1909-1929

Rebecca Coulter

In 1920 sixteen year old Albert B. was sent to Canada by his father presumably to seek his fortune but the twenty-five dollars the boy had in his pocket when he left England did not last long in his new homeland. Albert was arrested in a rural area of Alberta, charged with vagrancy, convicted and sentenced to four months of hard labour at the Fort Saskatchewan Gaol. His case would likely have passed unnoticed except for the fact that a police magistrate sympathetic to the child saving movement angrily wrote to the Attorney-General's Department to complain about the harsh sentence handed down.

> It is to me an almost incredible story. A boy of only sixteen, about six thousand miles from home, without work and needing to eat — could he be blamed if he stole something, or are there not some other people in the world more responsible for the theft than he would be?[1]

The letter went on to suggest that Albert should have received a suspended sentence, been found work on some farm and "helped to do the right thing, as probably, with a full stomach, he would not have any temptation to steal".[2]

In defense of the original sentence and the magistrate who imposed it, Superintendent Bryan of the Alberta Provincial Police informed the Deputy Attorney-General that Albert had actually stolen a car and when apprehended had given "a lot of evasive and contradictory statements as to his movements". In addition, argued Bryan, the man's conviction would "probably have the effect of stopping other cases of a like nature".[3]

It is not clear whether Police Magistrate Primrose's intervention on Albert's behalf resulted in a suspended sentence[4] but this anonymous youth's life, revealed in some fragmentary correspondence, serves to illustrate the conflicting views of childhood and juvenile delinquency prevalent in the early part of this century. Was Albert a boy or a man?[5] Was the environment responsible for delinquent behaviour or must individuals be held responsible for deviant acts? Should the courts be concerned with reforming or with punishing delinquents? Answers to satisfy all parties were never found (indeed, have yet to be found) but in Alberta, at least, the social reform position which argued for a prolonged, protected childhood, for the paramountcy of environmental influences as a determinant in child life and for the need to reform juvenile delinquents pre-dominated between 1909 and 1929. That is not to say that the practice of juvenile justice always reflected the social reform position nor even that the child savers were always consistent in their explanations or actions. Conflicting interpretations and practices existed and over the course of twenty years Alberta's child welfare officials, like those elsewhere, became more and more enamoured of efficiency and "scientific" and "professional" social work. Nonetheless on the whole it is safe to say that the sentiment and ideas of social reform continued to inform practice in a major way throughout the period.

Of the many social problems facing the new province of Alberta, juvenile delinquency was among the first to be tackled. In 1908 the Legislative Assembly of the Province passed the Industrial Schools Act in order to make provisions for the treatment of juvenile delinquents. This act empowered the Attorney-General to appoint a Superintendent of Industrial Schools. He chose R.B. Chadwick for the position and immediately instructed the new appointee to investigate and bring in recommendations about the best way to deal with delinquent and neglected children in the province. In preparing his report, Chadwick toured the North American continent and investigated forty-five industrial schools, visited fifty-five juvenile courts, and looked at various other institutions.[6]

In the end, he recommended that the Province of Alberta enter into an agreement with the Province of Manitoba in order that delinquent boys needing industrial school training could be admitted to the school at Portage la Prairie. He felt that the costs involved in building a modern cottage system [7] in Alberta would be prohibitive and, since Manitoba was willing to accept boys from Alberta, this arrangement ought to be pursued. In addition he recommended a broad system of child welfare laws for Alberta. Both his recommendations were accepted, the latter one being incorporated into law as An Act for the Protection of Neglected and Dependent Children (1909), and more commonly referred to as The Children's Protection Act. With its passage, the Act became the first major piece of welfare legislation in the province.[8]

Although the Alberta Act was modelled very closely on its counterpart in Ontario, it was understood, according to its initiator, R.B. Chadwick, "that amendments would be made from time to time in order that the Act would become workable under conditions as found in the Province of Alberta".[9] Chadwick also noted that Alberta's Act was regarded as the "broadest" on the continent. This was because Alberta's Act defined "neglected child" in a way which was "sufficiently broad to meet almost any condition or contingency which may arise in reference to the question of what constitutes a neglected child".[10] According to the Act,

> "Neglected child" shall mean a child who is found begging, receiving alms, thieving in a public place, sleeping a night in the open air, wandering about at late hours, associating or dwelling with a thief, drunkard or vagrant, or a child who by reason of the neglect, drunkeness or vice of its parents, is growing up without salutary parental control and education, or in circum-

stances exposing such child to an idle and dissolute life; or who is found in a house of ill-fame, or known to associate with or to be in the company of a reputed prostitute; or who is a habitual vagrant; or an orphan and destitute; or deserted by its parents; or whose only parent is undergoing imprisonment for crime; or why by reason of ill-treatment, continual personal injury or grave misconduct or habitual intemperance of its parents or either of them is in peril of loss of life, health or morality; or in respect to whom its parents or only parent have or has been convicted of an offence against this Act, or under *The Criminal Code*; or whose home by reason of neglect, cruelty or depravity, is an unfit place for such child, and "neglected children" shall mean two or more of such children;[11]

The normative nature of this definition allowed officials of the Department and Children's Aid Societies to intervene in nearly any situation they wished, an advantage they felt was particularly appropriate when it came to protecting children. The Act was further strengthened in this regard in later years by the addition of two clauses so that the definition of a neglected child also included one

. . . who is incorrigible or cannot be controlled by its parents; or who is employed anywhere between the hours of ten o'clock p.m. of one day and six o'clock a.m. of the following day . . .[12]

Additionally, the Act was extended by changing the definition of "child" from "a boy or girl actually or apparently under sixteen years of age" (1909), to seventeen in 1910 and eighteen in 1916. Furthermore, Chadwick noted,

The problems of dependent and delinquent children are so closely interwoven that they have been made as one as far as circumstances will permit, in the Province of Alberta.[13]

Thus both dependent and delinquent children were considered to fall under the more inclusive term "neglected".

As well as defining the clientele, the Act provided for the establishment of an administrative framework. To encourage, direct and supervise the work of the Children's Aid Societies[14] and to act in place of these societies where none existed, the Lieutenant Governor in Council was entitled to appoint a Superintendent of Neglected Children. Every city or town with a population over 10,000 (changed to 5,000 in 1916) was instructed to provide a home or shelter where children could be temporarily housed prior to placement in a foster home. The children placed in a shelter were to be supervised and managed by the Children's Aid Society, if it had been established, or, by the Superintendent, if it had not. Municipalities were held responsible for the maintenance of children although they or the Children's Aid Societies could apply for a court order to force parents to contribute to a child's upkeep.

The Act went on to outline the procedure to be followed in apprehending children and placing them in foster homes. The municipal police, the Royal North West Mounted Police, officers of a Children's Aid Society (authorized by a district judge) or the Superintendent could apprehend a child without a warrant. If a judge[15] found the child to be neglected within the meaning of the Act, the child was transferred to the care of the Children's Aid Society or the Superintendent of Neglected Children, either of which then became the legal guardian of the child and responsible for its placement in a suitable foster home. Foster homes and shelters were both subject to inspection by the Superintendent or his designate.

In this way The Children's Protection Act managed to legally define provincial, municipal, parental and voluntary activity in the field of child welfare. While various amendments were made throughout the years, mainly to expand the administrative machinery, the basic intent of the Act remained the same. Wide ranging powers were necessary to deal adequately with child welfare problems argued Canadian social reformers. Alberta's legislators apparently agreed and so do many historians.[16]

To put into practice the provisions of The Children's Protection Act, the Attorney-General promoted R.B. Chadwick to the position of Superintendent of Neglected Children. In appointing Chadwick, the Attorney-General ensured that Alberta would enter into the mainstream of current child welfare thought and practice. Chadwick, a native of Ontario, had come to Edmonton in 1906 to serve as general secretary to the Young Men's Christian Association. He had had previous experience in boys' work both in New York and Toronto[17] and throughout his tenure as Superintendent of Neglected Children retained and enlarged his contacts with social reformers throughout North America, Europe and Australia. By 1913 he was Vice President of the American Prison Association and Assistant Secretary of the Canadian Conference of Charity and Corrections[18] and in 1914 he sat on the national council of the Canadian Welfare League[19] along with such notables as J.S. Woodsworth. The network of contacts Chadwick established was maintained by his successors who continued to attend conferences in both Canada and the United States, often presenting papers while there. Additionally, Alberta hosted visiting reformers. For example, in 1909, J.J. Kelso, the well-known Superintendent of Neglected Children in Ontario, visited Alberta.[20] In 1918, the Annual Meeting of the Canadian Conference of Public Welfare was held in Edmonton[21] and in 1922, C.C. Carstens, Director of the Child Welfare League of America, spoke to the Annual Conference of the Department of Neglected Children.[22]

Chadwick was frank in acknowledging his indebtedness to the work of social reformers elsewhere. As has been already noted, The Children's Protection Act nearly replicated Ontario's, and in the early annual reports Chadwick notes the contributions of the United States, Australia, Germany, France, Scotland, Great Britain, Norway, Sweden and Austria. It is not surprising, then, that Alberta, as a member of the trans-national and international network[23] should develop policies and procedures for dealing with child neglect and juvenile delinquency very much like those in operation elsewhere in Canada, and especially in Ontario where, Rutherford claims, a small group of central Canadians were mainly responsible for articulating the theories and tactics of the national social reform movement.[24] But if central Canadians selected one idea from here and one idea from there to construct a child welfare system that they *knew* was superior, as Sutherland[25] suggests, then Albertans, at least, exhibited that same smug attitude towards Ontario's system. Ontario's system was good but Alberta's was better.[26]

How did the last, best west deal with the problem of juvenile delinquency? By 1912 Alberta had a functioning system of juvenile courts. Thus children charged with juvenile delinquency would appear before a Commissioner of the Juvenile Court. These commissioners most often had no legal training but had been appointed to the position because of their interest in child saving. Often they were ministers like Bishop H. Allen Gray or Rev. Michael Murphy, local businessmen in small communities or women like Alice Jamieson or Annie Langford. The approach used by these commissioners was closely modelled on the court procedures adopted by the famous Judge Ben Lindsay of Denver, Colorado,[27] a man who was frequently quoted with approval by the Superintendents of Neglected Children.

Juvenile courts were held separately from the proceedings of adult courts in keeping with the child savers' views that children must be protected from any contact with adult vices. Hearings were conducted informally without juries and commonly without benefit of counsel. It was understood that the presiding commissioner would, in the manner of a kind, concerned adult, inquire into the events surrounding the charge and determine what should be done with the child. A.M. McDonald, the man who became Superintendent of Neglected Children after Chadwick's death in 1915, likened the juvenile court procedures to medical ones when he quoted, with obvious approbation, an analogy made by Judge James Hodge Rocks of Richmond. When a child is physically ill, he goes to a doctor who examines the youngster, diagnoses the ailment and prescribes the remedy. Similarly, the juvenile judge should minister to the "morally ill" delinquent in the "moral clinic", the court.[28]

In the matter of delinquency, three remedies were open. The child could be placed on probation, made a ward of the Department of Neglected Children or lastly a boy could be sent to the Industrial School at Portage la Prairie or a girl to one of the provincial social service homes.

In keeping with the social reformers' emphasis on the efficacy of family life, the preferred course of action was probation. Thus the child would be left in his natural home but would be supervised by a probation officer who, in the cities, was usually the agent of the Children's Aid Society. The probation officer was expected to oversee the probationer's pursuits, friends and amusements.[29] This concept of probation was designed to meet Section 31 of the Dominion Delinquents Act which stated in part "that as far as practicable every juvenile delinquent shall be treated, not as a criminal, but as a misdirected, misguided child, and one needing aid, encouragement, help and assistance."[30]

If probation proved to be unworkable or unsatisfactory, the child could be made a ward of the Neglected Children's Department and would then be "placed out" in the hopes that a suitable home would turn the child into the right paths of behaviour. Placement in an institution was seen as the last resort to be employed only in cases of the "more hardened type of child" who needed "the rigid system of discipline offered in an Industrial Training School".[31] The "hardened" child was one

> . . . who is in the habit of defying authority, an habitual thief, an incorrigible or a child who does not respond to the milder treatment or probation or to the influences which are thrown around him by the Department of Neglected Children . . . .[32]

While a few juvenile court commissioners seemed bent on sentencing children who appeared before them in a way which would set an example for others, deterrence and retribution were not supposed to be considered as motives when bringing down a judgement.

> The old attitude of "an eye for an eye, and a tooth for a tooth" is frequently met with in those going through the channels of the Juvenile Court, but for this attitude there is substituted, as far as possible, the idea that preventive and educative reformation are the ends sought, and as far as possible records and terminology eliminate the idea of criminality.[33]

This issue of punishment versus reformation was the source of some friction between the Department and the Alberta Provincial Police. Superintendent McDonald wrote to the Deputy Attorney-General on September 5, 1918 with a request that the relationship between the A.P.P. and the Department of Neglected Children be clarified.[34] McDonald accused the police of dealing with juveniles without consulting the Department and further complained of the tendency of members of the A.P.P., acting as commissioners, to sentence children to the Portage la Prairie Industrial School unnecessarily.

While part of McDonald's concern no doubt arose from financial considerations,[35] it is, nonetheless, true that the child savers' conviction that unsatisfactory home conditions generally caused delinquency gave them an attitude towards youthful offenders that was more sympathetic than that of most police officers. Child savers often described delinquents as "more sinned against than sinning" and for this reason much of the work of the Department of Neglected Children and the Children's Aid Societies tended to blur the distinction between dependent and delinquent children as Chadwick had originally intended it should. The police, on the other hand, were more inclined to draw a line between delinquent and neglected children. The Constables' Manual used by the Alberta Provincial Police was unequivocal.

> A delinquent child is one which breaks the law and therefore is liable to punishment; a neglected child is one which has been neglected or abandoned, and therefore to be cared for and pitied, not punished.[36]

Police officers were reminded, however, that neither class of children was to be allowed to mix with other criminals.

Susan Houston[37] has argued that the tendency of child savers to treat both types of children — the dependent and the delinquent — as one indicates that the real motivation for child welfare work was social control. She claims that by seeing dependent children as potentially or actually delinquent, the child savers were able to justify their interference in the lives of poor children and their families in terms of "the common good". There is no doubt some justification to this argument, especially for nineteenth-century Ontario, but it does ignore the two-edged nature of the child savers' position. If failing to distinguish between dependent and delinquent children resulted in harsher treatment for the former, it might also be argued that it resulted in a more humane treatment for the latter. Given the reality of institutional life in the early twentieth century, it seems likely that young delinquents and their families would be quite happy to trade incarceration for home supervision.

In any event, while probation theoretically meant that a probation officer could supervise both the delinquent and his parents, the simple fact was that financial considerations prevented it. Both provincial and municipal governments were extraordinarily parsimonious and even with the assistance of volunteers, the Department of Neglected Children was never able to come close to thoroughly supervising the cities, never mind the rural areas.[38] Lack of funds also meant that child welfare officials had practical as well as ideological reasons for trying to keep delinquent and neglected children in the parental home. Department officials claimed they tried to avoid apprehending children because "The home of the child is the natural place of protection and the parents are its natural guardian."[39] They might have added that it was cheaper to let families feed, clothe and house their young than to have children's shelters or reformatories take on the responsibility.

This is not to imply, however, that those involved in child welfare work were duplicitous characters propounding the benefits of home life as a cover-up for monetary concerns. The financial imperative was not of their making but they had to live within its constraints. Thus, for example, the third Superintendent of Neglected Children, K.C. McLeod, opposed staff cuts in his department by arguing that it was important to have an officer of the department present at all juvenile cases because otherwise

. . . many Magistrates become incensed against boys and wish to send them at once to the Reformatory, without the chance of probation. Our Officer there, accepting charge of the boy on probation, can . . . save him from being sent to Portage, and the Province from the expense of at least $2000.00[40]

Similarly the most compelling argument made against raising the age of children coming under the Dominion Delinquents Act was the financial one. If the age were raised by two years from 16 to 18, a significant increase in the number of children coming into care would be experienced and the Department had neither the facilities nor the staff to cope. Indeed, throughout the 1920s the Department of Neglected Children was constantly under pressure to reduce spendings and decrease staff.[41]

While child and family welfare work, like other reform measures, can be shown to have an important role to play in legitimizing capitalist society, it is clear that in Alberta the mediating influence of social service work was to be restricted by more immediate pecuniary concerns. It was simply impossible, given the available resources, for social reformers to effect a wholesale super-vision of the lives of the children of the working class, much less their parents as well. The impact of their work was to be felt not so much in what they actually did but in how they contributed to what Sutherland has called the "twentieth century consensus" but others have called the ideological hege-mony of capitalism.[42]

The approach to the causes of juvenile delinquency is a case in point. Because of the emphasis on environmental factors as the primary cause of delinquency, it became easy to blame poor families for crime. Child savers used the following model of the three stages of child development to explain the centrality of an appropriate family life. The first eight years of life, said Chadwick, were distinguished by an absolute dependency on adults and the child simply reflected the home. If the home were good, then *ipso facto*, the child would be good. Conversely, bad homes made bad children. The second period of childhood occurred between the ages of nine and thirteen. It was at this stage, Chadwick felt, that the child was learning habits and morals by imitation. Thus it was important that wholesome adult models be available to the child. The third stage of childhood was from the age of thirteen to the age of seventeen and this period, warned the Superintendent, was fraught with danger. Chadwick quotes freely from the works of G. Stanley Hall to show that adolescence is filled with emotional upset, that this is the impulsive age. In explaining adolescence Chadwick said

During this period the child is up against the most serious time of its life. Rapid physical and mental growth, lack of knowledge of how to conduct itself under new conditions and circumstances, the ambitions and desires of men and women with the experience of children to carry them through this trying time, are but a few of the many trials to which the child is subjected.[43]

Furthermore, while the religious impulse was considered to be strong at this age so was the tendency towards criminal behaviour. If firm and loving parents failed to correct misbehaviour, the child would become a criminal for life.

Since most juvenile delinquents in Alberta were twelve years of age and older[44] and since a large proportion of them came from working class homes, homes often beset by unemployment, the loss of one parent, or very marginal incomes,[45] it was easy to create an explanation for delinquency based on the psychopathology of both adolescents and working class families. While some delinquent activity was part down to "the desire for fun" or "mischief-making", much more was blamed on the failure of parents to provide the proper home life. This was especially true in the case of the delinquent girl who

> . . ., as a rule, comes from a home where immorality and vice are more or less common and in the majority of cases she is compelled to house herself in crowded and unsanitary quarters with others of her kind. As a general rule these girls are stubborn and untractable.[46]

Thus both the families and the girls were to blame. Chadwick was also critical of parents who sent their girls out to work and of these working girls themselves because they sought some pleasure in life by attending dances, parties and dinners. Chadwick seemed particularly distressed with young girls who eschewed domestic service for jobs elsewhere. He was critical of girls who

> . . . prefer to work as waitresses in cheap restaurants, or even in the capacity of dishwasher, in order that they may have their evenings free, that they may be able to enter and leave their rooms at their own discretion, bring in their own companions, and entertain whom they will.[47]

In instances such as these, Chadwick seemed more concerned with the degree of independence of the young women rather than with anything else. Did he favour domestic service because employers in this situation could be seen as surrogate parents for the girl who had been allowed or encouraged to leave her own home and was not yet under the protection of a husband? Certainly, girls were seen as in special need or protection because they became women and women became mothers. As the "Angels of the Home" they then were responsible for the proper rearing of the next generation of children. In other words, the future of the country lay in the hands of mothers so it was important that they themselves be brought up correctly.

The reformers were also concerned about the sexual activity of girls because girls could lose "all that was valuable in their lives" before they realized "the sacredness of preserving the purity of their bodies and of their

minds".[48] Reformers recognized the double standard of sexual morality existing in society but simply acceded to it.

> A boy who makes a mistake is welcomed back into society, and there is
> rarely any difficulty in finding a good private home for him. A girl who has
> gone wrong has lost so much that it would be difficult to regain her place
> in society, even if society were as ready to welcome her as her erring brother.
> The fact is that she is not so welcomed.[49]

Chadwick had noted in 1911 that one of the reasons girls received harsher
treatment in the matter of "sex crimes" was the fact that the consequences of
their behaviour were so glaringly obvious[50] and, indeed, throughout the years
illegitimate children became a growing concern for the Department of
Neglected Children.

Among working class families, the immigrant family, especially, was subjected to close scrutiny. Despite the fact that the majority of the immigrants
in Alberta were English-speaking, the Department defined "immigrant children" as those who could not speak English. Consequently, Superintendent
Chadwick felt able to claim that immigrant children, "lacking knowledge of
the language, . . . readily fall into mistakes, violate the laws and commit
many misdemeanours . . ."[51] That they could not speak English was thus
considered an essential part of the explanation for their delinquent behaviour.

On the other hand, once these same children learned English they were a
threat of another sort. When they could speak English and their parents could
not, these children were suspected of devising "schemes under the eyes of the
parents" who were too ignorant to realize what was going on.[52] Additionally
the children were seen as able to "indulge in many habits and actions which
are incomprehensible to their parents"[53] because the parents did not understand the ways of the city. Thus, whether the immigrant children knew English
or not, they were viewed as more prone to delinquent behaviour. An additional
problem with the children of the foreign born as opposed to the Canadian
born was alleged to be their precociousness in sex matters and their tendency
to "succumb more readily to immorality".[54] Furthermore, their parents were
often seen as forcing the children out of the home to work — the girls in
unskilled restaurant and hotel jobs and the boys in street trades, both of which
endeavours it was said led rapidly to the criminal life.

On some occasions the reformers recognized that the average immigrant
had come to Canada to better his life and that immigrants had contributed to
the opening of the west. However, the faster they could be brought to a "high
grade" of Canadian citizenship, the better it would be. Chadwick felt so
strongly about the necessity of absorbing immigrants into the Canadian way
of life, that he was able to cite this story seemingly unaware of how it contradicted his other notions about the respect owed by children to their parents
and the importance of human dignity in general.

There has been a tendency for the Canadian-bred child to look down upon the child of the foreign-born as not so fortunate as he, owing to the fact that he has not been born a Canadian. This all has a good effect in bringing the child of foreign-born parents to be a good Canadian. The sentiment is best expressed in the attitude of a small boy who, after having been punished by his father, said he did not object to being punished when he needed it but he hated to be thrashed by a dirty foreigner.[55]

An uncritical analysis of the delinquency statistics of the Department tends to support its assertion that the delinquency rate was higher among immigrant children than among others. With the exception of the years 1910 and 1911 when 15.57% of the population had its origin in non-English speaking lands and 15.58% of the delinquents had a similar origin, children of the "foreign-born" were overrepresented in the delinquency statistics.[56] Several explanations can be postulated. More immigrant children may have been committing acts considered delinquent because in the troubled economic times after 1912 their families likely were the ones to suffer first from unemployment. On the other hand, the "self-fulfilling prophecy" may have been at work. The child savers and police assumed immigrant children were inclined to be delinquent and, therefore, may have spent more time looking for delinquents in the immigrant neighbourhoods and thus found more. There may have been a tendency, exacerbated by prejudice, to deal more firmly with immigrant children than with other children so that immigrant children would be placed on probation while English-speaking children would be let off with a warning. This state of affairs has been noted in the historical context by Gillis and Platt and in the modern one by, among other, William Ryan.[57] Unfortunatey the evidence for the Alberta situation does not allow for a firm conclusion on this matter at this time. What we can note, however, is the fact that by the end of World War I, the Superintendent of Neglected Children was less inclined to single out the children of the "foreign-born" for special mention when he was discussing juvenile delinquency.[58]

What forms did juvenile delinquency take in Alberta between 1909 and 1929? According to the statistics included in the Annual Reports, most cases of delinquency seem to have related to theft for boys and sexual offences for girls. From the evidence available, it can be postulated that, while some of these delinquencies were "childish pranks" and "mischief making", many of them resulted from adolescents trying to meet the necessities of life. A large number of the recorded thefts, for example, were of articles of clothing such as sweaters, boots and socks. This was particularly true in the winter. The testimony of girls charged with sexual offences shows that they had often lost their jobs, had been unable to find a job, or had felt forced into a sexual relationship in order to keep a job.

J.E. Robbins points out that between 1911 and 1931 wage earners, on the whole, were gaining financially, with the exception of the young and the old.

He notes a continuous gap of about two years between the school leaving age and the attainment of economic independence. Robbins further claims that the loss of independence was especially severe among the boys whose relative earning capacity dropped by 35% from 1911 to 1931.[59]

With this increasing dependency, the strain on poor families must have been noticeable. While hourly wage rates were increasing, so was the cost of living. Moreover, much of the work was seasonal in nature. In 1921, for example, in Calgary, labourers worked an average of only 40.87 weeks in the year.[60] Children in families such as these would need to go out to work as early as possible in order to support themselves or add to the family income. Yet the young were experiencing increasing difficulty in finding jobs. Thus it is not unreasonable to expect that, when work was unavailable, they and their families would have to survive as best they could.

Louis Chevalier has argued in his book *Labouring Classes and Dangerous Classes* that the city houses a segment of the population that lives in the twilight zone between crime and unskilled labour, working when work is available but turning to crime when it is necessary for survival. Stephen Humphries, in looking specifically at juvenile delinquency, convincingly argues that much juvenile crime was "social crime".[61] By this he means that a great part of youthful stealing was done in order to supplement family economies. Pilfering, from the corner store or raiding a vegetable garden, for example, brought in additional food. Shoplifting or stealing from a clothesline added clothing to the family wardrobe. Other forms of illegal activity also helped a family get by as the case of an Edmonton boy shows. He was eventually caught shoplifting but he had begun his life of "crime" by sweeping up the wheat left in railroad box cars. This he would sell for a little money and it was only after this route to additional income was closed that he turned to stealing from stores. In summarizing this case in his 1932 thesis on juvenile delinquency, Hermin Lewis King observed "As the family was large and the father's income small, it appeared to me as though the boy was to some extent forced to 'sweep up the grain', and this led to his subsequent antisocial acts."[62] Here is an example of how the family was held responsible for a son's delinquency. He was "forced" into illegal activity by his parents. No blame is attached to the economic system which allowed unemployment and poverty.

Of course not all delinquent behaviour was directed towards the noble cause of family survival. Young males of all classes stole cars in which to go "joy riding" and at least one adult wondered if boys were contributing to their own delinquency by acquiring "French safes".[63] Rather trivial cases also appear in the records. For example, a local school board charged a young lad with throwing a stone through a school window. The boy was acquitted, the school board appealed to the Attorney-General, an inspector was sent out to investigate and, after a volume of paperwork, a settlement was finally reached.[64] Childhood scraps seem to have sometimes ended in court too. A young lad, L., in Peace River called one of his peers a "son-of-a-bitch", a bit of a brouhaha ensued, and the boys ended up in juvenile court. A police report summarized the results of the case.

> His Worship in reviewing the evidence stated that the accused had received a great deal of provocation, and that to the majority of people the words used by L. _____meant "Fight". The parents of the two boys were present in Court, and his Worship lectured them rather severely on their attitude in the latter, stating they should exercise more control over their children.[65]

The accused boy was given a suspended sentence pending good behaviour.

This last case indicates an interesting trend in community attitudes towards youthful behaviours. As the formal structure of a juvenile justice system took hold in Alberta more and more adults seemed to be turning to this formal state mechanism to control the pranks and indiscretions of children. For example, Hallowe'en tricksters who over-turned outhouses, rolled away garbage barrels or hid front gates could easily find themselves facing police questioning and possibly a juvenile court hearing.[66] Adult attitudes in the 1920s, especially, began to harden when middle class youths appeared to increasingly involve themselves in a variety of delinquent acts. Delinquents from well-to-do families were a puzzle. Their family life — so very much like that of the child savers themselves — could obviously not be blamed. These young criminals were, of course, tainted by their adolescence but firm and loving parents were supposed to be able to control the raging emotions of this life stage. Part of the blame fell on "the gang" but working class youths had gangs too. Thus, more and more, juvenile delinquents of the "better class" who, it was felt, committed crimes for "thrills", found a hardened attitude awaiting them. This particular type of juvenile offender, blessed with the fortunes of life, was clearly a perverse, intractable individual — a "bad seed".

Newspapers of the 1920s reflect a growing concern on the part of adults for the "wayward youth" of the land. Fears about the loose and immoral behaviour of the young grew and cigarette smoking, drinking, dancing and movies all had to accept their share of blame for delinquent behaviour.[68] With the arrival of the depression and a corresponding increase in crime rates, "respectable" citizens, primarily out of fear for their property, demanded harsh treatment for young "hoodlums". One prominent Edmonton financier, commenting on a rash of crime, demanded the return of the lash and said

> Most of these would-be bandits are probably boys in their 'teens who dread the lash and it would soon end these hold-ups.[68]

Despite some public outcry, however, child savers were able to hold to the notion of reformation rather than punishment[69] although they, too, continued to be exasperated with incorrigible youths.

Between 1909 and 1929 large numbers of Albertans also worked in ways designed to prevent delinquency. While the Children's Aid Societies and the Department of Neglected Children "rescued" children from the more desparate circumstances, most churches and many men's and women's service clubs and organizations involved themselves in boy and girl work. Much of this work was designed to provide healthy recreational activities for young people under the supervision of trustworthy adults. The Young Men's and Young Women's Christian Associations and community leagues afforded opportunities to participate in a wide range of athletic pursuits including swimming, gymnastics and basket-ball. Service clubs such as the Rotary International and church-related groups like the Canadian Girls In Training provided summer camping experiences. Through these forms of recreation it was hoped that young people would use their time profitably and would, through the example and training of adult leaders, behave "decently", eschewing the diversions of the street and alley which, it was thought, ultimately led to delinquency. It must be noted, as well, that many prominent social reformers devoted themselves to improving social services in general so as to lend support to families which were the victims of poverty. The struggle for Mothers' Allowances is one case in point.

Throughout the twenty years from 1909 to 1929, juvenile delinquency continued to trouble child welfare workers. Despite the child savers' best efforts in both prevention and treatment, young people persisted in breaking the law. In 1927 a note of pessimism, born of frustration, was heard at the Social Service Conference held in Edmonton. Perhaps the boys and girls of 1927 were inferior to those of twenty years ago. Not so responded Brother Rogatian. Parents must simply learn to adjust to current conditions and be prepared to guide and control rather than drive and coerce the young. Other speakers reiterated the old faith. The time-worn cliches, "Give the kid a chance" and "More sinned against than sinning" were rolled out and delegates were sent on their way to promulgate and practice the precepts of child welfare much as they had been established in Chadwick's day.[70] Indeed, despite developments which have occurred since 1929, it is clear that the fundamental philosophy of child life and child care enunciated early in this century by the child savers has left an indelible mark on current thought and practices. This is especially true with respect to the view that a family home is the natural and proper place in which to rear children and that with the proper environmental influences young offenders can be reformed.

Notes

The author wishes to acknowledge the support of the Social Sciences and Humanities Research Council of Canada and the Alberta Heritage Scholarship Fund.

[1]P.G.H. Primrose to A.G. Browning, 2 December 1920, Department of Neglected Children, File 6-C-5, Box 124, Acc. No. 75.126, Provincial Archives of Alberta (hereafter PAA).

[2]*Ibid.*

[3]Supt. Bryan to A.G. Browning, 8 December 1920, Department of Neglected Children, File 6-C-5, Box 124, Acc. No. 75.126, PAA.

[4]Primrose also demanded that his colleague who had imposed the sentence be struck from the rolls. A decision on this was avoided because the sentencing magistrate died four days after Primrose wrote his complaint.

[5]In the strictly legal sense, at 16 Albert was no longer a juvenile delinquent but an adult criminal.

[6]Alberta, Department of Neglected Children, *Annual Report*, 1912, p. 7. These reports will be cited hereafter as AR.

[7]A cottage system generally involved the construction of one main building with kitchen, laundry, school rooms and other facilities along with several small "cottages" in which the boys would live in a setting thought to be more like a real home situation.

[8]For a discussion of the early history of welfare legislation in Alberta see David Edgar Lysne, "Welfare in Alberta, 1905 - 1936" (M.A. thesis, University of Alberta, 1966).

[9]AR, 1912, p. 8. Discussions of Ontario's act can be found in Neil Sutherland, *Children in English-Canadian Society: Framing the Twentieth Century Consensus* (Toronto: University of Toronto Press, 1976) and in Andrew Jones and Leonard Rutman, *In the Children's Aid: J.J. Kelso and Child Welfare in Ontario* (Toronto: University of Toronto Press, 1981).

[10]AR, 1911, p. 12.

[11]Alberta, *An Act for the Protection of Neglected and Dependent Children, 1909*, 9 Edward VII, c.12, *Statutes of Alberta*, pp. 206-207.

[12]Alberta, *An Act for the Protection of Neglected and Dependent Children, 1922*, 12 George V, c.217, *Statutes of Alberta*, III: 2674 (s.2, s.s.h.).

[13]AR, 1909, p. 9.

[14]A Children's Aid Society was a society approved by the Lieutenant Governor in Council and having as one of its objects the protection of children and the care and control of neglected children.

[15]Because of the wide powers assigned a "judge" in the Children's Protection Act, it is worth noting that, according to Section 2, subsection (e), "'Judge' shall mean a judge or a retired judge of the Supreme Court or of the District Court, or a police magistrate, or a justice of the peace appointed as a commissioner for the trial of juvenile offenders, or two justices;".

[16]For example, see the sympathetic view of Canadian child savers and their work in Sutherland, *Children*; Jones and Rutman, *In the Children's Aid*; and H.C. Klassen, "In Search of Neglected and Delinquent Children: The Calgary Children's Aid Society, 1909 - 1920," in *Town and City: Aspects of Western Canadian Urban Development*, ed. Alan F.J. Artibise (Regina: Canadian Plains Research Center, 1981), pp. 375-391.

[17]C.W. Parker, ed., *Who's Who and Why* (Vancouver: International Press, 1913).

[18]*Men and Makers of Edmonton, Alberta* (n.p., 1913?).

[19]J.S. Woodsworth to H.M. Tory, 26 June 1914, Henry Marshall Tory Papers, University of Alberta Archives.

[20]Reported in *Calgary Daily Herald*, 15 January 1909.

[21]Department of Neglected Children Files, Box 123, Acc. No. 75. 126, PAA.

[22]AR, 1922, p. 16.

[23]For a discussion of these networks see Sutherland, *Children*; Paul Rutherford, ed., *Saving the Canadian City: The First Phase 1880 - 1920* (Toronto: University of Toronto Press, 1974); Tamara Hareven, "An Ambiguous Alliance: Some Aspects of American Influence on Canadian Social Welfare," *Histoire sociale/Social History* 3 (April, 1969): 82-98.

[24]Rutherford, *Saving the Canadian City*, p. xiii.

[25]Sutherland, *Children*, pp. 236-237.

[26]See, for example, AR, 1912, p. 8.

[27]The work of Judge Ben Lindsay and the American juvenile justice system in general has been the subject of much study. See, for example, Joseph Hawes, *Children in Urban Society: Juvenile Delinquency in Nineteenth Century America* (New York: Oxford University Press, 1971); Robert M. Mennel, *Thorns and Thistles: Juvenile Delinquents in the United States, 1925 - 1940* (Hanover, N.H.: University Press of New England, 1973); Anthony M. Platt, *The Child Savers: The Invention of Delinquency* (Chicago: University of Chicago Press, 1969); Stephen Schlossman, *Love and the American Delinquent: The Theory and Practice of "Progressive" Juvenile Justice, 1825 - 1920* (Chicago: University of Chicago Press, 1977).

[28]AR, 1919, p. 28.

[29]AR, 1914, p. 13.

[30]*Ibid.*, p. 12.

[31]AR, 1911, p. 18.

[32]*Ibid.*

[33]AR, 1914, p. 12.

[34]A.M. McDonald to A.G. Browning, 5 September 1918, Department of Neglected Children, File 6-C-5, Box 123, Acc. No. 75.125, PAA.

[35]It was far more expensive to keep a boy in the Industrial School than it was to put him on probation or place him in a foster home and the records of the Department of Neglected Children make frequent reference to this cost consideration. The figure most often mentioned was $2000 for a two year term.

[36]"The Constables' Manual," Alberta Provincial Police Files, File 1302, Box 81, Acc. No. 66.166, PAA.

[37]Susan Houston, "Victorian Origins of Juvenile Delinquency: A Canadian Experience," *History of Education Quarterly* XII (Fall, 1972): 254-280.

[38]Rebecca Coulter, "Alberta's Department of Neglected Children, 1909 - 1929: A Case Study in Child Saving" (M.Ed. thesis, University of Alberta, 1977) p. 68.

[39]AR, 1912, p. 13.

[40]K.C. McLeod to A.G. Browning, 12 May 1923, Department of Neglected Children Files, File 6-C-5, Box 123, Acc. No. 75.126, PAA.

[41]See continuing correspondence in Department of Neglected Children Files, Box 123, Acc. No. 75.126, PAA.

[42]Sutherland, *Children*. For a brief summary of arguments about the concept of hegemony and its application to schooling and crime see Peter Seixas, "From Juvenile Asylum to Treatment Center: Changes in a New York Institute of Children 1905 — 1930" (M.A. thesis, University of British Columbia, 1981), chapter 2.

[43]AR, 1911, p. 8.

[44]See statistics in AR, 1909 — 1929.

[45]See Hermin Lewis King, "A Study of 400 Juvenile Delinquent Recidivists Convicted in the Province of Alberta During the Years 1920 — 30" (M.A. thesis, University of Alberta, 1932).

[46]AR, 1911, pp. 26-27.

[47]AR, 1913, p. 25.

[48]AR, 1918, p. 38.

[49]AR, 1916, p. 14.

[50]AR, 1911, p. 26.

[51]AR, 1913, p. 17.

[52]AR, 1912, p. 19.

[53]*Ibid.*

[54]AR, 1913, p. 19.

[55]AR, 1914, p. 26.

[56]In making these calculations it was assumed that immigrants from the United States and Great Britain could speak English.

[57]John Gillis, *Youth and History: Tradition and Change in European Age Relations 1770 — Present* (New York: Academic Press, 1974); Platt, *The Child Savers*; William Ryan *Blaming the Victim* (New York: Vintage Books, 1976).

[58]In 1914 the term "foreign born" was replaced with the expression "Canadians To Be".

[59]Canada, Dominion Bureau of Statistics, "Dependency of Youth," by J.E. Robbins, *Seventh Census of Canada, 1931: Monographs*, Vol. 13 (Ottawa: King's Printer, 1942) pp. 377-439.

[60]Canada, D.B.S. *Sixth Census of Canada, 1921*, Vol. 111 (Ottawa: King's Printer, 1927) p. xvii.

[61]Louis Chevalier, *Labouring Classes and Dangerous Classes*, trans. Frank Jellinek (London: Routledge and Kegan Paul, 1973); Stephen Humphries, "Steal to Survive: The Social Crime of Working Class Children 1890 — 1940," *Oral History Journal* 9 (Spring, 1981): 24-33.

[62]King, "A Study of 400 . . .," p. 38.

[63]F.B. Rolfross to J.E. Brownlee, 13 June 1922, Department of Neglected Children Files, File 6-C-5, Box 123, Acc. No. 75.126, PAA.

[64]"Earl F. Case," Department of Neglected Children Files, File 6-C-5, Box 124, Acc. No. 75.126, PAA.

[65]"APP Report," 21 January 1922, Department of Neglected Children, File 6-C-5, Box 124, Acc. No. 75.126, PAA.

[66]See, for example, "Damage Done Hallowe'en Night," City Police Department Special Report, 28 November 1930, Commissioner's Files, Police-Crime 1926 — 1966, Box 195, Acc. No. 73-52, City of Edmonton Archives (hereafter CEA).

[67]See, for example, "Report of Gerald V. Pelton to the Government of Alberta on Enquiries Instituted in Colorado, California, Oregon, Washington, and British Columbia, into Some of the Causes and Cures for Juvenile Delinquency Among Boys," Premier's Papers, File 235, Acc. No. 69.289, PAA.

[68]"Citizens Demand Swift Action . . .," 6 November 1930, "Edmonton Crime" File, Newspaper Clippings Collection, Box 17, Acc. No. A77/18, CEA.

[69]See, for example, M. Gutteridge to City Commissioners, 22 November 1927, RG11, Class 3, File 1, CEA and T.S. Magee to City Commissioners, 16 November 1935, "Children's Shelter," uncatalogued City Commissioners' Papers, CEA.

[70]"Social Service Conference Held in Edmonton,", *Western Catholic*, 17 February 1927, p. 6.

"We can't live on air all the time":
Country Life and the Prairie Child

David C. Jones

One of the most significant influences on the child life of any generation is the endlessly recapitulated adult attempt to dictate for youth various priorities, ideals and forbidden fruit. In sundry historical eras it would seem possible to isolate a paramount issue, a principal adult message. Often this message is supported by an array of educational agencies, mutually complementary and reinforcing, melding together to generate a cohesive and insistent set of ideas. Revolving on the core message, these ideas constitute an ideology which specifies the assumptions behind the message, the presumed results of heeding the message, and the consequences of ignoring it. Youth's reaction to such prescriptions is related not only to the seemingly inherent perversity of the young but also to the salient features of child life in the period.

For youth on the Canadian prairies life has long centred on agriculture. As the modern West evolved from roughly 1900 to 1925, a country life ideology grew apace touching the lives of thousands of settlers and their families. Anchoring this ideology was a powerful imperative — the injunction for prairie children to stay on the land.

Youth were literally assailed with this message — from the agrarian press, contemporary fiction, women's institutes, university extension people, school reformers, parliamentarians, speakers at agricultural institutes, and from agricultural colleges, schools of agriculture and departments of agriculture. An explicit theme in the wealth of promotional literature attending the settlement of the West, moreover, was the goodness of the land and its suitability for rearing families.[1] All the above agencies and others combined to create a supportive ideology which idealized agricultural life, the calmness and peace of the country, the power of the land to elevate ethically, emotionally and intellectually, the tendency of rural environment to engender better morals than the city, and the strength of the soil to create the foundation of all wealth and prosperity. The farm was the ideal setting for the maturity of youth; it taught industriousness, resourcefulness and improvisation; it instilled perseverance and frugality. Providing honest work and genuine satisfaction, it most significantly brought children closer to nature and to God.[2]

In this well orchestrated scenario the essence of evil was created, a bogeyman to terrorize children and adults alike — the city. How it drained energy, frayed the moral fibre, and dazzled the mind with imitations, veneers and thoughtless excitement! "With its great white ways and its snares of pain," the city was a trap.[3] It was a maelstrom which swallowed up farm boys and girls, choked them with limited opportunities in foul factories, and broke them with unhappiness and unfulfilment. It was a repository of ugliness and uselessness. It sheltered and pampered the degraded and the debauched, the lazy and the parasitic — the prostitutes, food profiteers, and speculators. Fundamentally, the city was a place for neither honest farm folk nor, especially, their impressionable offspring.

Buttressing the propaganda was a potent reform movement which proposed to so vitalize and enhance rural life that its superiority over urban life, as a haven and workplace for adults and as a nesting ground for children, would be secured for all time.[4]

Why the country life ideology developed so dramatically on the prairie West was related to the agrarian destiny the region had established. In this sense the ideology was a supportive mechanism brought forth by the nature of society. The fact that the percentage of prairie population designated urban rose from 19.3 percent to 28.8 percent from 1901 to 1911 and that for Canada as a whole jumped from 37.5 percent to 45.4 percent, gave substance to warnings that fewer and fewer people on the land threatened the nation's developing identity and its ability to feed itself.[5] Intensifying the alarm was the spectre of severe agricultural crisis after 1916 when the large dry belt region of Alberta and Saskatchewan began its descent into disaster.[6] To some extent the pooling of foreigners also heightened the country life message. A nagging immigrant problem with its attendant language difficulties indicated to many anglophone rural zealots that they would not be able to spread their gospel of self improvement and enhanced rural living as quickly as they would have liked.[7]

Whatever the reasons for the country life message, which pivoted on the injunction to stay on the land, the fact that there *was* such a message and that it literally dominated the propaganda of the period is ineluctably clear. Equally apparent is the fact that the message was often unheeded. The rural population on the prairies never stabilized for long. In Manitoba between 1901 and 1926 the population designated rural declined from 72.4 percent to 56.4 percent. In Saskatchewan it dropped from 84.4 percent to 70.5 percent, and in Alberta, from 74.6 percent to 61.5 percent.[8] While it is impossible to tabulate precisely, many of the thousands who became urbanites in the space of a generation were adolescents and young adults.

This chapter is devoted to explaining why the rural life propaganda which issued from so many sources fell on deaf ears, why, is fact, prairie youth left the farm. To understand why so many young people ignored the dictates of the age one needs to assess crucial aspects of the lives of rural children in the first twenty-five years or so of this century — their major outside influences, their interaction with parents, and their perception of a future as adults on the farm.

Consider first a major influence on both sexes — the school. Any movement of as broad a scope as the country life campaign was bound to permeate virtually all institutions of society. Thus the prairie school too was affected. In the heartland of the plains, Saskatchewan, three powerful campaigns were mounted in the second decade of the century to relate school curricula to the world of work.[9] The result of these efforts was a modest shift in school orientation. For a time nature study became more popular, school gardens abounded, and special agricultural instructors were employed. School fairs emerged along with Farm Boys' and Girls' Camps and junior clubs. In the process, Supervisors of School Agriculture, Fred Bates and Harry Saville, actively promoted the scientific principles of farming and the country life outlook.

In Manitoba a similar movement occurred, focussing on boys and girls clubs and club fairs as part of University extension work. Alberta emphasized new agricultural schools which were far more vocational in tone, seeking somewhat more to create good farmers than an attitude toward a way of life. These schools then established the most vibrant and long lasting school fair movement in the West. Over time all these organizations and institutions spawned by the country life spirit reached thousands of prairie youths.

But the effect of the movement on the school itself was less than promoters had hoped. As the gardening mission fell to pieces amid drought, gophers and neglect, the focus of junior agricultural work often shifted away from the school to the home where interested parents, generally more informed about the land than teachers, picked it up. While parents were often divided on the issue of agriculture in schools, many in time came to the viewpoint of one Alberta farm wife. ". . . The boys and girls of a farming community," she wrote, "are saturated already with agriculture lore. The farmer's work is his life, sleeping and waking." Moreover, the claim that agriculture in the schools would keep youth on the farms was shortsighted.

> All the boys will not be needed on the farms. If one boy in each family that has been blessed with boys and girls elects to remain to work with father, and maybe one day takes his place, it is all one could expect or wish. The outside world needs the remainder of the boys. In other walks of life all the boys in a family are not expected to follow their father's vocation. Not every country boy, even if taught agriculture, would make a good farmer. A misfit here is as pitiable a sight as in any other occupation or calling. *"Some men are born farmers, some achieve farming, and some have farming thrust upon them."*[10]

In Manitoba the opposition to the linkage between the school and the world of work was pronounced. As the chairman of the committee on educational policies of the Canadian Society of Technical Agriculturalists reported in 1927, "It appears that many farmers in Manitoba, far from desiring to have the teaching of elementary agriculture made compulsory in the higher grades of the public school, do not wish their children to be taught agriculture either for its educational or for its vocational value."[11]

Even in the most popular of the agricultural spinoffs — the school fair — the actual connection with the school program was often tenuous. A special federal committee appointed to inquire into agricultural conditions in 1923 dealt with the problem of articulation and with the significance teachers attached to school fair work. One witness noted of the prairie school fair — "in the advancement of the child from one grade to another *that* is not counted."[12]

One result of the failure of agriculture to gain a foothold on the curriculum was a distance between teacher and pupil, a lack of a common reference point, and a kind of teacher alienation from the community and its fundamental agrarian reality. In the drought and depression of the early twenties which undermined practical school agriculture, this distance was accentuated, especially in the extensive dry belt regions of southwest Saskatchewan and southeast Alberta. There school districts often operated as unofficial extensions of the normal schools as teachers sought experience before landing a city job. There teacher transiency was worst and pressure on young and inexperienced school marms to provide secondary education greatest. More than one parent lamented how pupils suffered, especially the little ones, when a young teacher had to instruct high school subjects as well. In these areas, because of her training which ironically underplayed rural postings, or because of her city background, or the destitute social conditions, the teacher was often an outsider. She usually had little or no influence on public sentiment and she was often obsessed with getting out. As schooling became more general throughout the twenties, her pupils underwent great trauma — wondering where they would be educated in a region rapidly depopulating, where they might find dormitories, how they might be transported, or if their parents could make arrangements with neighboring school boards or resolve petty quarrels rife under harsh economic conditions. Children in these large regions lived in a chaotic and fleeting world wherein little was constant — where school district boundaries changed overnight, where schools were transported across the plains at a moment's notice, where their friends or they themselves were threatened with expulsion if their parents were late paying a neighboring district their tuition or sometimes if parents simply owed impecunious boards money.[13]

For the many parents who finally abandoned their farms partly in search of better schooling for their children, there were several years of profound poverty as they struggled to their feet. Here again their children faced the consequences of bone shattering deprivation — malnutrition, improper health care, and few diversions.[14]

If both youthful sexes encountered a school system which at best downplayed and at worst ignored the country life imperatives, the work-a-day life on the farm did the same. Consider first the life of boys.

In the early war years a western farmer's speech to his twelve year old son circulated as follows:

Now, Jimmy, hurry up, you've got to clean out the stable, bed down the horses, milk the cows, separate the milk, and chop some wood for your mother. And don't forget to feed the pigs. I've got to go to the schoolhouse to give a lecture on 'How to keep the boys on the farm.'

Apparently the rest of this man's sons had already left for the city, the certain destiny of young Jimmy.[15]

The joke masked a serious problem. "We lose thousands of farmer boys every year," wrote E.L. Vincent, "just because home is not a home, but just a place to stay nights and run on chores day times." Vincent gave the example of a young lad he had visited on a farm. The boy's father said that the lad was a good worker, a statement that pleased the boy. "But," said Vincent, "that boy was a little bit of a chap for his years, stunted and dwarfed by years of work he had already done." Moreover, he was not attending school. "It was work all the time in the field and in the barns," regretted Vincent. "The day will come when he will miss the good he might have gotten from the farm, and if he is not very bitter toward the one who thus cramped and narrowed his life down it will be a wonder."[16]

The editor of the *Farmer's Advocate* related the experience of "two boys and two farms." Fred, the first lad, had overfed a pure bred young mare and the animal was in serious condition. Before strangers, Fred's father told Fred "plainly, even vulgarly, just how little he thought of his son's ability for a boy of his age." Fred's humiliation was acute and visible. Said the editor moved by a sense of injustice: "We wonder if the father ever noticed the boy's affection for the filly or knew that he thought a lot more of her than he did, that the feed of grain had been given in a moment of indulgence, and upon seeing the results that the boy regretted his action very keenly." Missing the chance to teach a lesson in scientific feeding, "the father had lost a share of Fred's confidence. . ." What would happen in eight or nine years, wondered the editor, if Fred received "the same rebukes for all his mistakes. . . Will he stay on the farm or will he leave it?"

Harry was the second boy. Owner of the first pure bred calf born on his father's farm, Harry knew "the name of every pure-bred animal on the place, and the sire and dam of most of them." He also knew the history of the breed. Not long before the war Harry and his father travelled several hundred miles to buy stock. "Needed his judgement," said his father simply. As a result, the editor wrote, "Harry at twelve has it firmly rooted in his mind that the farm could not get along without him." Ten years hence the farm would really need Harry. "Somehow," mused the editor, "we cannot see him leaving that herd of cattle."[17]

"Many a boy grows up, gets little education, works hard, and is never consulted about the business of the farm," agreed Nellie McClung in an address before the Annual Convention of Manitoba Home Economics Societies. Seeing nothing ahead but more of the same, such lads were soon driven by a sense of independence to strike out on their own. "This free service," wrote a British Columbian, "is at the root of most of the discontent amongst the young people on the farms."[18] Many other annoyances — such as lack of a horse, family quarrels and unreasonable parental restrictions on adolescent social lives — fueled the discontent. On the last matter, said Nellie McClung, "I heard once of a boy who had to hide his Sunday clothes in the hay-mow when he wanted to go anywhere."[19]

In late 1918 the *Farmer's Advocate and Home Journal* carried "The Story of a Farm Boy" in four parts, a true account of a graduate of Ontario Agricultural College by a friend of the graduate and of the *Advocate*'s editor. The story is important for two reasons: first, it concerns a small, but significant coterie of young people who both believed and later tried to implement the country life message; second, it highlights the powerful forces which often thwarted even these dedicated converts.

As a boy of eighteen, Jimmy remembered a visit his father received from an old friend who had left the farm in his youth to become a big stockholder of a city manufacturing concern. "John," said the friend, "you should have left the farm." The comment impressed the boy.

> There was "Dad" with his horny hands and stooped shoulders, after years and years of drudgery, and yonder sat "Mother," broken in health, but not in spirit; tired, yet hopeful. Compared with these . . . were the neat, trim, straight, agile, soft-handed, alert, business man and his over dressed, polished wife. The work of father, mother and son combined on the farm had yielded in the best year $900 to pay on the mortgage. Some years it returned only a living and the average day's work ran from fourteen to sixteen hours in summer . . . Yet the man who had left the farm for the city business made thousands twice over where his industrious farmer friend got only hundreds for several times the effort.

Added to these thoughts was the advice Jimmy himself had received to leave the farm. "All his teachers from the first to the last advised him to, just as they advise thousands of other boys."[20]

Reared close to nature, Jimmy had an intimate knowledge of the farm animals, especially his own sheep. With "an inherent love of nature, agriculture, livestock, and all things rural," he resolved, despite warnings, to go to the agricultural college at Guelph, Ontario.

Jimmy's description of his philosophy as a young man reflected the sustained effort of many educational agencies to keep youth on the land. But it was written years later, after his crucial encounter with the Ontario Agricultural College — perhaps the greatest promoter in Canada of the country life outlook.[21] "While he almost worshiped the land," the description went,

He believed that to give the man thereon a chance, something which he did not then understand thoroughly, was necessary. He disliked the city just as ardently as he loved the soil. He understood fully that big cities are necessary to the welfare of the nation, but he had no desire to be confined in one. True, bright lights and bustle had some attraction for him, as they have for every youth of spirit. But city pleasures were to him largely superficial. He had not been molded in the proper groove to make a satisfied city citizen.

While he had a friend who was city bank clerk, better dressed than himself, and while he remembered his father's plutocratic comrade, he also believed as he had been educated to believe "that the great rank and file of the boys who leave the farm for the city's bright lights, sociality and opportunity, ultimately find themselves facing limited opportunities." Aware of the drawbacks of hand or machine labor, he resolved "never to join the dinner-pail brigade of factory workers; not that it did not offer honest toil, but because it offered nothing more than this and moving pictures." As he summed it up, "He preferred to sweat in God's fresh air, rather than in man's foul factories."

At college he was green, but not so green "as to go to the pig pens to register . . ." After a rusty start he did well. When he returned home for the spring and summer he noted the beginnings of a new problem: "His boy friends began to hold aloof, inclined to criticize the "educated farmer." No doubt because of this estrangement and because of a growing attraction for the life of the college, he began to feel after another year that if he returned to college again he would not return to the land. Undecided, he sought the advice of his parents. His mother left things to him, but his father said: "If I had your ability and chance, I'd never farm." A personal letter from the President of the College, urging him to return, helped make up his mind.

During the third summer he revealed indirectly the kinds of pressures that city bred youths or remittance lads interested in agricultural degrees might expect. One of each he had as roommates. Deciding to try his college acquired knowledge in a job, he found it useful but without his practical experience, he would often have been lost.[22]

After graduation he discovered why so many rural lads of high ideals who earned agriculture degrees still left the farm. Some believed that the College of Agriculture itself educated boys off the farm, encouraging them to enter professional agriculture rather than practical agriculture. Discrediting this notion, the author blamed the lack of capital. "When they get through [college]," he said, "their financial condition is such that they cannot farm unless as hired men." To young men who had studied scientific agriculture for four years the prospects of apprenticeship as underlings to those who could well have known nothing of science were grim. There was more than this to what professional agricultural training had done to a young man's mind.

The average college graduate hesitates to start farming with small capital. There are too many doubting Thomases in the average rural neighborhood for one thing — men who are more ready to criticize than to aid. And while graduates of the stuff that men are made, as Jimmy was, care little for criticism and what the people think, nevertheless it is a comparatively stiff proposition for a young man fresh from his books and full of enthusiasm on scientific farming, to withstand the "gaff" of the gray-headed wiseacres who are prone to see all failures and di[l]ate upon them, while they utterly disregard the successes. Practical farmers have, in the past, been too ready to poke fun at the college-educated farmer.

One might ask why the fathers of these young graduates so seldomly staked them. "The plain fact is that the average farmer cannot give his boys the start he would like," wrote the author. "The old farm is enough to keep the old folks. They need it until they have passed to the Great Beyond." Most parents did not clear the farm of debt until they were nearly sixty and they needed everything they had saved. Jimmy's parents were no exceptions.

It was thus little wonder that Jim, like so many other B.S.A.'s chose a career in professional agriculture, a consulting job in the city. And despite the claims of Jim's biographer that the Agricultural College did not educate boys off the farm, it seems clear that Jim's decision was abetted by the service mentality the college inculcated.[23] One could obviously be of more service to humanity as a professional reaching scores of farmers than as a self contained, self involved farmer.

The last installment of the story revealed that after Jimmy spent several years reaching out from his city post, he married a country girl and in time, after a family arrived, he and his wife prepared to return to the land. "Boys are a problem in the city," wrote the biographer, "and Jimmy had two of the liveliest sort. He knew the gloss, glitter and hollowness of the life that lay ahead of the lads if they remained in the city." And he remembered the last line of an article a friend who had travelled the same road had written: "It's character counts; and character grows strong and sturdy on the land."

Both Jim and his biographer were clear examples of the country life enthusiasts emerging at the end of the First War. As the latter wrote, Jim "hoped by returning to the land to become a "booster' for organized agriculture. He believed that through co-operative union farmers could advance their calling and greatly improve their position. Besides, the revelations of the Great War had shown the man on the land to be the first essential of the race."[24]

The story ended at the height of the back-to-the-land propaganda, but one wonders how the family fared in the next years as agriculture fell on hard times and crisis overtook the land. The generality is known: people like Jimmy stopped preaching the country life message which — amid agrarian depression, a fizzling farmer revolt, and in large areas, wholesale depopulation — appeared strangely out of touch, like a fancy that had passed.

If the lot of farm boys was often influenced by less deliberate and devoted parents than Jim, hundreds of articles, editorials and letters on youth in the agrarian press suggest not only that farmers worried more about boys than girls but also that the outlook for the latter could be very bleak. "Many a girl does a women's work on the farm from the time she is fourteen years old," wrote Nellie McClung, "and if she gets a cow and a feather-bed when she gets married, every one feels that the claims of justice have been fully met." McClung then related the typical story of Martha, eldest of four children. Needed at home, Martha was denied the educational advantages her three brothers enjoyed. Helping to bring up the boys, she labored on and never married. When father died the property was divided thusly:

> Each boy got a farm. The will stipulated that the mother was to have her keep, until she died — no sum specified, just her "keep' — this from the son who got the old homestead! Martha, who is an old woman at forty, gray, hard-handed, bent, received $100! The poor old mother, left dependent, after her years of hard work, fretted out her life in a few months and now no longer is in need of 'keep'.

Wife and daughter, undeniably were victims of "wrong-thinking," discriminatory and deeply imbedded. For most of the period on the prairies women were viewed as chattels virtually extinct of property rights. It was legally possible for an irresponsible husband to run off with another women and sell the farm to finance the spree, forcing the wife and family to leave the homestead penniless and fend for themselves. "Is it any wonder," McClung asked, "that girls like Martha leave the farm when they know what is ahead of them?"[25]

In May 1913 the *Grain Grower's Guide* revealed in greater detail the torments of the farm for young women. The author's struggle symbolized the plight of farm women everywhere, not just on the Canadian prairies, and set the context in which parent-child interaction unfolded. The story was long, but revealing.

Eleanor and Louis were married not long before the turn of the century in the former's city home. By spring they were in a new cottage on Louis' farm. Said Eleanor:

> All water was drawn from a well in the yard; there was no sink in my kitchen — and of course,no bathroom or furnace, no built in china-closets, linen-presses or bookshelves; but at that time not half a dozen country houses in our whole county had any of these things . . .

Despite the lack of amenities, the farm was very valuable. More paradoxical was a relationship Eleanor noticed between a farmer's wealth and his wife's labor: the more he made the harder she worked. "The comparatively poor had no hired hands to feed, did not keep so elaborate a table, had fewer chickens, put up little meat and therefore escaped soapmaking, had much less milk and fruit to care for, and, in fact, lived very much as women in the same station live in town. The rich man's wives were the overworked drudges."

This realization did not come at once. Determined to make country living work, Eleanor managed an orderly household, excelling as a cook. "The beautiful country life," she wrote, "compensated me . . ." Loving the country, she invariably went strolling in the late afternoons. Often Louis accompanied her. When they returned, sometimes laden with wild flowers, they felt the peace of rural life. "I never failed to return rested," wrote Eleanor, "no matter how tired I had been upon starting out." At night she would then read to Louis or play the piano for him. Untroubled by hired men, milking or heavy garden work, she kept herself and her house immaculate, believing that she "had solved the farm-life problem easily and well". She looked forward to the time when Louis would lighten her load even more by providing modern conveniences.

Some foreshadow of times to come had appeared, but Eleanor had dismissed it. When, for example, she showed Louis' mother the hemstitched monogrammed sheets she had sewn, the lady remarked disdainfully, "What do you think these will look like after the hired hands have slept on them a while?"

"We will not have the men in the house," Eleanor answered. "There are two tenant houses on the farm and it is much better to let them live outside our home."

"That will do for a year or two," the mother persisted, "but you will see that Louis will want them in the house after a while. He can get 'em out earlier when they are right in the house and it saves some on their wages."

Unhappily Eleanor's optimism and energy failed in the first winter and she grew ill, compounded by pregnancy. The setback brought her face to face with the servant problem in the country. After scouring the region, she and Louis soon realized that even the unemployed scorned household service. Work was too hard and life too lonely. When a domestic was finally procured, "a timid, ignorant creature, inhumanely treated at home by a cruel stepmother," Eleanor had to put up with incredible ineptitude. "My precious china was smashed; silver spoons were found in the ashes, burned and ruined, and my best napkins were occasionally taken for dish rags when nothing else conveniently offered." Because a replacement was unavailable, the girl stayed.

As the birth of Eleanor's child approached, the roads grew impassable and a doctor could not be reached. The result was that they "had to send for an ignorant stupid quack" who nearly killed the mother. Louis' playful remark to the baby shortly after was ironic but prophetic: "Well, young lady, this old farm has got to get up and hustle after this to provide for your future."

Throwing herself into work as did Louis, Eleanor raised more and more chickens and preserved more and more fruit. Tending to the baby too, she soon found that her health was not returning and that Louis was not always helpful. Many men in farming communities, indeed, were inconsiderate.

She remembered a neighbor, the second wife of a wealthy, university educated ex-legislator. "Their cook stove was so old and dilapidated," she wrote, "that three of its four legs were gone and had been replaced by bricks, and it leaked ashes at every pore." Like Louis, the husband rarely had the wood chopped. The wife, however, was too proud to cut it herself. "I have been in her kitchen," said Eleanor, "when she had one end of an old tree-branch stuck in the stove for fuel, the rest of the branch projecting halfway across the room and supported by two chairs. As the end in the stove burned off, the remainder was gradually fed into the fire until the supporting chairs could be safely removed." Then another log, spurs and all, would be lugged into position. "Poor woman!" lamented Eleanor. "She is now dead, like her predecessor; and their well-preserved husband is industriously seeking a third wife."

That summer Eleanor went nowhere. Fatigued, she and Louis stopped going to church, stopped their afternoon walks and stopped reading together evenings. The following winter Louis bought an adjoining quarter section. In spring, as he hired new hands, he remarked, "Eleanor, can't we let two of the men eat in the house for the next three months. They can sleep over the toolshed and you will not be bothered with them except at mealtime." The move, he thought, would get the men out earlier. To Eleanor's look of dismay he commented: "You know we have got to work harder to pay for that land."

As a result, the family began rising at four o'clock. For Eleanor the four extra men to feed instead of two were a constant irritation:

> They brought mud and bad odors into the house; they only half washed their faces and hands and wiped the rest of the dirt on the kitchen towels, so that I was obliged to change them after every meal. They ate in a slovenly manner, so my table no longer presented its usual attractive appearance. What little conversation they held was about crops and crop conditions. Our dining room had become only a part of the farm workshop.

Eleanor began to plead with Louis to buy modern kitchen conveniences. Invariably he wished to wait until they were out of debt. Alas for big farmers the wait could be long, for they were forever making more improvements or buying more land or more equipment. None of the last however included labor saving devices in the house — no bath, kitchen sinks, furnaces, or lights — despite "the fact that the women of the family must do the work in the house, while that elsewhere is done by hired labourers."

As Eleanor sagged under this customary rural arrangement, she began to look disheveled and despondent. "You work too hard by trying to keep things so clean," Louis remonstrated. "Let things go more. Eat off an oil cloth. Let the men eat their dessert on their plates. That is better than they are used to."

After a bountiful crop which nearly paid for the quarter section, Louis promptly bought another eighty acres and some feeder cattle, the latter necessitating "hands in the house all winter, as feeding requires great care — else much money may be lost". Since the men could not sleep above the toolshed in winter, Eleanor had to prepare extra bedrooms for them. "After the democratic manner of farmers," she noted, "they sat in our living room when not at work. The farm had now invaded the whole house."[26]

To be thrifty, said Eleanor, "You have to kill your own hogs to have hams, bacon and lard of the best quality. After the nightmare of hog-killing time is safely over, the unused fat must be made into soap or utterly wasted." Milk had to be skimmed for the young pigs, cream had to be sold and butter made. Vegetables had to be grown abundantly and great care taken to make them appear fresh on the table.

Till now Eleanor had been swept by her husband's ambition. But she began to feel the strain of farm life and when Louis, "already owning more than five hundred acres of land, promptly bought eighty more without providing me even a kitchen sink," she confessed, "my spirit broke a little."

The next summer the regular hands stayed in the house because Louis placed unused machinery in the room above the toolshed. When extra hayhands and threshers were brought in, Eleanor sometimes had to contend with thirty men at a time. The visit of her brother and sister added to her consternation. "After they had been with me a few days," she wrote, "they began to treat me as we unconsciously treat a well-beloved member of the family suddenly stricken with an incurable malady." Eleanor recalled the jokes they had made about marrying a farmer and she sensed that their worst predictions were coming true.

One afternoon her sister encountered her in the hot kitchen, perspiring profusely over a steaming washtub of towels. Furious, the sister hissed: "You have already done enough work today to exhaust a stevedore. And your husband is a — —."

After the sister and brother left, Eleanor's mother invited her and Louis to visit. Amid harvest, Louis commented: "Much they know about farming — to ask us to visit them now." No sooner had Eleanor refused the invitation than she fell into a "peculiar" state: "I grew nervous and self-conscious; when my old friends came to see me, which they still occasionally did in spite of the fact that I never returned their visits, I felt as if I was in a different world from other people — a world where nothing counted but rushing work." She resolved to get away from home more. Unfortunately her horse was used in the fields and there was a "strange prejudice among country people that [equated] a woman walking to see a neighbour . . . with a tramp".

One Sunday afternoon Eleanor thought how she might get away. She suggested that the men take "Kitty," a fine mare never worked, and that they free "Bird," her horse.

"Kitty is too valuable and raises too fine colts for me to risk hurting her with hard work," replied Louis.

"Then it is only the human female who runs no risk of hurting herself and her offspring by hard work?" Eleanor responded despairingly.

"If you did not want to work," said Louis quietly, "you should not have married a farmer."

Early in the fall Louis and one of the men who had been drinking water from an old well on the new property fell ill with typhoid. The hired man soon died and Louis lay for weeks close to death. The best doctors were summoned and a woman was procured at great cost to handle the kitchen and child. In Eleanor's great solicitude for Louis nothing else mattered. As she wrote, "I became almost a stranger to my own little child."

One morning, at the top of the stairs, Louis appeared, "a shadow of his former self — but alive . . ." As soon as Eleanor was not needed at his bedside the high priced help was dismissed. Scarcely had Louis recovered before Eleanor's second child was born. Again there was the servant problem and the work load suddenly shifted entirely on Louis' shoulders. Caring for the children, cooking, washing and sweeping, Louis tried, but grew more and more irritated with the little girl and less and less attentive to Eleanor and the baby.

One day, recalled Eleanor, "in frenzy at the continued crying of our oldest child — a mere baby — [Louis] slapped her flat on the floor and dragged her from my room. I lost all control of myself and broke into wild hysterics. My shrieks and the young baby's wails, mingled with the lusty howls of our oldest child, no doubt sounded to Louis like Pandemonium broken loose." As her paroxysm wore down, Eleanor's mind became lucid and she saw how speedily her husband had succumbed to the torment she had endured so long.

After Louis fled to town the next day, Eleanor groped about, catching her reflection in a mirror: "Wrinkled, hollow-eyed, worn to a shadow, was the sad, cowed looking creature who stared back at me . . . Twenty years of ordinary living could not have done to me what less than five years on the farm had done!" Pondering the causes of her discomfiture, Eleanor refused to blame Louis. Instead, she concluded that "women on the farm today are caught between the upper millstone of present enlightenment and the nether stone of past necessity". That is, the enlightened woman understood something about health and nutrition and these imperatives drove her to see that her children were "properly fed, clothed, bathed, and that they have pure air, attractive rooms, and sanitary surroundings . . ." As well, the home, like those of the past, was "a hotel, laundry, meat and soap factory, canning factory and poultry plant" managed and conducted solely by the woman.

Beaten, Eleanor resolved to leave, with Louis if possible, without him if not. Appealing to his insatiable demand for land, she procured numerous real estate and railroad folders advertising cheap lands to the west. Soon Louis

198 *Studies in Childhood History: A Canadian Perspective*

was moved to leave in search of vaster estates. At the same moment, a buyer offering good profit appeared, taking most of the farm, and a very good renter took the rest. In their travels a desperate Eleanor played on another of Louis' weaknesses. "Knowing his energetic disposition and his horror of spending money without any source of immediate income," she wrote, "I really expected that he would be led into trying to "make our expenses' in town." Her secret hope that Louis would accept a business position there while amassing his treasury of properties was realized. In time the escape from the farm was consolidated and the family became permanent city folk.[27]

The essence of rural existence, as revealed by this and similar tales, was that the farm as much as the city could be a trap, that life on the land too could offer little more than tedious and tiresome drudgery, an endless apprenticeship for a calling both scorned and demeaning.

Despite the claims of promotional immigration literature, domestic service was not viewed highly by most adolescent girls, and likely few anticipated cheerily a lifetime of such meniality. To even the most unobservant the clutch of economic circumstances on both the quality and tenure of employment would soon have been apparent. Given the bleak prospects there was some tendency for domestic service to attract misfits of the sort Eleanor had encountered during her first pregnancy.

As for farm daughters, it would not have been long before the complaints of mothers like Eleanor and Nellie McClung took their toll. Activating the enormous discontent of women in the period, these criticisms seeped everywhere. The collective agrarian press, for example, the most comprehensive repository of prairie social attitudes, fears and hopes, was sprinkled annually and liberally with the very reasons young girls would do well to escape the farm. At first sight these reasons often seemed to apply to adults. Yet the way of life of children can often be seen through the rigors and obsessions of their parents. Not only can the pressures of adults rebound on children in bad temper and intolerance, but also the things that adults perceive to debilitate and crush them can indelibly impress children old enough to understand. Had Eleanor and Louis stayed on the land, it would have been difficult to see how love for the farm might have been instilled in the minds of their harried children. And it would have been surprising after the first child's initiation into the onerous work rhythms of the household, if the girl did not perceive something of the life of McClung's character, Martha, stretched out before her.

Each generation of youth has its characteristic way of renouncing the dominant adult wisdom. Over and over, youth in the first generation of this century heard what would happen if they went to the city, what it meant about their sense of values, and what character weaknesses it revealed. The endless reiteration was often given less in a spirit of altruism than in one of condemnation. As Donald Stewart wrote *The Farmer's Advocate* in 1920, "Our people, especially the young and those not rooted securely to the soil, have been seared by the excitement of war. They want crowds, the roar of city traffic, and the stuffy twilight of moving picture shows. Moreover, our young people are not so ready to accept responsibility as they once were."[28]

Aside from the tone of such statements, there were other explanations of why youth rejected the advice to stay on the land. Their school system, despite some innovation, had little to do with its socio-economic setting, and their teachers, with exceptions, were usually transient agents from an alien environment. As models for students, such teachers no doubt influenced many farm students by their advice and example. More important than the school were problems in the agrarian way of life — the often unsatisfactory parent-child interaction, the loneliness, the long hours and the drudgery, the shortage of domestic help and of labour saving devices, and the utter marginality of so many farm operations. Even those driven by the imperatives of the country life movement to attend agricultural college faced the difficulties of lack of capital when they finished, farmer attitudes toward agricultural experts, and the pressures to enter professional agriculture rather than private farm life. It was thus little wonder that so many youths failed to heed the country life message. In rejecting the dominant advice of the age, some did so mindlessly, others knew what they were doing, and still more had little choice.

As farming difficulties mounted after the First War, the movement off the land, especially in the dry areas, accelerated. It had always been so — the disenchantment whenever the long lauded virtues of rural living seemed submerged by economic adversity. A poem submitted to *The Nor'-West Farmer* by a Scotsman, farming near Edmonton in 1912, captured this relationship and accentuated an inherent frailty in the country life imperative.

The Simple Life

I'm only a tenderfoot, new to the West,
And not even raised on a farm;
No, it wasn't the dollars that drew me out here,
The free, open-air life was the charm.

I bought a half-section — Alberta black loam,
The soil and the climate are prime,
And just yet I ain't going to make tracks for home,
But one can't live on air all the time.

I put in my crop, and the weather-clerk smiled,
The wheat on the prairie came strong,
All my fears for the future were surely beguiled,
And life was one long, glad, sweet song.

The frost and the hail and the damaging rust
We escaped, and the wheat golden grew:

We harvested, threshed, thanked the Lord for the crop;
It was all far too good to be true.

I hitched up the team and post-haste drove to town;
Elevators soon showed up ahead.
The buyer fixed on his most critical frown;
"Waal, yes, sure! It's number one red."

"Yes, it's just what we're wanting; send all that you've got, —
How I envy you darned farmin' gents, —
The price? Waal, we likes to encourage new blood,
You may leave it at — thirty-five cents."

And now, Mr. Editor, it's all up to you.
To champion the poor farmer's pleas,
And out on the Grand Trunk, up Edmonton way,
We have surely been caught in a squeeze.

From the Old Land we've come, left our home o'er the sea,
To farm in the West's golden prime,
The country, the soil, and the climate are right,
But we can't live on air all the time.

Cold Feet[29]

In the nature of things children heard this message too, and when they tried to square it with the more insistent country life propaganda the insightful must have wished that the adult generation would get its story straight. The children, however, could hardly know how dominant the criticism of the land would become. Many in the settlement period and shortly after were carted from the land by parents who had tried the country life propaganda themselves and found it wanting. Later, a contrary and imposing reality would discredit the rural ideology and subsequent generations of youth to leave the land, either of their own volition or of their parents', effected the desertion for similar reasons but perhaps with a diminished sense of guilt.

Notes

[1]See Doug Owram, *Promise of Eden* (Toronto: University of Toronto Press, 1980); John Warkentin, "Steppe, Desert and Empire," in A.W. Rasporich and H.C. Klassen, eds., *Prairie Perspectives* 2 (Toronto: Holt, Rinehart and Winston, 1973),

pp. 102-36. Note David C. Jones, "Jack Canuck, John Bull and Uncle Sam — Blending in the West," unpublished paper, 1981.

²Note Jones, "'There is some power about the land' — Country Life Ideology and the Western Agrarian Press," *The Journal of Canadian Studies,* forthcoming.

³"Back to the Farm," *Farm and Ranch Review,* Apr. 1908, p. 5, hereafter *Review.*

⁴Jones, "Agriculture, the Land and Education," Ed.D. thesis, University of British Columbia, 1978; Jones, "Better Schools Day in Saskatchewan and the Perils of Educational Reform," *The Journal of Educational Thought* 14 (Aug. 1980): 125-37.

⁵*Census of Prairie Provinces,* 1936, vol. 1, pp. 4, 359, 832; *Census of Canada,* 1931, vol. 11, p. 141. See Jones, "'The Little Mound of Earth' — The fate of School Agriculture," in George Tomkins, ed., CSSE *Yearbook* 1979, pp. 85-94. It was this demographic trend exhibited throughout North America and elsewhere which gave such impetus to the country life message.

⁶Jones, "We'll all be buried down here in this dry belt," *Saskatchewan History* 35 (Spring 1982): 41-54.

⁷Jones, "Better Schools Day in Saskatchewan and the Perils of Educational Reform."

⁸*Census of Prairie Provinces,* 1936, vol. 1, pp. 4, 359, 832.

⁹See the *Commission on Agricultural and Industrial Education,* 1915; the Better Schools Day Campaign, 1915-16; and the Foght *Report,* 1918.

¹⁰"Star," Alberta to editor *Farmer's Advocate,* Oct. 29, 1913, p. 1589, hereafter *Advocate.* Italics in the original.

¹¹"Report of the Chairman of the Committee on Educational Policies," *Scientific Agriculture,* 7 (Aug. 1927): 476.

¹²Special committee appointed to inquire into agricultural conditions, minutes and evidence no. 14. Apr. 10, 1923. Pamphlets 6, box 4, Special Collections, University of Calgary; underscoring mine.

¹³For a full development of this argument see Jones, "Schools and Social Disintegration in the Alberta Dry Belt of the Twenties," *Prairie Forum* 3 (1978): 1-19; Jones, "A Strange Heartland: The Alberta Dry Belt and the Schools in the Depression," in D. Francis and H. Ganzevoort, *The Dirty Thirties in Prairie Canada* (Vancouver: Tantallus, 1980), pp. 89-109.

¹⁴See throughout the drought files of the Alberta Premiers' Papers, 69.289. Alberta Provincial Archives. Note also Jones, "We'll all be buried down here in this dry belt."

¹⁵Editorial, "Keeping the Boys and Girls on the Farm," *Grain Growers' Guide,* Oct. 20, 1915, p. 5.

¹⁶E.L. Vincent, "What is home to your boys and girls," *Advocate,* Aug. 12, 1914, p. 1097.

¹⁷Editorial, "The Boy that Leaves the Farm," *Advocate,* May 6, 1914, pp. 625-26.

¹⁸S.G., B.C., to Editor, Third Prize, *Review,* Nov. 10, 1928, p. 7. The comment was part of a prize winning essay on how to keep youth interested in the farm.

¹⁹Nellie L. McClung, "Why Boys and Girls Leave the Farm," *The Nor'-West Farmer,* Sept. 5, 1913, p. 1106, hereafter *NWF.*

²⁰BSA, "The Story of a Farm Boy: Part I — Why the Boy Left the Farm," *Advocate,* Nov. 20, 1918, pp. 1815, 1838.

²¹See Douglas Lawr, "Agricultural Education in Nineteenth-Century Ontario: An Idea in Search of an Institution," in Michael B. Katz and Paul H. Mattingly,

eds., *Education and Social Change* (New York: New York University Press, 1975), pp. 169-192; Jones, "Agriculture, the Land and Education," ch. 4.

[22]BSA, "The Story of a Farm Boy: Part II — Why the Boy Chose an Agricultural College Course," *Advocate*, Dec. 4, 1918, pp. 1888, 1909.

[23]BSA, "The Story of a Farm Boy: Part III — Why the Boy Entered Professional Agriculture," *Advocate*, Dec. 18, 1919, p. 2029.

[24]BSA, "The Story of a Farm Boy: Part IV — Why the Boy Planned to Return to the Land," *Advocate*, Dec. 25, 1918, p. 2063.

[25]McClung, "Why Boys and Girls Leave the Farm," p. 1106.

[26]n.a., "Why We Left the Farm," *Guide*, May 7, 1913, pp. 7, 18, 19.

[27]n.a., "Why We Left the Farm," *Guide*, May 14, 1913, pp. 7, 18, 19.

[28]D. Stewart to Editor, "The Back-to-the-City Movement," *Advocate*, May 19, 1920, p. 878.

[29]n.a., "The Simple Life," *NWF*, Mar. 5, 1912, p. 310.

Part III

Conclusion

Childhood Rescued and Restrained
In English Canada

R.L. Schnell

The preceding chapters reflect some of the chronic problems in history of childhood. As conventionally practised, history is concerned with public actors and events that are deemed to be significant in the unfolding of future public actions. Historians of childhood not only study one of the conspicuous mutes of history but also a stage of life seemingly invincibly private and trivial. Nevertheless, scholars generally are committed to the significance of the pre-adult years for several reasons. First, it seems a counsel of prudence to assume that how one is reared has something to do with one's adult behaviour. Second, the general acceptance of a rational, if not deterministic, view of human nature demands causal relationships within human behaviour. Finally, actions within the limits of private life seem bound up with the most basic human instincts and needs. Understanding how these basic elements are satisfied promises insight into the sources and nature of our most deeply held social values.

Although constrained to believe in a connection between childhood experiences and adult character and behaviour, historians and social scientists have faced great difficulty in demonstrating those links. Even the social science evidence associating experience and subsequent behaviour in the aggregate is cold comfort for historians dealing with scattered and often idiosyncratic material. As might be expected, historians have turned to psychological theories and psycho-biographies for explanatory frameworks in which to embed their evidence. If psychologizing childhood history has given structure to data, it has also introduced new problems. The most notable difficulty is the tendency to treat the theory as given and the evidence as illustrative examples, causing the work to become increasingly ahistorical and law-like in character. This is not to deny that psychological studies can be used effectively to interpret specific bodies of historical data[1] but that the imposition of psychological theories destroys the very basis of historical inquiry that is predicated on the individual — if very similar — characters of human actors, societies, culture, and events.

Related to the search for a link between childhood and adult life is the effort to understand how popular ideas have influenced adult perceptions of child life and in turn what kinds of adults would children raised by such parents become. Since these ideas were often promulgated by leading philosophers and scientists who wrote both for a scholarly and a popular audience, historians have analyzed these writings for insight into how adults may have perceived and reared children and for prediction about the sorts of adults that would develop under such practices.[2]

There are, of course, major difficulties in using such evidence in understanding specific individual or group behaviour. We know from a whole range of human activities about the difficulty of establishing an empirical link between specific knowledge and action. Even apparent connections may be spurious since behaviour consistent with one knowledge base may in fact be derived from quite a different one. The difficulty in deducing specific and unique pedagogical practices from markedly different philosphies of education illustrates the problem. Even it it were possible to assume the link between knowledge and behaviour, we are still faced with the problem of establishing the connection between child rearing practices and the specific enculturation of the young.

What we do have are the writings of the major proponents of intellectual traditions that have been acknowledged as having considerable impact on the manner in which we understand the world. What Michael Zuckerman has said about parental advice literature pertains as well to the utilitarianism, pragmatism, and psychologism as ways of understanding human development.

> So we must eschew all efforts to divine what parents did see in the advice and address ourselves instead to what there was to be seen. We must seek a re-construction of the prevading assumptions and injunctions of the text. . . . We cannot get inside the minds of . . . audiences . . . except by interpretation. We have only the texts. Yet if we are not too chary of interpretation . . . the text may be sufficient.[3]

The first three chapters address themselves "to what was there to be seen" in the "texts", i.e., the writings and lives, of exponents of utilitarianism, pragmatism, and psychology, who have played major roles in shaping our attitudes and perceptions. Many of their ideas, usually diluted and adulterated, have entered popular culture. Although as with the advice literature, it is virtually impossible to demonstrate direct links between the "texts" and the popular perceptions, we are able to analyze the writings and to establish what understandings were available to those who sought to act in light of their ideas. Many will reorganize bits and pieces of the traditions of our own thought and actions and in the language and ideology of the educational and helping professions.

As is clear from the chapters, the traditions had different channels for entry into popular thought, spoke to different audiences, and rested on different assumptions. The chapters provide us with an understanding of the models of childhood that have shaped our thinking about child life for nearly two centuries.

Major theorists help us to see the world in ways we could not without their assistance and hopefully our authors will initiate us more thoroughly into those ways of seeing.[4] Since the themes of utilitarianism, pragmatism, and psychologism are, of course, tremendously shapeless, the authors have attempted to provide specificity and clarity in their analysis by focussing on one or two representatives of each tradition. In the case of Jeremy Bentham and John Dewey, the representatives are synonymous with utilitarianism and pragmatism respectively.

Bentham possessed sufficient intelligence and ambition to conceive a world in which disorder, waste, and superstition would disappear as the results of the well ordered society, prison, and school. Scholars have debated Bentham's influence on early nineteenth century British social reform. Although we are faced with the same questions regarding child rearing practices and education, Professor Taylor's discussion of Bentham's utititarian child tells us much about the manner in which one master sought to bring order to his world and consequently about the ideas and assumptions that are still espoused by advocates of utilitarian education.

Unlike Bentham, John Dewey is primarily remembered as an educational theorist and particularly as the leading exponent of educational progressivism in the United States between 1890 and 1950. Indeed, Dewey's reputation (for good or bad) in education has been so overwhelming that his work in logic, aesthetics, ethics, and the philosophy of science have been largely overlooked. Coming of age in an newly industrialized America, Dewey was concerned with the decline of traditional modes of enculturation and the growth of individualism and social disorganization. If the home and community were no longer able to educate and socialize for cooperative and socially responsible life, then Dewey argued the school must be reorganized and given new purposes and power to ensure the existence of a society that was democratic, cooperative, and scientific. Professor Orteza's analysis of Deweyan pragmatism illumines the problems of educating for Dewey's ideal society.

In examining psychologism, Professor Miller has chosen two remarkably different representatives: Homer Lane and J.B. Watson. Lane remains a minor figure in the history of education. Indeed, the man with whom he is often linked, A.S. Neill, at least had the advantage of a long career as a successful schoolmaster of an unorthodox school. Lane on the other hand was dogged by failure and scandal and left no substantial body of writings. Watson's success in academic psychology was followed by a long career as an advertising executive. Although representing — and proxies they truly are — very different themes in psychology, education, and childrearing, Lane and Watson speak for enduring traditions in psychologism. To what extent they influenced or reflected values and practices remains a matter of analysis and interpretation. We must recognize that psychological ideas about childrearing and education were frequently popularized by less controversial figures than Lane and Watson. Dewey, who had come out of nineteenth century philosophy, paid considerable attention to social psychology. One would suspect that his views like those of more conventional psychologists and medical advisors such as E.L. Thorndike and Dr. Spock were those accepted as authoritative by teachers and middle class parents.[5]

Yet Lane and Watson were signs of the profound shift in sentiment and sensibility of the late nineteenth and early twentieth centuries whereby psychological ideas entered the consciousness of modern educated classes. In Lane's case, the psychological tradition tapped included the concern for unconscious motivation exemplified by Sigmund Freud. Here we see the intricate web of drives, reasons, and inter-personal relationships that is always at risk. Indeed, Lane's efforts were primarily therapeutic.[6] Drawing on an older positivist and deterministic view of human nature, Watson's world was less problematic. Although human nature had its drives and needs and individuals had their particular characteristics, human nature was ultimately amenable to socialization, training, indoctrination, and conditioning. For Watson, the problematic area is more limited and tidy and the necessary adjustments are individual and not societal.

The geo-cultural studies of Part II move from the intellectual traditions to examination of institutional care for dependent children, public health campaigns, and juvenile delinquency, which are perennial themes in childhood history. Although not directly studied in the chapters, the establishment of systems of common schools can be usefully understood as efforts to impose a "childhood" on all children by forcing an extended period of psychological and economic dependence, insuring protection and segregation from the more questionable aspects of adult life, and granting delayed responsibility in social and ethical matters.[7]

As the most ordered of rescues, the common school worked best with children in stable natural families. During the nineteenth century, both government and voluntary relief agents had shown little interest in maintaining the integrity of psychologically sound but destitute families. The suspicion that economic distress and poverty were the results of social, if not moral, incompetence encouraged child savers to remove routinely children from their families for placement in institutions or in domestic and agricultural service. The epitome of this interventionist mentality was reached with the British Juvenile Emigration Movement that between 1869 and 1930 shipped some 80,000 children and young people to Canada. Although a few were "adopted," the great majority spent their childhoods and adolescents as indentured farm and domestic servants.[8]

By late nineteenth century, the debates over boarding out as against institutionalization, which had begun to surface in Great Britain as early as the 1850s, were gradually changing the views about child development. The boarding-out argument was predicated on the belief that institutionalization — except in cases of severe handicap and delinquency — was detrimental to the development of independent and self-supporting adults. As the practice of foster care gradually replaced institutionalization and its associated practices of binding out and indenture, the "reformers" were faced with the difficulty of securing adequate numbers of homes to receive such children. Moreover, the experience of child savers with institutionalized and boarded-out children demonstrated the strength of familial bonds in even the most exploitative families. The century long complaint about absconding children, well placed adolescents leaving their situations, and parents and friends endeavouring to assert control over children in or out of the institutions — not to mention the costs of payment to foster parents and of inspections and supervision — led child savers and their social work descendants to move towards an interventionist stance that stressed prevention over care and family maintenance over removal of children. The latest approach pushed the old slogan of a natural family for a natural child to its logical conclusion, i.e., that the truly natural family for a child was its own family and that removal could only be justified when the danger of the child's welfare was extreme.[9]

Such a position meant that family whose only "crime" was economic failure or inability to cope with illness and death would be supported psychologically and economically. Even situations that included such elements of irresponsibility or perhaps anti-social behaviour were no longer deemed sufficient reasons for family breakup. The success of such family maintenance programs — when connected with public efforts to sustain family incomes in times of distress through such means as mothers' allowances — helped to ensure "childhoods" for more children and to compel their attendance at the common school.

Dr. Norah Lewis' study of the child health care movement in British Columbia during the inter-war years documents the efforts both to improve the physical well-being of children and to contribute to "building wholesome attitudes and social consciences." Such efforts, of course, reached well beyond the child and required the education of parents — particularly mothers — to ensure proper home conditions. The reformation of manners and morals — not to mention the inculcation of industry, honesty, and self-reliance — had been a theme both of evangelical children's literature and child rescue societies of the early nineteenth century. Issues of good health and adequate care seem so uncontestably desirable that few can see in the child health campaigns the same self-interested efforts of the bourgeoisie to impose their social values on the masses. Like her mentor, Neil Sutherland, Dr. Lewis concludes with a positive assessment of a movement that had science on its side.[10]

Although the child health movement was directed at chronic areas of illness and disability among the depressed classes, it brought considerable benefits to all classes of children. Efforts to ensure pure milk and to eradicate communicable diseases foster the development of all children — even if the lower classes, given their poorer standards of housing, clothing, and personal hygiene, might be singled out for rough treatment in the school and public health campaigns to control these plagues. Juvenile delinquency was an entirely different matter. The benefits to middle class society were indirect, indeed, namely the protection of its property and person but, more particularly, of its children from moral and physical contamination. Reformatories and training schools housed the poor, the working classes, immigrants and native peoples. Children of the middle classes hardly appeared in juvenile courts and even less in penal institutions. By the 1960s, critics of juvenile justice systems were challenging conventional, if liberal, interpretations of "delinquency" and the efforts to control it. Powerful critiques such as Antony Platt's *The Child Savers* probed the personal motives and class interests of men and women who campaigned for a separate juvenile justice system.[11] Other historians examined the optimism surrounding the establishment of asylum and the subsequent disillusion as the promise of rehabilitation turned to incarceration.[12]

Alberta's experiment with juvenile justice came well after the first flush of asylum founding and at the beginning of the general Canadian movement to de-institutionalize "normal" dependent children. Rebecca Coulter's study of juvenile justice in the new province of Alberta, 1909-1929, tells the curious Alberta method of de-institutionalization of delinquents, i.e., farm placements, and the use of other provincial facilities for difficult cases. Alberta had the distinction of being the first province to declare the 1908 Juvenile Delinquents Act in force for an entire province. The centralization of social services that became a mark of Alberta politics is clearly foreshadowed in the handling of juvenile delinquency. The Alberta perchance for provincial control, which was to infuriate Charlotte Whitton and her Canadian Welfare Council in the 1930s and 40s, gave a false impression of an efficient and effective social welfare system;[13] however, as Coulter notes, social workers were aware as early as 1927 that the Alberta system failed to rehabilitate.

In attempting to understand what the prairie experience must have meant to adults and children, David C. Jones has probed the country life movement in the popular press during the period 1900-1925. Like Norah Lewis, he examines an educational and propaganda campaign that was aimed at parents and children. The myths were intended to attract and hold the right kinds of settlers, i.e., Anglo-Celtic and worthy citizens of the True North. In the case of western settlement, parental response to the country life movement made little difference in the ways in which their children reacted when the ideal failed to square with the reality. The essential element of Jones' account is that the myth of the land was never fully accepted and that it had attraction only for those who hungered for property no matter what its value. The rural experience was noted principally for its negative force in confirming the undesirability of rural life on the prairies.

Whether the emphasis is on child health care, juvenile justice or dependent children, the case studies demonstrate the rapid transition from child rescue to child welfare during which old notions of voluntary service and Christian charity gave way to therapeutic services professionally staffed and scientifically administered. The studies by Lewis and Coulter coming at the beginning of the move to science and professionalism naturally do not examine the ways in which the two traditions played dialectically on each other.

The most obvious examples of the inter-play of forces and institutional modification are the Protestant Orphans' Homes established in nineteenth century British North America from St. John's to Victoria. The history of the Atlantic institutions recounted in "Guttersnipes and Charity Children" represent the founding period of the POHs. During the twentieth century, POHs across Canada were forced to modify their practices in the face of sustained criticism of institutionalization, generated by public and private preventive services aimed at maintaining family integrity and the rise of social welfare professionalism. Given the economic and social stagnation of much of the Atlantic region, these children's institutions were among the most stable representatives of the old tradition of religious benevolence.[14]

Leslie Savage's study of the Sisters of Misercordia in Edmonton around 1900 is an instructive example of organizational adaptation. The establishment of the Misercordia in Montreal in the 1840s represents an example of Christian stewardship and service within the Roman Catholic tradition. As an exemplary representative of French-Canadian society, the Misercordia's twin objectives of preserving the spiritual and temporal well-being of illegitimate infants and securing the spiritual and social reformation of their mothers could be satisfactorily combined with a religious community life. Moreover, maintenance of such facilities for mothers and children remained a significant social service throughout the nineteenth century.

The failure of the Misericordia in Edmonton to attract unwed mothers or to hold on to the children born in its institution raises some interesting questions about transplanting institutions. In addition to the social, cultural, and economic conditions of Edmonton, the Sisters had to operate within an essentially anglophone and protestant milieu. The curious thing about the rapid transformation of the Edmonton Misericordia into general nursing and health care is the absence of any specific decision about such a shift. Of course, since as Savage notes such missionary activites were to be self supporting, the Edmonton foundation might be understood as simply adaption to socio-economic conditions in order to survive. The position of a small community beset by financial anxieties and lacking the leisure to contemplate organizational transformation might also help to explain the failure to discuss the issue.

Unlike the POHs that despite their transformations remained essentially children's institutions, the Misericordia soon became a general purpose institution. Although it has been suggested that the change derived from the radically different conditions of Western Canada, it might also be seen as a result of the unique nature of infants' as opposed to children's institutions. As a society catering to illegitimate neonates, the Misericordia had none of the educational and resocialization aims of the POHs with regard to their children. Instead, these objectives were transferred to the unwed motthers for whom the Sisters held hopes of moral and social reformation.

If the Misericordia underwent a rapid and uncommented transformation from care for unwed mothers and their offspring to general hospital and nursing care, one might understand the development not so much a result of the opportunities for marriage on the part of such women as their unwillingness to submit to convent discipline. On the other hand, as Savage demonstrates, the Misericordia was able to establish an orphanage and to require the same total surrender commonly demanded by the POHs. This insistence of total wardship, which ran quite counter to examples of French-Canadian orphanages serving stable Quebec communities, surely must have been related to the kinds of women who surrendered their children. The use of orphanages as temporary homes for children of families in difficulty seemed to be common among both Roman Catholic and Protestant homes. What evidence there is on French-Canadian institutions suggests a much less judgmental relationship with parents and kin than their POH counterparts who generally assumed the worst of motives.[15] Consequently, the insistence on total wardship by the Edmonton Sisters strikingly supports Savage's muted contention that they were much more suspicious of their clientele than the Sisters had been in Montreal.

These five case studies have illustrated issues within the history of childhood in Canada from the establishment of the first institutions for dependent children in mid-nineteenth century to the campaign for child health care as well as the more general problem of the relationship between children and their social and physical environment. If this relationship remains largely uncharted, it is a result of inadequate historical evidence or appropriate methods of dealing comprehensively with discrete data.

Nevertheless, we must acknowledge that the study of the deviant and vulnerable as well as the comfortably situated provides us with insights about our most cherished social values and our unexamined perceptions of our world. If these chapters have helped us to see more of our everyday world as problematic, then they will have served us well.

Notes

[1]Patricia T. Rooke and R.L. Schnell, "The 'King's Children' in English Canada: A Psychohistorical Study of Abandonment, Rejection and Colonial Response (1869-1930)," *Journal of Psychohistory* 8 (Spring 1981): 387-420.

[2]Bernard Wishy, *The Child and the Republic* (Philadelphia: University of Pennsylvania Press, 1968).

[3]Michael Zuckerman, "Dr. Spock: The Confidence Man," in *The Family in History,* ed. Charles E. Rosenberg (Philadelphia: University of Pennsylvania Press, 1975), p. 182.

[4]Good examples of such work are Philippe Aries, *Centuries of Childhood* (New York: Vintage Books, 1965); and Michel Foucault, *Discipline and Punish* (New York: Vintage Books, 1979).

[5]John Cleverley and D.C. Phillips, *From Locke to Spock* (Melbourne: Melbourne University Press, 1976.

[6]For modern British public schools with therapeutic tendencies, see Robert Skidelsky, *English Progressive Schools* (Harmondsworth: Penguin Books, 1969).

[7]R.L. Schnell, "Childhood as Ideology," *British Journal of Educational Studies* 27 (February 1979): 7-28.

[8]Kenneth Bagnell, *The Little Immigrants* (Toronto: Macmillan of Canada, 1980); and Joy Parr, *Labouring Children* (London: Croom Helm, 1980).

[9]Patricia T. Rooke and R.L. Schnell, "From Binding to Boarding Out in Britain and English-Canada: A Transformation in Childhood Sentiment and Practice," Calgary, 1982. (Typewritten).

[10]Neil Sutherland, *Children in English Canadian Society* (Toronto: University of Toronto Press, 1976); and "Social Policy, 'Deviant' Children, and the Public Health Apparatus in British Columbia Between the Wars," *Journal of Educational Thought* 14 (August 1980): 80-91.

[11]Anthony Platt, *The Child Savers* (Chicago: University of Chicago Press, 1969); Joseph Hawes, *Children in Urban Society* (New York: Oxford University Press, 1971); Robert M. Mennel, *Thorns and Thistles* (Hanover, N.H.: University of New England, 1973); Steven Schlossman, *Love and the American Delinquent* (Chicago: University of Chicago Press, 1977); and Ellen Ryerson, *The Best-Laid Plans* (New York: Hill and Wang, 1978).

[12]David J. Rothman, *The Discovery of the Asylum* (Boston: Little, Brown, 1971), and Conscience and Convenience (Boston: Little, Brown, 1980); and Gerald N. Grob, *Mental Institutions in America* (New York: Free Press, 1973.

[13]Patricia T. Rooke and R.L. Schnell, "Charlotte Whitton Meets the 'Last Best West.'" *Prairie Forum* 6 (Fall 1981): 143-162.

[14]Patricia T. Rooke and R.L. Schnell, "Childhood and Charity in Nineteenth Century British North America," *Histoire sociale/Social History* 15 (May 1982); and "Child Welfare in English-Canada, 1920-1948," *Social Service Review* 55 (September 1981): 484-506.

[15]Bettina Bradbury, "The Fragmented Family," Canadian Historical Association Annual Meeting, Montreal, 1980.